Art Therapy in Prisons and Other Correctional Settings

DRAWING TIME

Art Therapy in Prisons and Other Correctional Settings

Edited by David Gussak, M.A., A.T.R.-BC &
Evelyn Virshup, Ph.D., A.T.R.

Magnolia Street Publishers

Library of Congress Cataloging-in-Publication Data

Drawing time: art therapy in prisons and other correctional settings
　　/edited by David Gussak & Evelyn Virshup.
　　　　　p.　cm.
　　Includes bibliographical references and index.
　　ISBN 0-9613309-9-6
　　　1. Prisoners—Mental health services.　2. Art therapy.　3. Prisoners as artists.
I. Gussak, David.　II. Virshup, Evelyn.
RC451.4.P68D72　1997
616.8'5156'086927--dc21　　　　　　　　　　　97-44591
　　　　　　　　　　　　　　　　　　　　　　　　　CIP

Copyright © 1997 by **Magnolia Street Publishers**

All rights reserved. No part of this book may be
reproduced by any process whatsoever without the
written permission of the copyright holder.

Published by
Magnolia Street Publishers
1250 West Victoria Street
Chicago, Illinois 60660

ISBN: 0-9613309-9-6
Cover Design: Evelyn Virshup
Book Design: Sarah Reinken

Printed in the United States of America
　2　3　4　5　6　7　8　9　10

This book is dedicated to the warm and loving memory
of
Bernard Virshup, M.D.

The Third, Silent Editor

I would like to take this opportunity to give special recognition to William Fox, MSW, LCSW, who was more than just a contributor with his article "The Hidden Weapon." All the contributing authors heard me at one time or another refer to "the third, silent editor." Because of his many years of experience as an editor himself, he was an extraordinary source of feedback and critical review of all articles submitted. He also helped me overcome many obstacles with my own writing and never tired of the many questions I posed regarding this book.

Thank you, Bill.

DG

Table of Contents

A Vignette
   Deborah Good..v
Introduction
   Evelyn Virshup ix
A Brief History
   David E. Gussak xv

PART ONE: Presenting the Dilemma

Chapter 1: **Breaking Through Barriers:** Advantages of Art Therapy in Prison
   David E. Gussak 1
Chapter 2: **Insider Art:** The Creative Ingenuity of the Incarcerated Artist
   Will A. Ursprung 13
Chapter 3: **Creativity & Incarceration:** The Purpose of Art in a Prison Culture
   Nancy Hall 25
Chapter 4: **The Hidden Weapon:** Psychodynamics of Forensic Institutions
   William M. Fox 43

PART TWO: Some Solutions

Chapter 5: **The Ultimate Hidden Weapon:** Art Therapy and the Compromise Option
   David E. Gussak.. 59

Chapter 6: **No Artist Rants and Raves When He Creates:** Creative Art Therapies and Psychiatry in Forensic Settings
Stephen Rojcewicz 75

Chapter 7: **Suspending Normal Prison Taboos Through the Arts**
Jack Cheney 87

Chapter 8: **Art Therapy in a Managed Care Environment**
Janis Woodall, Pamela Diamond & Anne Hanson Howe 99

Chapter 9: **Surviving One's Sentence:** Art Therapy with Incarcerated Trauma Survivors
Elizabeth Day & Greg Onorato 127

Chapter 10: **Easing the Transition** from Prison to the Community
Dorrie Mosel-Gussak 153

PART THREE: Special Forensic Populations

Chapter 11: **The Lucky Ones:** Probationary Students in a Special Education School
Claudia Ronaldson 167

Chapter 12: **A Barbed Wire Garden:** Art Therapy in a Maximum Security Prison for Adolescents
Linda Milligan 175

Chapter 13: **Helping Criminally Insane Men Who are Hearing-Impaired**
Renu Sundaram 187

Chapter 14: **Growing Old, The Hard Time Way:** Art Therapy as an Intervention in Gerontology and Criminology
Marcia Taylor 197

PART FOUR: Healing Ourselves Through Art

Chapter 15: **Red Rope and Blue Veins:** The Inportance of Self-Monitoring in a Prison Setting
Beth Merriam 213

Chapter 16: **Mandala Healing:** My Recovery from a Hostage Crisis
Joan Pakula 219

PART FIVE: Other Arenas

Chapter 17: **What One Museum Does for Prison Art**
  Carol Wisker 231
Chapter 18: **In The Future:** Art Therapy Research in Prisons
  Linda Gantt 241

About the Editors 245
Contributors 247
Index 253

"After all, this is an intern— an art therapy intern"

Deborah Good, Ph.D., A.T.R., LPCC, LPAT

As an intern for my master's degree in art therapy, I worked in a medium security prison.

In my first group of five male inmates, all under age twenty-five, three were incarcerated for assault and battery crimes, and two were serving sentences for murder. They admitted they had committed their crimes while they were drunk or on drugs. They seemed so young, yet very old at the same time.

During the first session, they drew individual pictures to tell me something about themselves.

One young man drew a time bomb in the middle of the page with a short fuse, lit with sparks. I needed more information to know if this client was a potential danger, or if I was being conned so I asked the group to take their pictures one step further and draw picture stories to embellish the original.

He drew his second lit time bomb clearly in a stylized form, putting it at the top of the page in the upper left hand corner. Then leaving space, he drew a rope noose. In the upper right hand corner he drew a razor blade, and in the very center of the page, he drew a large equal sign. Below that he drew a stereotypical tombstone with RIP written on it. The client handed the drawing to me saying that he really did not know what it meant, but he felt agitated after drawing it.

After the group was over, I showed my supervisor the picture. He was concerned and immediately talked to the psychologist in charge of mental health services. That night my supervisor reported that the psychologist was not alarmed. The inmate in question was doing very well and scheduled to be released to a minimum security placement at the end of the week. The psychologist did not want to jeopardize the transfer. My supervisor felt the art work was not taken seriously. He was told, "After all, this is an intern—an art therapy intern."

Over the weekend, my supervisor called again and asked if I still had the drawing. When I asked why, he told me the warden wanted it.

The inmate had been released to minimum security and escaped the day after the transfer. He then kidnapped a woman, tied her up, assaulted her with a razor blade and left her to die.

Let us hope that incidents like this don't happen and art therapy becomes more valued, not only as a predictor of violent behavior but as a valuable intervention in prison settings.

INTRODUCTORY SECTION

Introduction

Evelyn Virshup, Ph.D., A.T.R.

Since prison has become a major industry, with more money being spent on incarceration than education and mental health care, and mentally ill people are being committed to prisons rather than hospitals, more humane and helpful strategies are needed to prepare prisoners for their release into the free world, to give them more skills and internal resources. Art therapy is one of those strategies, a powerful tool that has been proven effective.

What is it like to do art therapy with inmates in a prison? How effective is art therapy in such a milieu? How do the prisoners respond? How do the guards respond? What sort of art activities are being done with inmates that are safe and therapeutic at the same time?

What problems arise for the art therapists? How do they deal with issues an art therapist on the outside would never think of, like the length of pencils, which might be long enough to be weapons, the strength of thread, possibly to be used for strangling or hanging, the use of clay to hide contraband or mold keys, mask-making, possibly to be used for escape, the unceasing need to count supplies over and over again so no one walks off with a potential weapon? Are these problems consistent from prison to prison, state to state?

How is art regarded by the correctional staff? Do they understand its power? How do the guards feel about the "sissified" work of drawing and painting? How do they feel about possible competition between them and the therapists for the prisoners' attention?

Drawing Time: Art Therapy in Prisons and Other Correctional Settings deals with these questions and more and gives many examples of how art therapy is practiced in American correctional settings today.

In a poignant yet frightening introductory anecdote, art therapist Deborah Good demonstrates the importance of using the process of art therapy both to help the incarcerated express themselves nonverbally in prison and guide the staff in reading the unspoken messages in their art.

Then art therapist David Gussak gives an overview of the history of prisons in Europe and the United States, noting the current trend of mixing psychiatric patients with criminals, due to mental hospital closings, and hypothesizes about the future of many inmates under these

DRAWING TIME

conditions. He refers to past studies showing that art-making in prisons has decreased violence and cut the recidivism rate, a much desired goal.

In PART I: *Presenting The Dilemma*, Gussak relates how prison inmates build rigid defenses and put on 'masks' ensuring survival in the correctional subculture. In "Breaking Through Barriers," he illustrates how art therapy goes behind these masks, unbeknownst to the prisoners, and allows them to resolve many of their conflicts on paper, without engaging in verbal therapy. Art therapy under stringent prison conditions is effective because the art process can be completely nonverbal; the inmates can draw out their anguish and resolve internal conflicts without even knowing how they are helping themselves.

Art therapist Will Ursprung's main thesis, in his chapter, *Insider Art*, is that by supporting art in prison, we help the artists find solace and transform themselves via the power of making art, readying them for life in the free world. In his text, he shows how through the ingenuity and resourcefulness of the inmates, they transform "straw into gold," using flotsam to create their art and humanize their dehumanizing environment .

Working in the sixth largest maximum security prison in the United States, Graterford State Correctional Institution in Pennsylvania, Ursprung has developed a series of exhibition opportunities for inmate/artists, bolstering their self esteem and recreating their image.

Nancy Hall spent five years working as an art therapist in a maximum security prison "of legendary stature" on the east coast. In her chapter, *Creativity & Incarceration: The Purpose of Art in the Prison Culture*, she tells how she structured her art therapy groups with the most severely mentally ill men, focusing on autobiographical work, past and future. She reports on her interventions, what worked for the inmates, what didn't, and why.

In her major focus, Hall tells how many men spontaneously use artmaking to control their rage and get absorbed in the process, helping them pass the interminable time, how they produce desirable products for sale or barter, from portraits and pornographic drawings to picture frames from woven potato chip bags. She shows how art provides a safe means of escape from the environment, how it creates bonds between the artists and their jailers. She decries the fact that no matter how important art is to the inmates and their jailers, and how it permeates the prison, in her experience, it happens with little or no support by the authorities.

William Fox, licensed clinical social worker, elucidates in his chapter, *The Hidden Weapon*, the dynamics of the relationship between the prisoners and their captors and the hypervigilance which neither group can sustain. The theory is based on a paranoid, primitive relationship. Applying psychoanalytic, object-relations theory to the basic forensic situation, whether that institution be a prison, state hospital or jail, he looks at the socio-dynamics of these people and institutions and explains why there seems to be ingrained opposition to any form of therapeutic intervention, including art therapy.

In the following section, *PART II: Some Solutions*, David Gussak considers his associate, Bill Fox's chapter about the conflict between jailer and jailee, and describes the clinician's dilemma as third entity in the equation. In *The Ultimate Hidden Weapon*, he outlines the options, makes recommendations based on his experiences and reiterates the art therapist's mantra, "the act of making art allows therapy to happen."

INTRODUCTION

Demonstrating the value of poetry therapy in a dehumanizing environment, psychiatrist Stephen Rojcewicz shares in his chapter, *No Artist Rants and Raves*, the poetry he has found effective not only in helping inmates gain insight and motivation for change, but recognizing and accepting responsibility for what led to their incarceration. He describes the various formats of group poetry sessions which have enabled inmates to express feelings never expressed constructively before. He talks about the inherent interplay between freedom of expression, raw emotions and a highly organized structure accounting for much of the therapeutic benefit of the creative arts therapies in prisons.

Through the use of the arts, singing of songs, playing of instruments, drawing, imagining, sculpting and talking, Jack Cheney, in his contribution, *Suspending Normal Prison Taboos Through the Arts in a Prison Psychiatric Setting*, gives an account of his unique ways of helping these prisoners not only outlive their sentences but develop coping skills and insights to find direction and meaning in their lives.

In *Art Therapy in a Managed Care Environment*, Janis Woodall and her associates contribute an outline of their art therapy program in a managed care psychiatric facility in Texas. The writers define the many nuts and bolts of the program designed by their multi-disciplinary team including music therapists, occupational therapists, recreational therapists and drug counselors. The chapter describes their pre- and post- measurements, time-limited art psychotherapy groups, and is complete with exercises, treatment team objectives and goals, inmate objectives and what to look for in the inmate/patients' art. In addition, they include a contract clearly delineating the commitment from both the client and the therapist of the art therapy program, establishing the boundaries of the art therapy group process.

What happens to sexually abused girls when they grow up? Many of them find their way as trauma survivors to prison, unable to deal with their unspoken rage and confusion. In *Surviving One's Sentence*, Elizabeth Day and Greg Onorato, working with these trauma survivors in a female correctional environment, discuss in detail how they run the art therapy groups with this under-served population.

Dorrie Gussak describes her psychiatric hospital's multi-disciplinary approach in *Easing the Transition*. Using a variety of creative arts therapies to help their mentally ill patients learn how to rejoin their communities, the staff trains them in much needed social skills. Through these therapies, inarticulate and isolated patients are reached, socialized and their feelings and needs are expressed. Ms. Gussak discusses the conflicts arising from teaching how to make choices as well as acting as auxiliary egos, and setting boundaries.

Special Forensic Populations are presented in Part III. Seriously emotionally disturbed (SED) boys are clients of art therapist Claudia Ronaldson who describes her art as therapy/art therapy program at a residential treatment center/special education school. In her chapter, *The Lucky Ones*, she recounts conflicts arising from the addition of boys with conduct-disordered behaviors, which created an "uneasy mix of students" and of how effective their work in art has been to create relative harmony in the school.

In *A Barbed Wire Garden*, art therapist Linda Milligan describes how she uses art to help solve the many problems of incarcerated adolescents, ages 14 to 18, in a maximum security prison. Many are inner city gang members, described as predatory, struggling with their very real adolescent issues as well as the physical constraints of prison. Ms. Milligan uses Erikson's developmental levels as a guide to her clients' needs. She shows how she integrates art therapy projects into the healing process. She helps them explore their inner worlds, their relationships and feelings about others, their fear, rage and manipulative behavior, all using the process of art.

To be diagnosed as criminally insane and to be hearing-impaired as well makes for difficult times in prison. Renu Sudaram, an art therapist who is hearing-impaired herself, communicates well with these patients and acts as an intermediary between them and the staff. She describes her work in her chapter, *Helping Criminally Insane Men Who are Hearing-Impaired Through Art Therapy*, noting that the traditional approaches don't always work with this population. She recounts a case study in a group setting, showing how effective the art process is in creating effective support groups.

The problems, now and even more so in the future of the aging in prisons is related by Marcia Taylor in *Growing Old the Hard Time Way*. She outlines art therapy interventions with this growing population which help them pass "dead time" when they are in their cells. The art experiences allow them to withdraw into privacy in an accepting supportive environment, hard to find in prison, and learn skills to cope with their fate.

PART IV: *Healing Ourselves Through Art* suggests tools for dealing with potential burnout of staff. Constantly hearing tragic stories of abuse told by incarcerated women wears away at prison mental health workers. So much exposure to inhumanity, pain and trauma as a steady diet is hard to digest.

Beth Merriam, art therapist in a Canadian federal prison, found a way to deal with feelings aroused by these "case histories." She took her clients' life experiences and transformed them into a poignant short story, *Red Rope & Blue Veins*, turning her sense of horror into a creative experience. It gave Merriam a vessel to contain the helplessness and pain she felt listening to their stories, as well as the strength and will to continue working with them.

Joan Pakula described her experience of being taken hostage in a prison, by a pencil-wielding inmate and how she helped to heal herself through the process of drawing mandalas to recover from her trauma.

Of particular importance, Pakula's article, *Mandala Healing: My Recovery From A Hostage Crisis*, demonstrates the reality that those working in these facilities must face, as well as the tools an art therapist inherently has, to regain stability after such a traumatic incident.

In *PART V: Other Arenas*, some possibilities for future work in art and art therapy for prison settings are suggested.

In *What One Museum Does for Prison Art*, Carole Wisker compares museums to prisons and makes a good case for the juxtaposition as well as for the efforts the Philadelphia Museum of Art is making for promoting and displaying prisoners' art as well as educating both the prisoners and the public about their efforts.

And in the final chapter, *In the Future: Art Therapy Research In Prisons*, Linda Gantt tells us what is needed to make others aware of how art therapy works. She suggests qualitative and quantitative analysis of inmates' products across the country in order to identify and read the

INTRODUCTION

underlying language of prison art.

Is there a basic universal graphic vocabulary? Can covert symbolism be translated, to forestall riots, suicides, or attacks on the staff? In addition, can recidivism or suitability for job training be correlated to artwork? Her article points us to a future rich with research ideas for art therapists to improve prison life for both staff and inmates and extend the use of art therapy in forensic settings.

We hope our book, *Drawing Time*, an exploration of how's and why's of art therapy with correctional populations, will answer questions and suggest more to continue the work already begun, and help resolve the tremendous dilemma of how to help the incarcerated help themselves.

A Brief History

David E. Gussak, A.T.R.-BC

After interviewing for an art therapy position in a prison, I was given a tour. An art therapist working on the acute psychiatric unit told me, "You'll see more here in four weeks than most therapists see in one year in any other place." At the time, I believed she was exaggerating; I had worked in other settings with difficult patient populations. However, after just a few months, I reluctantly admitted she was right.

Prison is a stressful place to work. For example, in order to get to my office, I must first enter the kiosk-like entry where I am greeted by an officer who looks at my I.D. and my briefcase. He then pushes a button that opens a small gated enclosure, which I enter. Once the first door is locked electronically, an officer in a forty-foot tower pushes a button that opens an electric gate, leading me to the lobby of the prison. I enter a large room protected by thick glass while an officer behind it electronically opens a large steel-barred door. Then I enter another room protected by thick glass. Again I show my I.D. Again the officer opens yet another large steel door that finally leads onto the prison mainline.

I then walk one-eighth of a mile through throngs of inmates. While walking the "line," I continuously look around me, hypervigilant to potential danger. After going through several other locked gates, I reach my unit. After an officer lets me into my unit, I walk to my office, the first door for which I have a key. I am one of the lucky few since most offices are tiny, converted cells. It is then I realize the tension I felt since entering the prison. I relax the muscles in my neck. It is just 15 minutes into my day.

While in this facility, I have seen examples of nearly every DSM IV diagnosis, from malingering and adjustment disorder (understandable), to acute, exacerbated psychosis. These inmate/patients vary in their depth of criminality, ranging from petty thieves to multiple murderers, serving from eighteen months, to 'life without.'

I have learned a great deal about the prison culture, and the role of the clinician within this setting.

Brief History of Prisons

As literature on the history of penitentiaries and prison systems is extensive, a brief summary

DRAWING TIME

does not do it justice. However, to have basic understanding of what led to the modern penal systems, and consequently modern concerns for the mentally ill in these facilities, a short overview is important. I urge interested people to read the available texts listed in the bibliography.

Although history reveals that different forms of imprisonment existed since before Roman times, modern prison was not recognizable until the eighteenth century. In Europe, imprisonment was a means to house a "criminal" until punishment could be carried out, i.e. transportation (to colonies), banishment, workhouses, or public execution. However, by the 1790s, imprisonment became the main form of punishment.

Initially, prisons began as "disciplinary institutions meant to deal with problems of poverty and marginality" (Morris and Rothman, 1995, p. 65). A "criminal" could have been someone who was poor, a vagrant, someone "politically incorrect," a child who was thought to be incorrigible, or someone with a mental illness. The convicted were all housed together in crowded conditions, in dungeons, "hulks" (floating ships transformed into detention centers), and asylums. Children were with adult convicts, women with men, the sick with the well. Lives were unnecessarily lost due to epidemics that ran rampant. Prisoners were frequently beaten and tortured for the sake of security.

Generally prisons were run as private enterprises charging fees to the relatives. Consequently, many prisoners were neglected when they had to rely on their families for care.

Indifferent wardens also created neglected prisons. However, this often worked to the prisoners with families' advantage. Since visitors were rarely monitored, families were permitted to deliver food and other necessities. Consequently, the care given to prisoners by their families could be considered quite superior to what institutions provide today. Woe be unto the imprisoned who had no family; they would have to rely on the kindness of the institution. Prisons were privately owned, wardens inheriting their positions, ensuring the continuation of this neglect.

Early Prison Development in America

Invoking the Act of Transportation, convicts were often sent to the American colonies. Colonists of the 17th and 18th centuries dealt with the criminal element in the same way as their predecessors. As sin was considered an inherent trait, punishment was a means of deterrence with no thought to rehabilitation. Punishments ranged from fines to executions. Punishment depended on the prisoner's status in the community and how much property he or she held. Incidentally, Massachusetts in 1736 had their version of the three-strikes edict: first offense and conviction brought about a whipping and a fine, the second conviction involved sitting at the gallows with a noose around the neck for an hour, and then 30 lashes, the third conviction resulted in hanging.

In the late 18th century, during an early period of reform, alternate means of punishment were considered but incarceration remained the primary form. Throughout the early 19th century, prisons were built at a rapid rate, primarily to eliminate the gallows while keeping the public safe.

Early prison life was unstructured and chaotic—prisoners lived together in large rooms, with few rules and controls. However, in the 19th century, facilities became more structured with

A BRIEF HISTORY

various means of control, including isolation of prisoners, rules of silence, and military-like administration. Yet, as time went on, this structure, too, broke down, and the post-Civil War era was once again witness to disorder, overcrowdedness and brutality.

Drug use, a common element of prisons today, began to run rampant in the early 20th century. Morphine was the drug of choice, with innovative methods used to smuggle it inside.

Prison Reform

As in most reformations, prison modification occurred gradually, in recurring waves, beginning as early as the 16th century. As ideas were formulated to improve and refine prisons, interest would disappear, only to emerge again later, stronger and with more far-reaching results. Significant experiments using current reformers' innovative ideas were attempted, with varying, and not always acceptable results.

In the ebb of reform, conditions became even worse than before. Budgets dictated prison life, and corruption and cruelty became the rule. Reformation involved hit or miss methods where a form of punishment or care was attempted for the betterment of the inmates, only to be discarded and replaced by another approach.

It wasn't until the 19th century that reformation became serious. Starting in facilities for women and children, it soon encompassed all types of prisons. Indeterminate sentencing developed, wherein the actual term served was dependent on the inmate's behavior and how well the inmate proved his reformation.

The focus of these institutions changed from punishment to corrections. The intent was rehabilitation. Campaigns to make prisons safe and healthy were begun. Systems of classification were established to separate convicts by sex and crime. The definitions of "criminal" became more narrow, and proper sentencing began, with length of stay to match the crime committed.

During one strong period of reform, DeFord (1962) indicated a current purpose of incarceration:

> ...the objects and methods of imprisonment should be, first, the protection and safety of the persons and property of noncriminal people, and secondly, the remedial treatment of the convict himself. 'The shift from theories of revenge, retribution, expiation, and deterrence to a theory of reformation of the offender, with its ultimate aim the protection of society,' is the aim of today's enlightened penology. (p.110)

Ironically, this idea immediately preceded what was deemed by Sullivan (1990) as "the decline of treatment" (p.61).

Today, legislators are being asked to address the issue of crime, resulting in an increase of jails and prisons. The tide of rehabilitation has turned once again. People firmly believe in retribution, and that, in today's prisons, inmates are being coddled and are living a 'country-club life.'

With the growth of the prison industry, there has been an equally loud outcry from those concerned with poor prison conditions. Those involved with human rights protest overcrowding, low standards of health and cleanliness, and inadequate mental health care.

DRAWING TIME

The number of prisons and the level of care established is up to the discretion of the legislators of their particular states. California alone, at the time of this writing, has 31 prisons, while four more are in the building or planning stages—yet mental health facilities are being closed.

Health Care and Rehabilitation
In the mid 17th century, institutions specifically for the insane began to appear. Previously, unable to support themselves, these 'insane lunatics' were often left in prison basements with little attention given to their needs, unless their family members provided care. Needless to say, some of the most ill-treated "prisoners" were the mentally ill.

However, with reformation came attention to health care, and later, mental health care. Reformers believed that catering to the prisoners' individual needs could "cure" the convicted as if crime were an illness; therefore, treatment staff were employed in prisons.

In the early 20th century, the "therapeutic model of rehabilitation" was used primarily as a form of labeling. Sociopathy that ran rampant in these institutions was believed to be a primary illness, and thus required treatment. Once an inmate became 'classified' by the psychiatric staff of the facilities, individual treatment programs were developed, and these "mentally defective" inmates were segregated from the general population. By the 1950s, there was a dramatic increase in experimentation in the treatment of "patients."

As Sullivan writes, "It was the heyday of experimentation in techniques Progressives had only dreamed about. For one facility, Paxtutent Prison in Maryland, indeterminate sentencing was set by doctors; once the psychiatrists believed an inmate had been 'cured,' he was released from the facility." By the 1950s, "...psychiatric group therapy techniques infiltrated most state institutions." By this time, all of the penitentiaries and reformatories attempted to establish a form of the 'therapeutic milieu.' The end of the 1960s witnessed another radical shift in the rehabilitation of prisoners due to changes in political, social and racial events. The focus on health care began to decline, and an increase in housing for the sake of punishment dominated. By the 1980s and early 90s, because of conservative moral values in society, "...penology shift[ed] greatly towards harsher punishment and tighter methods of social control," (Sullivan, 1990, p.136).

What Happens to the Mentally Ill Today?
Today, as psychiatric programs are eliminated, and prisons are being built, mentally ill patients who commit even minor crimes are becoming criminalized (Gibbs, 1987). At the same time, prisons often worsen already existing psychiatric problems (Morgan, 1981), creating more irrational and "illegal" behavior, which inevitably lead to longer prison stays. Once paroled, inmates, still unable to obtain help, return to the facilities. Consequently, the treatment setting for the mentally ill is shifting towards prisons.

As an example of progress towards mental health care reform in prisons, a position statement in 1988 was prepared by the APA Task Force on Psychiatric Services in Jails and Prisons of the Council on Psychiatric Services. It specifically outlined the importance of providing psychiatric care to those inmates that need it. It reminded the APA membership that "...the supreme court has ruled that it is the obligation of correctional officials to ensure that the civil rights of the mentally ill are protected. This obligation includes the right to adequate mental health care," (Weinstein, et al., pg. 1244). The panel outlined six principles to be followed to ensure adequate mental health care in a prison or jail setting.

These were:

1) The fundamental goal of a mental health service should be to provide the same level of care to patients in the criminal justice process that is available in the community.

2) The effective delivery of mental health services in correctional settings requires that there be a balance between security and treatment needs. There is no inherent conflict between security and treatment.

3) A therapeutic environment can be created in a jail or a prison setting if there is clinical leadership, with authority to create such an environment.

4) Timely and effective access to mental health treatment is a hallmark of adequate health care. Necessary staffing levels should be determined by what is essential to ensure that access.

5) Psychiatrists should take a leadership role administratively as well as clinically. Further, it is imperative that psychiatrists define their professional responsibilities to include advocacy for improving mental health services in jails and prisons.

6) Psychiatrists should actively oppose discrimination based on religion, race, ethnic background, or sexual preference, not only for mental health services but for all activities in the judicial-legal process.

There remains a challenge for clinicians to achieve therapeutic excellence in a generally non-therapeutic environment.

Art Therapy in Forensic Facilities

Creativity and artistic expression are qualities inherent in this setting, as seen through prison crafts shops, inmate-painted wall murals, decorative envelopes that inmates can "buy" from each other to send letters to loved ones, and intricate tattoos designed and displayed with pride. The ability to create "good art" becomes a status builder.

Awareness of the advantages of art programs within forensic settings is spreading. A study of the Arts in Corrections program in four northern California prisons demonstrated the advantages of the creative arts in prisons. In 1983, political science professor Larry Brewster of San Jose State University found that fewer disciplinary reports were written on inmates who participated in the program; in one institution the reduction was 80%. A more recent study conducted in 1987 (California Department of Corrections) revealed a more successful parole outcome for those participating in the Arts in Corrections program, showing an 88% favorable outcome within 6 months, and 69.2% after two years.

An abundance of literature about the arts in prisons exists. Many arts organizations focus primarily on bringing the arts inside, including the Arts In Corrections. However, these efforts differ greatly from exploring the therapeutic qualities of the arts from a clinical point of view.

There have been few recorded resources for art therapists in prisons. As Elizabeth Strait Day and Gregory Thomas Ontario said, "The correctional arena is one barely explored by art therapy"(1989, p.126). Although some literature exists, up until now, no comprehensive account of art therapy in prisons in the United States has been published.

Our goal is to present a comprehensive text, through chapters contributed by art therapists and various clinicians throughout the United States, focusing on a helpful and realistic view of what is happening in art therapy in an historically difficult and non-therapeutic setting.

References

American Psychiatric Association. (1994). *Diagnostic and statistical manual of mental disorders.* (Fourth Edition). Washington D.C.

Brewster, L.G. (1983). *An evaluation of the arts-in-corrections program of the California Department of Corrections.* San Jose: San Jose State University.

California Department of Corrections (1987). *Research synopsis on parole outcomes for arts-in-corrections participants paroled December 1980-February 1987.* Sacramento: CDC

Day, E.S.,and Onorato,G.T. (1989). Making art in a jail setting. In H. Wadeson, J. Durkin and D. Perach (eds). *Advances in art therapy.* 126-147, New York: John Wiley and Sons

DeFord, M.A. (1962). *Stone walls: Prisons from fetters to furloughs.* Philadelphia, PA: Chilton Co. Book Division

Gibbs, J.J. (1987). Symptoms of psychopathology among jail prisoners: The effects of exposure to the jail environment. *Criminal Justice and Behavior, 14* (3), 288-310.

Morgan, C. (1981). Developing mental health services for local jails. *Criminal Justice and Behavior, 8* (3), 259-62

Morris, N. and Rothman, D. (Eds.) (1995). *The Oxford history of the prison: The practice of punishment in western society.* New York/Oxford: Oxford University Press.

Sullivan, L.E. (1990). *The prison reform movement: Forlorn hope.* Boston: Twayne Publishers

Weinstein, H. C., Hoover,J.O., Kagan, B., Metzner, J.L., Sadoff, R.L., and Zimmerman, V.H. (1989). Position statement on psychiatric services in jails and prisons. *The American Journal of Psychiatry, 146* (9), 1244

Part 1

PRESENTING THE DILEMMA

Breaking Through Barriers
Advantages of Art Therapy in Prison

David Gussak, MA, A.T.R.-BC

As a rule, therapists help lower an individual's protective barrier in order to rebuild a healthier ego. However, prison inmates build rigid defenses and put on 'masks' which ensure survival in the correctional subculture and maintain them to ensure their safety. Even nonverbal therapeutic techniques such as art therapy, valuable in reaching this difficult population, must be used differently than in the "outside" world.

Unlearning basic approaches of therapy applied in normal therapeutic environments is one of the most difficult tasks for clinicians in a prison environment. These fundamental approaches might influence their clients to behave in ways threatening to their actual survival in the penitentiary. What may be considered maladaptive defenses in the outside society are adaptive inside.

Most prison inmates are sociopathic individuals who, to varying degrees, will violate the rights of others for gain. Contrariwise, these people can be charming, especially when attempting to obtain something they desire. They are imprisoned because they cannot make it in a conventional social environment, where their behavior is not adaptive; in prison, their behavior is standard. If an inmate does not have well-developed psychopathic traits upon incarceration, he certainly will develop them. Even mentally ill inmates must adapt to the prison norm.

Inventing to Survive

Inmates must constantly be aware of their environment. How they are seen and what they say are always being evaluated by other prisoners. What may seem an innocuous disclosure on the outside may be used against an inmate inside. In the different strata within prison society, the level the inmate achieves may decide his chances for survival. For example, inmates learn not to reveal crimes of child molestation, or rape of a woman. So they invent more socially acceptable crimes appropriate for the sentence received. Arson or armed robbery, which may fit the given sentence, are considered more "legitimate."

Consequently, an inmate/patient learns that it is dangerous to trust others, including "prying" therapists. If a therapist tries to break through necessary barriers, the inmate/patient may become dangerous even if initially charming and cooperative. The inmate's defenses take over, making him anxious and angry, perhaps even violent, to a much greater extent in this setting than clinicians are accustomed to with the general population.

Adaptation To Prison Standards

Therefore, the best help therapists can give their clients is to promote adaptation to prison standards, not standards of the outside world. Although therapists may not understand what these prison norms are, they should trust the lead of the patient, and allow him to disclose what he feels safe expressing. Paramount in every clinician's mind should be that when a patient leaves a session or leaves the psychiatric hospital, he is going back to the general prison population. Therefore, treatment should focus on helping the inmate/patient increase the understanding of self while allowing necessary defenses and masks to remain intact.

Patients with acute psychiatric illnesses often do not have intact cognitive skills to adapt to norms during periods of decompensation. Therefore, even when treating a psychotic patient, the therapist should focus on helping the inmate/patient readapt to the prison norms.

Why Art Therapy?

Art therapy is invaluable for the prison population because it accesses concrete nonverbal responses no verbal therapy can reach. The process of art therapy employs tasks whose simplicity results in the expression of "...very complex material which would not be available for communication in any other form..." (Kramer, 1958 pp. 12-16).

Art therapy does not require that the inmate/patient know, admit or discuss what his artwork has disclosed. Since the environment is already so dangerous, any unintended disclosure of issues or insight can be quite threatening. Because people do not know how much they reveal when they draw their pictures, they don't defend against their revelations. The process of art bypasses even rigid defenses and dishonesty. Since the patient is unaware of his disclosures and is not compelled to discuss them, he is not left vulnerable.

However, these inadvertent disclosures, available to the trained art therapist, help guide the therapy so that the inmate/patient grapples with his problems on a valuable but unconscious level. As Florence Cane indicated, "...a great number of our normal problems are attributable to some inhibition which needs release through the arts. Fixations and fears buried in the unconscious are... brought up through fantasies, and when they are expressed in a person's art, they act as a cathartic, they are a cleanser" (1983, p. 304).

Art therapy takes advantage of creativity inherent in the prison society and to the inmates' intense need for diversion and escape. The process of art allows their minds to escape the monotony and boredom rife in prison. Using art materials permits the inmate/patient to express himself in a manner acceptable to both cultures, inside and outside. For example, if he were to express anger verbally, those around him would react adversely because they interpret the expression of anger as an assault. But since an "angry" work of art is not generally regarded as threatening, they can draw out their hostility and rage on paper, with little fear of retribution.

Art therapy is especially helpful in this environment, given the low levels of education and/or illiteracy, organicity, and other obstacles to verbal communication.

Case History: Mr. M

The following case study of Mr. M illustrates the advantages of the art therapy process. Here Mr. M, through his drawings, unconsciously dealt with his many unspoken fears on paper which he previously had not discussed and did not even discuss during the art therapy treatment. Some of the art was done with other art therapists at different times during his term. Looking at the following drawings, although by no means a complete and sequential collection of his artwork, one can see how the art therapy process dealt with his issues and helped Mr. M.

Mr. M was in art therapy treatment with me for approximately six weeks, primarily in individual sessions. Forty years old, obese and balding, he wore thick glasses, had a plate in his hip, and severe arthritis, which caused him to move slowly. A quiet man, he interacted little with peers, and disclosed limited information about himself.

Before being arrested, he was homeless. His history revealed that he had been sexually abused as a child, subjected to incest, and forced to have sex with visitors to his home. His records disclosed his incestuous relationship with his five stepbrothers and sisters and his sex with animals. He had an extensive drug history, starting with glue-sniffing at age 14. He said he had no intention of quitting drugs, because "...when I get out, that's how I want to end it."

His long criminal history started at age five, setting fires. Among his convictions were 2nd degree theft, battery on person and theft, burglary, and sex with minors, when he molested a girlfriend's daughter. He was married at one time.

His immediate crime was mayhem and second degree robbery. Apparently, when drinking with a fellow transient at a homeless campsite under a bridge, he passed out. He woke up when he was being forced to orally copulate his drinking companion. He beat the transient, robbed him of what he had, and cut off his penis.

Mr. M was admitted to the mental health unit in the prison after he made suicidal gestures. His history revealed 8-10 other attempts. Initially it was believed that he faked these suicidal gestures for secondary gain, i.e. single cell placement, a locked and safe unit, and access to medication. Despite this concern, he was given an Axis 1 diagnosis of Dysthymia, and an Axis II of Borderline-Antisocial Mixed (originally under the DSM III-R). During an initial intake interview, Mr. M stated that he considered himself "psychotic at times, but really just eccentric." He complained of feeling anxious, paranoid and "like I might as well be dead." During Mr. M's short stay on our unit, it remained unclear how much of Mr. M's psychological problems were a result of his excessive drug use and organicity.

In the prison where I work, art therapists are called rehabilitation therapists, and belong to a treatment team consisting of a psychiatrist, a psychologist, a social worker, a registered nurse, and medical technical assistants (correctional nurses). The treatment team recommended art therapy for Mr. M due to his inclination towards drawing, and his general unwillingness to talk with staff. The goals determined by the treatment team were to:

- demonstrate a decrease of depressive symptoms as evidenced by increased energy level. He was to attend and participate in 80% of scheduled groups and activities.
- demonstrate a decrease of depressive symptoms through verbal reports of feeling more hopeful.

DRAWING TIME

- discharge him to a less restrictive environment. In prison, this means back to the mainline (general population) or to another prison psychiatric unit.

Prior to this admission, he had been on other psychiatric units in the prison, and had taken part in art therapy. The art therapists from the other units gave me some of his previous art and valuable information on how to work with Mr. M. It was fairly easy to convince him to attend the sessions.

Individual Treatment

Although most of the inmate/patients received art therapy treatment in group settings, if the treatment team decides, and it can be justified, occasionally patients can be seen on an individual basis. Sometimes approval is difficult due to security issues, time and room constraints. The justification, in the form of a written protocol, has to be approved by a program-wide clinical committee. Since Mr. M had already seen art therapists on an individual basis, the treatment team decided that Mr. M should continue due to his unusual crime and his tendency not to take part in group activities. The justification was to:

- provide a safe and structured means for self-expression and learn to redirect emotional and aggressive expressions and communications.
- address depression and negative tendencies on an individual basis.
- allow the provider a better focus on the patient's issues, and allow the free flow of expression, through one-to-one sessions.

The written protocol was approved.

We were not completely alone during our sessions, as a medical technical assistant (correctional nurse) had to be present. Despite Mr. M's willingness to participate in the one-to-one sessions, we rarely talked about his art work. I never gave him a specific topic or subject to draw about. Unlike most of the other inmate-patients on the unit, he was not in need of prompts or guidelines to get started and responded well to the free drawing directive. The sessions were structured only in that there was a time allotment (45 minutes), and through the size of the paper. When asked direct questions about his work, he would comment on artistic quality, and his success in completing the images. We never discussed the pictures, except whether he liked them or not. I provided closure after every session by having him sign his art pieces, and talking of the possibility that he might be discharged before the next session.

The drawings illustrated are but a few of the many pieces he completed.

Several Discrepancies

Figure 1 is an image of a pickup truck in what appears to be a farmyard, done on an 8 x 10 inch white paper with a felt tip ink pen. Drawn with a wavering, yet distinct line quality, it shows intense concentration on detail. For example, in the open doorway of the barn, a ladder leading up to the loft is seen, the interior cab of the truck is clearly visible to the viewer, and there are distinct textural qualities given to each object and area. There is also an attempt to convey perspective. It is a rather impressive and well rendered image. However, despite this attention to detail, or because of it, several discrepancies can be noted. Figuring in the perspective of the drawing and the distance of the truck from the open gate, obviously, the truck is too big to fit through the open gate. Despite the complexity of the scene, and all the signs of life and living area, there are no people or livestock.

BREAKING THROUGH BARRIERS

In another ink drawing (figure 2), we see a house in an open area. The line quality is clearer, and again, Mr. M pays a great deal of attention to detail. There are no living beings, but there is a suggestion of a person's presence. The ax in the bottom left corner is in the process of being used to cut firewood. Curtains are on the windows in the house and a relatively healthy-looking plant hangs from the porch roof. Apparently, most of the focus is on the "fortification" of the house, with detailed drawing of nails reinforcing the planks on the outside of the house and emphasis and detail on drawing the overlapping shingles on the roof, and the rock foundation of the house.

According to Groth-Marnat, a house "...might be perceived as a symbol of the self... it might also represent the body... In addition, the home is usually the place where nurturing and a

Figure 1: pen and ink

Figure 2: pen and ink

sense of security occur..." (1990, p. 389). Despite reinforcements, the house does not seem well protected. Mr. M's house floats off the ground in what appears to be an open field, with the trees in the background providing an insufficient barrier. The rail fence started on the left of the house does not continue onto the other side, allowing easy access to the house.

These two drawings are similar in style and begin to give a clear picture of Mr. M. The first drawing reflects feelings of not belonging, of not fitting in. The truck is too big to have fit through the enclosure, and is unable to go back through the gate. Since no person is available to drive the truck through, the scene suggests a feeling of being trapped and/or abandoned. The lack of people or animals may reflect antisocial qualities or perhaps feelings of abandonment. The wavering and static pen strokes at first were believed to have been caused by organicity from medication or extensive drug use. However, as later drawings were completed with bolder line quality, the initial wavering quality was probably created by anxiety.

Figure 2 displays this bolder line quality. This drawing may also indicate issues of abandonment. Although there seems to be some evidence of people having been there, (the green plant, the freshly chopped wood), there are none now. It is as if 'they' just left. Helplessness and vulnerability emerge (as seen by the floating images, the incomplete fence and the lack of protection by the trees). Despite an attempt to create a safe environment, the reinforcements and constructed barriers are inadequate. They do not provide a sense of security.

Intense Focus on Neatness

I consulted with a social worker who specializes in sexual deviance in crimes. He said he had noted that those who commit sex-related crimes usually display a greater attention to detail and a intense focus on neatness. He believes it is a defense mechanism against committing such a 'dirty' crime, and preventing others from seeing that side of him (W. Fox, personal communication, September, 1994). Hence the remarkable focus on detail, with evidence of vulnerability, anxiety and abandonment.

Figure 3 demonstrates a different style which he had incorporated in his drawings many times before. Drawn in chalk pastels, the image shows a unidentifiable humanoid, without expression or sexual identity, looking into a blank mirror. There is no recognizable background or setting, just a horizon line separating the "ground" from the "sky." The figure is quite slender. Despite a potentially messy medium (Virshup, Riley and Shepherd, 1993, p. 430), the drawing is meticulous and orderly. Mr. M's willingness or ability to draw a person, albeit in a familiar schema, may reflect a greater comfort, either with the pastels or with me. However, for this medium, he still displays a great deal of control and neatness.

The androgynous figure, the lack of any recognizable expression and no reflection in the mirror suggest a poor self and sexual identity. The lack of a background may again reflect a loss of connection with his surroundings.

Figure 4 was drawn in the same style as figure 3. However, there is a hint of a face emerging. The large, blank eyes are reminiscent of what can be described as 'extraterrestrial' or characteristic of embryos. With the lack of background, the figure also conveys a sense of alienation. Given his artistic ability, it is clear in this picture that he paid scant attention to the detail of the body form, which was distorted. This could also reflect a poor self-image.

Figure 5 (see color plate 1) was also drawn in this style, using chalk pastel in a relatively

Figure 3: chalk pastel   *Figure 4: chalk pastel*

controlled manner. He drew thick black lines separating people in what was otherwise an image of a tight group, possibly descriptive of family enmeshment, or incestuous relations he experienced early in his life. The combination of enmeshment and reinforced boundaries can also be due to his antisocial and borderline personality traits. The figures remain expressionless, demonstrating perhaps again the problem with identity, or expression. The inability to communicate with others in an emotional or expressive manner is portrayed. Again, there is no background.

Mask-like Faces

When Mr. M drew portraits with recognizable features, as in figures 6 through 8, the faces were generally expressionless, almost mask-like. Despite the apparent intent, the faces do not appear human. The woman in figure 6 is presented as pale and long-faced, reminiscent of his earlier slim E.T.-like figures. Of all his images, this one seems to have the most expression. Figure 7 has its eyes closed, and the head floats; it does not sit on a neck or shoulders. It seems to be a mask.

Figure 8 was completed in a session with another art therapist, who gave the directive of using a "mandala," a Hindu word meaning 'magic circle' (Jung, 1964, p. 213). Mr. M was given the directive to create an image in a circle, which Jung believed was "...a symbol of the Self." (p. 240). He used oil pastels creating a head which appeared inhuman, with the features pressed

DRAWING TIME

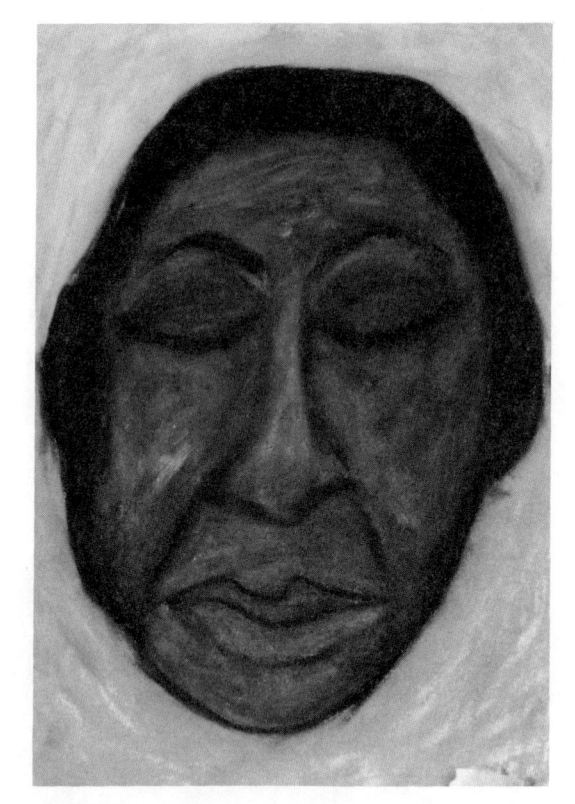

Figure 6: chalk pastel

Figure 7: chalk pastel

together forming a disturbing expression. Despite his apparent artistic skills, all three of these portraits appear to be caricatures of actual faces.

One lightly sketched drawing (not pictured), using a pencil, was of a strong, well-built man in a crouched position flexing his muscles, with a cleverly rendered "mask" of his own face for the head, indicating his ability to draw faces well. The image is floating on the page, with no ground line to support him.

Ten Hands

Figure 9 (see color plate 2) was completed in another art therapist's group on another unit. I have included it because it is his most disturbing piece, dramatically bringing together the themes suggested in his other works. It was done on a large sheet of paper, using chalk pastels. There are recognizable facial features, with an expression reminiscent of Munch's "The Scream," to which Mr. M made reference. The head is large compared to the "body." The only identifiable body features are ten hands, which emerge from the genital region. The image seems to portray internal anguish, and possibly reflects sexual dysfunction or deviance. This is suggested by the origin of the arms and hands which seem to be dragging the figure down, stifling him. Perhaps Mr. M was symbolically revealing the sexual abuse and rape that he had experienced as a child. His image certainly conveys powerful emotions clearly.

Discussion

BREAKING THROUGH BARRIERS

Mr. M was seen on an individual basis, contrary to the usual practice of working in a group. Despite this supposedly increased opportunity for safer disclosure, Mr. M did not discuss personal issues that could have put him at risk. However, Mr. M responded well to art therapy, dealing with his serious problems nonverbally.

What were the unique characteristics of art therapy that proved effective for Mr. M?

- Art therapy utilizes tasks whose simplicity result in the expression of "... very complex material which would not be available for communication in any other form..." (Kramer, 1958 pp. 12-16).

Using simple approaches and tasks with which Mr. M had experience, he revealed very complex issues, hidden by his bland, supposedly problem-free demeanor.

- Art therapy has the advantage of bypassing defenses, particularly rigid defenses, especially pervasive dishonesty.

Figure 8: chalk pastel

The art therapy bypassed Mr. M's defenses of denial, minimization, schizoid distancing and avoidance to deal with his issues of poor self-image, sexual identity confusion, feelings of inadequacy, and loss of connection to his surroundings—an alien quality. And, he did not have to lie or deny.

- Art therapy promotes inadvertent unconscious disclosure, even while the patient is not compelled to discuss therapeutic issues verbally, which might leave him vulnerable.

Mr. M was quite reluctant to disclose personal issues. Nevertheless, he produced clear concrete data about both his emotional problems and mitigation of them as he progressed through treatment.

- Art therapy does not require that the inmate/patient know, admit or discuss what he has disclosed. Since the environment is already so dangerous, any unintended disclosure of insight can be more threatening.

Mr. M's history make him a vulnerable target to those around him. His crimes and sexual deviance made him a potential victim to be killed in prison. Art therapy allowed the staff a better understanding of Mr. M while he expressed his fears and anxieties without having to talk. Using the art, he drew out his problems without realizing that he was actually revealing his issues.

9

- Art therapy takes advantage of the greater creativity inherent in the prison society, due to the intense need for diversion and escape.

Mr. M, already a talented artist, could take full advantage of the art therapy process. He was able to use his ability to create in an environmentally suffocating and uncreative place.

- Art therapy permits the inmate/patient to express himself in a manner acceptable to both cultures, inside and outside. For example, if he were to express anger, there would most likely be an adverse reaction from those around him who interpret the expression of anger as an assault. It allows the "blowing off of steam" in a productive manner.

Mr. M was admitted for dysthymia and repeated suicide attempts. Whenever he needed to release tension or express his anguish, he would turn it inward and harm himself through self-mutilation. His suicide attempts were viewed by those around him as weakness. His art allowed him to disclose his tension and anguish in a more reasonable and acceptable fashion.

- Especially important in the prison environment, art therapy can produce mitigation of symptoms without verbal interpretation.

By the time he was discharged from the unit, Mr. M had increased his interactions with others, and appeared brighter in affect. During the remaining stay on the unit, there were no further attempts at self-injury. He was able to be released to a less restrictive environment. He learned how to manipulate the talents he already had to develop and maintain new coping skills, and how to express himself in a more productive manner.

- Art therapy is especially helpful in this environment, given the severe disabilities of this population, such as low levels of education and/or illiteracy, organicity, and other obstacles to verbal communication

Despite manifold psychological and physiological difficulties Mr. M expressed himself relatively clearly and thoroughly through his art about the tragic burden he carried within.

Conclusion

As can be seen through Mr. M's case study, because of the inherent limitations of an institutional setting, it is not appropriate or necessary to "break through" prisoners' defenses, by trying to get them to reveal their many secrets. Rather, their art can do their talking. By talking through their art, they do not have to adapt to outside societal norms, and they don't have to make themselves vulnerable to their prison peers. When necessary, the art process allows them to express themselves and discharge much of their affect fearlessly and unselfconsciously.

Thus therapy can be given without destroying inmate/patients' defenses or succumbing to the limitations of the environment.

References

Cane, F. (1951, 1983). *The artist in each of us.* Craftsbury Common, VT.: Art Therapy Publications

Groth-Marnat, G. (1990). *Handbook of psychological assessment.* (2nd edition). New York: Wiley Interscience Publication

Jung, C.G. (1964). *Man and his symbols*. New York: Anchor Press/Doubleday
Kramer, E. (1958). *Art therapy in a children's community*. Springfield, Ill.: Charles C. Thomas
Virshup E., Riley S and Shepherd, D. (1993). The art of healing trauma: media, techniques and insights. In E. Virshup, (ed.) *California art therapy trends*. Chicago: Magnolia Street Publishers

Insider Art:
The Creative Ingenuity of the Incarcerated Artist

Will A. Ursprung, A.T.R.-BC, NCS

Prison art and art brut/outsider art converge in prison. The incarcerated artist's need to synthesize "new" artistic materials in response to a desolate, restrictive and often debilitating environment speaks to the wonders of creative expression and the resiliency of the human spirit against major odds.

The impetus behind this chapter evolved not so much from my clinical art therapy experience behind prison walls, but from an appreciation of the creative inventiveness I observed while curating inmate art exhibitions created by the general prison population for outside audiences. I was amazed at one venue to have five paintings sell before they were even hung on the wall! Experiencing this wholehearted acceptance reinforced within me my awareness of the expressive power of prison art, and the necessity to reveal its alchemy to the uninitiated.

> A man must create the world
> of which he is the center.
> This can be a masterwork:
> the painting of an artist,
> the piece of a cabinetmaker,
> the field of a peasant,
> the symphony of a composer,
> the page of a writer.
> It can be family.
> And when tragedy comes,
> as it will, we must take this
> suffering into our hands
> and, through willpower,
> transform it into a fruit
> that will nourish us
> as we begin life again.
> This is the fragile miracle
> hidden within us all.
>   (Martin Gray, 1975, pp. 271-3)

DRAWING TIME

The Setting

Thirty-one miles west of Philadelphia, PA, on seventeen hundred odd acres of rural farmland, the State Correctional Institution (SCI) at Graterford is surrounded by nine-sided, thirty-four foot high walls. These walls with nine gun towers, standing as sentinels evenly spaced, encompass sixty-two acres around the sixty-eight year old facility. Graterford was originally designed as a rural annex of the historic Eastern State Penitentiary of Philadelphia, built in 1829; the nation's first and prototype of the 'modern' penitentiary world-wide. When Eastern closed in 1970, Graterford received all transfers. Today, SCI-Graterford, the largest maximum security institution within the Pennsylvania Department of Corrections, (25 institutions, over 30,000 inmates) with a population of approximately 2,734, is the sixth largest maximum security prison in the United States.

Art Exhibitions

As a psychological services associate/clinical art therapist at the prison, I have attempted to nurture exhibition opportunities for a small cadre of inmate artists, (approximately 25) and we have had some successful shows. Most notable was an invitational exhibit at the American Correctional Association (ACA) Headquarters, in Laurel, Maryland, where SCI Graterford artists represented the State of Pennsylvania nationally. This show was very well received, with ACA staff enthusiastic about the talent they encountered.

Other highlights have been the inclusion of a large variety of works in the *Doing Time* exhibition at the Moore College of Art and Design's Levy Gallery in Philadelphia, an important regional exhibition that highlighted artworks created by inmate artists from several Pennsylvania state, local, and federal institutions within the last 150 years. Most recently, we had the good fortune to participate in the International Correctional Arts Network (ICAN) show held in conjunction with the American Correctional Association's '96 winter conference. Here again, Graterford artists represented the Commonwealth nationally, and in fact, internationally, as we shared exhibition space with the Prison Arts Foundation of Brantford, Ontario, representing all federal and provincial Canadian institutions.

In establishing venues for prison art shows, it helps to be connected in art circles such as regional art centers, art leagues, and other professional arts organizations (e.g.. National Artists Equity Association), as they may segue into possible leads. Area college and art school galleries often have an interest in exhibiting unusual works that are out of the mainstream, as do commercial galleries dedicated to "outsider" and primitive art.

Interestingly, retirement communities and nursing homes have been quite receptive to showing prison works, and often have exhibition spaces rivaling most in the public domain. Not only do these shows "liven up" such places psychologically, via prompting interaction of the residents with the art, but they also allow viewers to see the "human" side of the incarcerated artist, which is seldom experienced "outside the walls." Any exhibition opportunities are welcome, as they continuously bolster the inmate artist's self-esteem, allowing him to be valued as a person and as an artist.

To be successful in coordinating and curating such shows, one must be truly entrepreneurial in spirit, often working intuitively—exploring all possibilities—even "hunches." It is not uncommon to approach potential venues by way of what is termed in the business world as "cold calls." This is actually how a majority of opportunities have come to fruition.

Staging these exhibitions has had a positive effect, beyond the obvious impact on the inmate artists. Art shows generate "good press" for the prison, which, in these times of getting tough on crime and in corrections in general, is an unusual occurrence. It is important to break the barriers and stereotypes the general public has about the incarcerated individual in order to humanize an often inhumane environment. Another residual effect has been that prison employed staff carpenters have willingly donated their time and materials to construct frames for the successful presentation of artwork. This generosity has created a positive working environment, and is quite appreciated by the artists.

Despite a minimalist officially-sanctioned art program, inmate art graces the Superintendent's administrative corridor and many staff offices. Additionally, murals adorn the walls of the staff dining area, transforming the cold antiseptic environment.

Professionally, my civil service job classification is psychological services associate and entails wearing many hats aside from being a clinical art therapist. As a member of a psychology unit within a treatment department, I am responsible for providing group and individual psychotherapy and psycho-educational groups to the general population as well as assigned psychiatric cases. In this capacity, I also work with psychiatrists, correctional counselors, and correctional officers to realize the goal of care, custody, and control. I have held this position for five years.

As an art therapist, I consider it my sacred duty to nurture the creative and enhance the incarcerated person's quality of life via the transformative power of art. In my practice as an art therapist, I also subscribe to the philosophical duality in the field; that of the concept of art as therapy, where just involvement in the creative process is therapeutic, as well as the more clinical realm of art psychotherapy. Both have their place in prison, as in any other milieu.

My style of practice may fluctuate depending on the ego strength and level of functioning of a group or individual. Often, I employ what Kramer (1979) refers to as "precursory" activities for the lowest functioning inmates in my charge on the Special Needs Units. This type of "art in the service of defense" may include banal activities such as tracing, copying, and coloring pre-printed images. Individuals who have minimal experience in art enjoy the occupational activity.

Outsider Art/Art Brut

At this point, it is important to return to the premise of this chapter: when we support and coach the serious artist in prison, we help him to find solace and transform himself via the power of art.

Outsider Art, a term specifying the work of the artist "on the fringe" or the self-taught artist or auto-didact *outside* the mainstream art world, owes much to the vision of French painter Jean Dubuffet (1901-85) who coined the term "Art Brut," translated literally as *raw art* or *art in the raw*. Art Brut, as envisaged by Dubuffet, originally focused on such dissidents and nonconformists as psychiatric patients, eccentrics, recluses, and vagabonds, and is best exemplified in the Collection de l'Art Brut, Lausanne, Switzerland, a public museum which evolved from Dubuffet's personal collection spanning some 30 years.

Roger Cardinal, an international authority on the topic of Art Brut, and credited with the

DRAWING TIME

anglicized term, Outsider Art, in his landmark book of the same name (1972), defined these artists as "innocent of pictorial influences and perfectly untutored." As these artists are unencumbered by prior notions of what art is "supposed to be," much of the genre's vitality surrounds its honesty and naiveté.

Outsider artists are also known for their need to create, often appearing somewhat obsessional about their self expression, some remarkably prolific. One of the best illustrations of this phenomenon is Adolf Wolfli (1864-1930) who, throughout his thirty-odd years confined to a Swiss asylum, created thousands of intricate drawings (Cardinal 1979). Upon his death, a pile of drawings and writings over six feet high were recovered from his cell.

Derived from an irrepressible creative impulse, Outsider Art demonstrates that creativity means nothing less than getting in touch with what is most individual within oneself, with each work its own precedent.

Dubuffet stated:

> "We mean by 'raw art' the works executed by people untouched by artistic tradition—contrary to what occurs among intellectuals—so that their makers derive everything (subjects, choice of materials used, means of transposition, rhythms, ways of patterning, etc.) from their own resources and not from the conventions of classic art or the art that happens to be fashionable. Here we find art at its purest and crudest; we see it being wholly invented at every stage of the operation of its maker, acting entirely on his own," (MacGregor 1989, p.21).

John MacGregor (1989) qualified Dubuffet's rejection of established cultural values as understandable in an artist who, having witnessed the "rationality" of an insane world, sought the essential humanity that was found in the images of those who had turned their backs on the "real world" or who had never known it.

According to Cardinal (1979),

> "The lesson of Outsider art is that what is most uniquely personal to the individual can, if it is expressed without inhibition, be communicated to other individuals. These are works about intense experience which, if we are receptive, we will recognize as our own. The manner of expression may be abstruse, but the meaning is available if we try. We should not shy away from what these works are saying—no more than we should shun the expression of our own secret desires and dreams," (p.23).

Outsider Art/Art Brut has of late, come of age, realizing Dubuffet's belief in the power of raw expression. No longer hidden in obscurity, many mainstream galleries now represent Outsider artists, often commanding, and attaining high price tags. In addition, there are galleries specializing in Outsider Art, and a few in particular showcasing prison artists.

Also notable is the American Visionary Art Museum (AVAM) in Baltimore's Inner Harbor, which in 1992 was designated by unanimous vote of the U.S. Congress as America's official "national museum, repository and education center for the best in original, self-taught artistry."

The genre also boasts an annual art fair, The Outsider Art Fair, a three day event held in the Puck Building, New York City, where 35 galleries/exhibitors hawked their wares. Last year's fair yielded an excess of $1.5 million in sales.

Another indication of Art Brut's arrival is the London-based, *Raw Vision: The International Journal of Intuitive and Visionary Art*, a slick, glossy quarterly magazine published by editor John Maizels, who recently published a definitive text on the subject, *Raw Creation, Outsider Art and Beyond*, (1996).

Probably the most innovative evolution of Outsider art is the plethora of category-related websites on the Internet, where one can actively search for a specific artist's work or download articles germane to the phenomenon.

According to Lynn Bailey, a gallery director and collector, Saul Scalora, Assistant Professor of Art at the University of Connecticut, Kornfeld (1995), and Swislow (1993), the genre of "prison art" has a great affinity to the phenomenon of Outsider Art/Art Brut, naive art, folk art, etc.—the predominant commonalities being the essence of the self-taught idiom and a utilization of unorthodox materials, along with the necessity to create. References to being "outside" the mainstream, and creating in isolation are obvious.

> "The creative spirit is a wild bird that will not sing in captivity," (Van Dearing Perrine, 1936, p. 81).

Nothing can be more preposterous than the preceding quote. In prison as on the outside, creating is a basic human need, and nowhere is the urgency more evident than in prison. The incarceration experience, one of sensory deprivation, is a world of imposed controls, rigid regulations, tedium, minimum allowable risk, and consistent inconsistencies. It appears that the creative process (art-making) is a apt coping mechanism in order to survive such an oppressive dysfunctional milieu, especially to derive some sense of order out of the chaos.

According to Nachmanovitch, (1990):

> "There is nothing that can stop the creative...we have seen again and again how immense can be the power of limits, the power of circumstance, the power of life's pull in generating original breakthroughs of mind and heart, spirit and matter," (p.196).
> "...human imagination and feeling cannot be imprisoned..." (Lloyd, 1993, insert).

Kornfeld states:

> "Prison is a powerful place to work. It is a field of suppressed creative energy waiting to explode," (McDonald, 1991-2, p.8).
> "You cannot be human, and not be creative," (Cameron, 1993, cassette recording).

Silvano Arieti (1972) speaks of creativity as the supreme achievement of individuality which transcends the usual ways of dealing with the world and brings about a desirable enlargement of the human experience. Peter Breggin (1980) sees creativity as involving the full play of personal sovereignty and personal freedom; it is that area of life in which the individual as a self is most fully explored and expressed.

Likened to both free will and courage to which it is closely linked, creativity often seems to rise up in response to the most oppressive conditions, existing in opposition to self oppression. Adversity and turmoil throughout history have spawned many creative responses, enabling the human quality of hope to be undaunted. In times of repression, such as Restoration England, the Nazi Holocaust, Stalinist Russia and the Spanish Civil War, to name a few, history has repeatedly shown us that, despite the horrors of war, the inequity of prejudice, discrimination and oppression, creativity will not be stifled. Like a rose erupting from barren rocky soil, the human spirit triumphs to create beauty in despair.

Insider Art

Historically, the genre of Prison Art is probably as old as the prison itself. As prison is a microcosm of society, and society or culture cannot exist without art (culture's reflection), art is inevitable in prison. Recent archaeological excavation of Eastern State Penitentiary (1829-1970) has yielded early artifacts of inmate handicraft, specifically wooden toys, figurines and gaming pieces. Eastern State inmates were renowned in the neighborhood for their craftsmanship in fine woodworking, and would often refurbish castoff furniture and the like, for a nominal fee. Model ship-making was another popular pursuit to while away the time. In figure 1 (see color plate 4) (an example of work done at Eastern), an intricately carved match stick depicts the figure of William Penn atop Philadelphia's City Hall (circa 1965, artist unknown). It is an amazing piece of work, considering the painstaking detail—and is almost inconceivable in terms of labor intensiveness, and required patience!

For a number of reasons, unfortunately, art is difficult to create in prison. In most cases, basic or traditional art materials are not available in any quantity. Largely restricted in the name of institutional security, the most fundamental materials enjoyed by children "on the outside" are deemed taboo. For example, clay is considered "contraband" as it can make impressions of a lock, and be molded to make a key, or in an act of defiance, can render a lock unusable. Obviously taboo are scissors and other "sharps." Even long handled paintbrushes are forbidden. Although such restrictions can be annoying and frustrating, inhibiting the creative process, they are necessary. It is important that I never forget where I work—a maximum security prison—and security comes first.

The Pennsylvania Department of Corrections Administrative Directive 801 defines *contraband* as:

> "...possession of money, implements of escape, unprescribed drugs, or drugs that are prescribed, but the inmate is not authorized to possess, drug paraphernalia, poisons, intoxicants, materials used for fermentation, property of another, weapons, or other items which in the hands of an inmate present a threat to self, others, or to the security of the Institution."

The directive also specifies that contraband can be created by the altering of sanctioned materials from their original form or use (a potential infraction or misconduct for the inmate artist).

Other limitations are often financial. Although some rudimentary supplies (when scrutinized and sanctioned by the Activities Manager) are available in the prison commissary or ordered through an approved vendor catalog, most inmates cannot afford them. One of the more serious inmate artists, a lifer, and former graffiti writer, when queried on his process, said:

> "My works are derived from whatever resources are available. Financially, sometimes you can swing it; sometimes you can't. The objects and materials at many times are found or given. Certain denials and restrictions of traditional materials by the

INSIDER ART

Institution only compels one to be more creative and resourceful, wherefore overall works become more genuine and original in context. Creating for me serves to nurture strength of spirit."

As artists do on the outside, inmate artists often scavenge the institutional landscape to ferret out *found objects*, castoffs or any materials that may be incorporated into works of art. Much like the 'ready-mades' of Duchamp, or the "combine" painting/assemblage of Rauschenberg, this aesthetic of employing the "ordinary" object in the transformation into an object of art is truly alchemy. It is interesting to note that in the study of Greek myth, Hermes, the god of transformation, alchemy, and magic, was also the god of thieves and criminals.

In figure 2 (see color plate 3), *The Man in the Wall*, the artist uses a popular and readily accessible prison medium—a blend of Ivory bar soap (from the commissary), and State-issued toilet paper. When mixed with water and combined in the right consistency, this melange forms a modeling paste that can be molded like clay, and when dried, easily painted. He incorporates found objects including a broken radio antennae and string.

Often depersonalized, a prisoner may feel as if he is just a part of the surrounding landscape, or an article of State "property." The simulated prison "bars" of the antennae and barbed wire (string) further imply "prisonization." Obviously preoccupied with his incarceration, his work speaks to his alienated feelings.

Figure 3 (see color plate 5), by the same artist, again employing the same media, gives us more commentary on the banalities of prison life. This work, a parody on the "don't drop the soap" myth is about ego-dystonic homosexuality in prison.

Figure 4, entitled *Butterfly*, is a reference to "caged" freedom and transformation, (as caterpillar to butterfly/convicted felon to good citizen). Again, the artist puts into service found discards—wood scraps from the wood shop, old bits of telephone cable wire, and other items.

In figure 5, *Grandma and Grandpa Kettle*, the artist takes a novel approach compared to what we have seen thus far. Figurine heads, crafted from apples reserved from meals, were dried in his cell on a radiator.

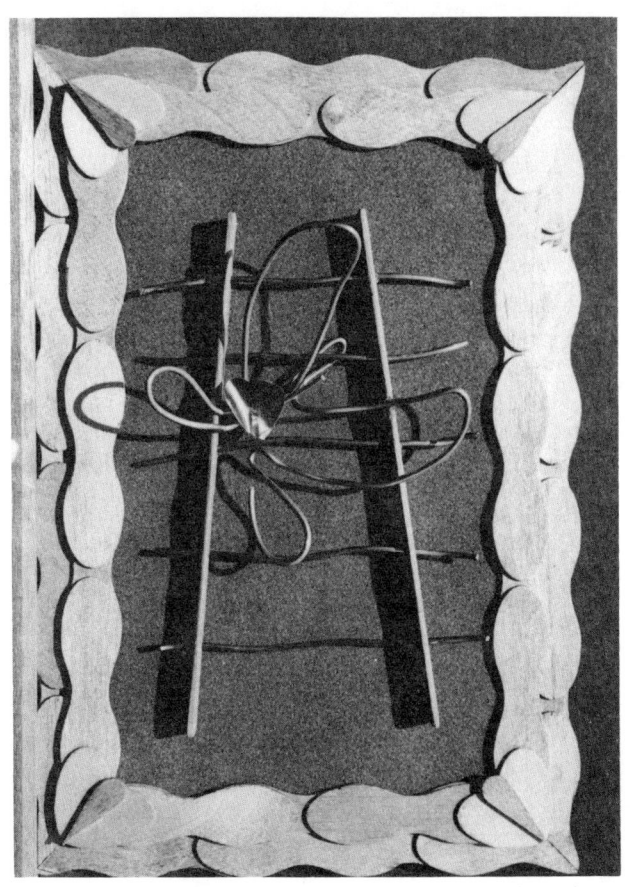

Figure 4: "Butterfly" Albert W. (1994) found objects, courtesy Ironhouse Inspirations, Clearfield, PA

DRAWING TIME

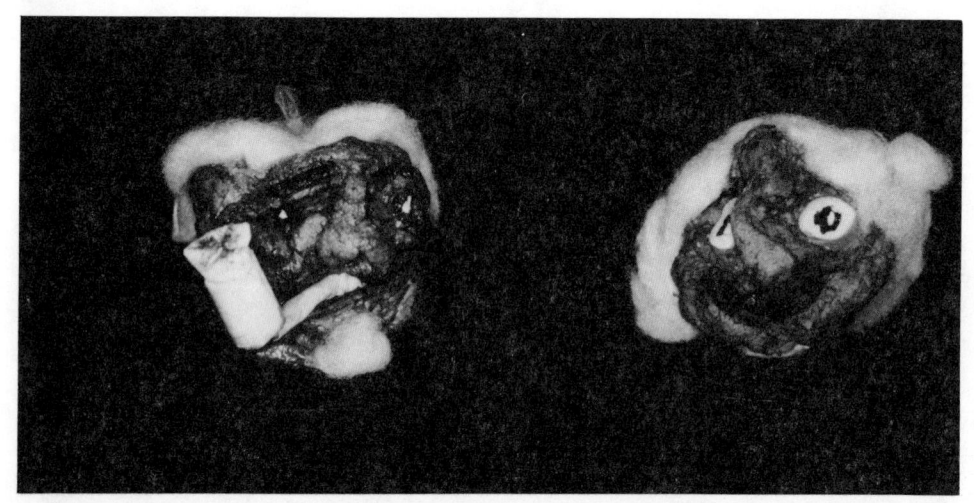

Figure 5: "Grandma and Grandpa Kettle" Robert Z. (1994) dried apples, cotton, acrylic and found objects

Cotton was used to simulate hair and beard, and an antenna fragment was fashioned into a pipe. The work was finished with an application of acrylic paint. This artist did not share much in terms of associations, but I learned that his father was a merchant seaman, which the male figure suggests.

Figure 6 represents another very popular technique/medium—dried and pressed flora—and combines an equally popular art form in prison—the "forget-me-not" card. Through the extensive horticulture/gardening program at SCI-Graterford, the men having the opportunity to work with the soil grow a wide variety of flowers and vegetables. Varicolored flower petals offer a different type of palette to work from—again, somewhat readily accessible materials for those sensitive to the beauty of nature in such a foreboding environment. Other manifestations of this appreciation are seen in works incorporating butterfly wings and the occasional found feather.

The last image, figure 7, a mixed media construction of found objects entitled *Untelevised*, is another work of the former graffiti writer. The artist writes:

"The piece (sculpture) was created after I completed my fourth year of imprisonment, the idea deriving from thoughts of how TV has played a part in our lives. The television is one of the biggest sources of information for many. Much is told about the world through

Figure 6: untitled card, James M. (1995) dried and pressed flowers

20

INSIDER ART

TV, but what is really told or really known about this world—the locked-down, dark one? Anything media-ized about prison is usually focused on violence, escapes, or how they're going to build more of these human warehouses. There's far more to be conceived than just this negativity: the educated, the talented, the kind and humble, and also the innocent are stored unseen, unheard. Let the 'Untelevised' tell a vision."

Straw Into Gold

In pursuing the literature during the research phase of my investigation, I was amazed at the myriad resources that inmates have available to use in their art making. The following is a partial listing at best: lye soap, foil potato chip bags, cloth scrap, cotton, socks, toilet paper, human hair, hickory nuts, Kool-aid and M&M candy sugar coating for pigment, cigarette wrappers, fast food containers, flowers, feathers, dried fruit, wood scraps, wooden match sticks, toothpicks, and magazines. Whatever a prisoner with a vision and a will to create needs, he can find.

The incarcerated artist has developed his own aesthetic, his own artistic language, in order to survive, to express the self, to be human. Here art making becomes a safe place to break the rules legally, a place where one can be in control when all other control has been relinquished.

Art is a commodity in prison as elsewhere, and can command any tender in return. In a prison economy, this usually translates into "packs" of cigarettes, but may include any desirable object or service. Inmates often barter their original artworks—be it cards, t-shirts, paintings, etc. for cigarettes, commissary food and toiletries, favors, etc.—whatever the market will bear.

On the more legitimate side, inmates are permitted to sell their art to staff for a nominal price that they set prior to sale. The proceeds usually are recycled back into the inmate's financial account in order to restore art supplies via approved vendor catalog orders. The more accomplished serious artists have made substantial sums selling their works to correctional officers, nurses, psychiatrists, and others. This commerce has had a positive effect on all parties involved and the institution at large. Here again, we see art as the catalyst for *humanizing* a dehumanizing environment. To personally experience the product of one's creative process appears to dispel preconceived notions and prejudice about who the inmates are, and often breaks down barriers. Such relationships, as mentioned above, may also nurture trust and as a result, encourage therapeutic alliances.

Figure 7: "Untelevised", SPEL (1994) mixed media and found objects

Conclusion

In this chapter, I have made a correlation between the genre of Outsider Art/Art Brut and Prison Art (Insider Art). The commonalities are the nature of the self-taught idiom, being removed from the mainstream art world, the necessity to create, and paramount to this writing, the use of unorthodox materials as artistic media.

The creative process of art making in prison as a coping mechanism is an important focus, as is the creative inventiveness of the inmate artist to overcome rigidly imposed limitations and restrictions of available art materials. The alchemy of the incarcerated artist, his ability to create something of beauty and value out of nothing (or objects of ordinary status), is truly remarkable. Pure self expression in art can credibly be created by those who are self taught, and is essential to the incarcerated.

References

Allen, H.E. & Simonsen, C.E. (1986). *Corrections in America: An introduction.* New York: MacMillan Publishing Company.
Allen, P.B. (1995). *Art as a way of knowing.* Boston: Shambhala Publications, Inc.
Allen, V. (1968). *Jean Dubuffet, drawings.* New York: The Museum of Modern Art.
Arieti, S. (1972). *The will to be human.* New York: Dell Publishing Company.
Arieti, S. (1976). *Creativity: The magic synthesis.* New York: Basic Books.
American Correctional Association (1978). *Arts in corrections: A summary of project culture: Handbook for program implementation* Laurel, MD: American Corectional Assoc.
Baroody-Hart, C. & Farrell, M. P. (1987) The subculture of serious artists in a maximum security prison. *Urban Life, 15,* 3-4.
Best, H. (1996). Going inside outside. *Art Matters,* May, 22-23.
Breggin, P. R. (1980). *The psychology of freedom.* Buffalo, NY: Prometheus Books
Cameron, J. (1992). *The artist's way: A spiritual path to higher creativity.* New York: Jeremy P. Tarcher/Putnam.
Cameron, J. (1993). *Meeting your creative myths and monsters.* (Cassette Recording No. 8230). Boulder, CO: Sound Time Recordings.
Cardinal, R. (1979). *Outsiders: Exhibition catalog.* London: Hayward Gallery/British Arts Council.
Carraher, R. G. (1970). *Artists in spite of art: A compendium of naive, primitive, vernacular, anonymous, spontaneous, popular, grassroots, folk, serv-ur-self art.* New York: Van Nostrond Reinhold, Co.
Chadwick, S. (1989, Dec. 16). Art Critique: Promising prison artist recommended for parole, *The Houston Post,* C4.
Cleveland, W. (1992). *Art in other places: Artists at work in Americas community and social institutions,* Westport, CT: Praeger.
Coburn, M. F. (1995). Insider art. *Chicago Magazine, 44,* 41-44.
Cohen, S.and Taylor, L. (1974). *Psychological survival: The experience of longterm imprisonment.* New York: Vintage Books.
Coleman, M. (1993). Fostering art behind bars. *New Haven Arts: the Arts Council of Greater New Haven,* 6, (9) 1.
Colman, D. (1995). Jailhouse art. *Vogue,* (Sept.) 374.
Congdon, K. F. (1984). Art education in a jail setting. *Art Education, 37,* 2.
Connor, S. M.(1995). Inspired in prison. *Correctional Arts Journal of the Connecticut Prison Association.* (Annual Publication), 1-8.
Courtney, J. and Gilens, T. (1995). *Prison sentences: The Prison as site/subject.* Philadelphia, PA: Moore College of Art and Design.

Day, E. S. and Onoratio, G. T. (1989). Making art in a jail setting. in H. Wadeson, J. Durkin and D. Perach (Eds), *Advances in Art Therapy.* New York: John Wiley.

Dewey, J. (1980). *Art as experience.* New York: G. P. Putnam & Sons.

Eisenhower, L. (1995). Art therapy with criminals, doing time, recidivism and sublimation. *Lecture in conjunction with the exhibit: Doing time,* Moore College of Art, October 18, 1995.

Ehrenzweig, A. (1967). *The hidden order of art: A study in the psychology of artistic imagination.* Los Angeles: University of California Press.

Finio, P. and Jackson, H. (1994). Women and children first! Emergency art from behind bars. *Exhibition Catalog, Esther M. Klein Gallery/ University City Science Center, January 19-March 31,* Philadelphia, PA: Pennsylvania Prison Society.

Fitzpatrick, J. (1995, July 2). Art in the cellblock, with futures in mind. *New York Times.*

Gardner, J. (1993). *Culture or trash?.* New York: Carol Publishing Group.

Goffman, E. (1961). *Asylums.* New York: Doubleday/Dell Publishing Group, Inc.

Goleman, D., Kaufman, P. and Ray, M. (1992). *The creative spirit.* New York: Penguin Books.

Grace, N. (1993). Arts related activities in prisons. *Convergence,* 26 , (3), 65-71.

Gray, M. (1975). *A book of life:To find happiness, courage and hope.* London: Seabury Press.

Johnston, N.; Finkel, K. and Cohen, J. A. (1994) *Eastern state penitentiary: Crucible of good intentions.* Philadelphia, PA: Philadelphia Museum of Art.

Kornfeld, P. (1995). Is this Outsider art or artists inside? *Art & Antiques,* 18, 20.

Kramer, E. (1979). *Childhood and art therapy, notes on theory and application.* New York: Schocken Books.

Kris, E. (1971). *Psychoanalytic explorations in art.* New York: Schocken Books.

Laing, J. (1984). Art therapy in prisons, in T. Dalley (ed.) *Art as therapy.* (pp. 141-156). London: Tavistock Publications.

Langer, S. K. (1980). *Philosophy in a new key: A study in the symbolism of reason, rite, and art.* Cambridge, MA: Harvard University Press.

Lasch, C. (1984). *The minimal self: Psychic survival in troubled times.* New York: W.W. Norton & Co.

Levy, B. (1978). Art therapy in a women's correctional facility. *The Arts in Psychotherapy,* 5, (3). 157-166.

Liebmann M. (ed.). (1994). *Art therapy with offenders.* London: Jessica Kingsley Publishers.

Lloyd, D. (1993). Inside out: Art Exhibition statement. *Connecticut Prison Association Journal of the Correctional Arts Program. (Annual Report),* insert.

London, P. (1989). *No more secondhand art, Awakening the artist within.* Boston, MA: Shambala Publication.

Lorch, D. (1996, July 28). Survival found at the tip of a paintbrush. *New York Times.* 25-6.

Maizels, J. (1996). *Raw creation: Outsider art and beyond.* London: Phaidon Press, Ltd.

May, R. (1975). *The courage to create.* New York: Bantam Books, Inc.

McConnel, P. (1994). *Guidebook for artists working in prisons. Arts in Education, Salt Lake City, Utah.* Flagstaff, AZ: Logoria.

McDonald, P. (1991-2). Flower and I. *Connecticut Prison Association Journal of the Correctional Arts Program. (Annual Report),* 8.

Morris, N. and Rothman, D. (Eds.) (1985). *The Oxford history of the prison: The practice of punishment in western society.* New York: Oxford University Press.

Nachmanovitch, S. (1990). *Free play: Improvisation in life and art.* Los Angeles, CA: Jeremy P. Tarcher, Inc.

Perrine, V. D. (1936). *Let the child draw, an experiment in culture building.* New York: Frederick A Stokes Co.

Quanne, M.(1985). *Prison paintings.* London: Joan Murray.

Read, H. (1969). *Art and alienation: The role of the artist in society.* New York: Viking Press.

Reid, W. H.; Dorr, D.; Walker, J. I. and Bonner, J. W., (Eds.) (1986). *Unmasking the psychopath: Antisocial personality and related syndromes.* New York: W.W. Norton and Co.

Riches, C. (1991). *There is still life: A study of art in a prison.* Unpublished M.A. Thesis. London Royal College of Art.

Rivenburg, R. (1994, Dec.7). Inmates discover prison sells. *Los Angeles Times,* E1C2.

Robbins, A. (1987). *The artist as therapist.* New York: Human Science Press, Inc.

Romig, M. B. (1994). Bars and stripes forever (prison art program in New Orleans, LA) *New Orleans Magazine, 29*, 34.

Samenow, S. (1984). *Inside the criminal mind.* New York: Times Books.

Scarborough, J. (1984). When prison is home: Challenging the creative spirit. *Fiberarts. 11*, 69-71.

Schoonover, B. (1986). The Captive audience. *Art Education, 39*, (3), 33-5.

Selz, P. (1962). *The work of Jean Dubuffet.* New York: Museum of Modern Art.

Skelly, T. (1992). On the yard: Prison art connects with the outside. *High Performance, 15*, 32-5.

Storr, A. (1976). *The dynamics of creation.* Baltimore, MD: Penguin Books

Swislow, W. (1993). From the inside out, Stateville prison artists, *Intuit, 2*, (1), 116-117.

Szekely, G. (1982). Art education in correctional settings. *Journal of offender counseling services and rehabilitation, 4*, 5-28.

Trantino, T. (1974). *Lock the lock.* New York: Albert A. Knoph, Publ.

Tuchman, M. and Eliel, C. S. (1992). *Parallel visions: Modern artists and outsider art.* Princeton, NJ: Princeton University Press.

Tully, J. (1996). Outside, inside, or somewhere in between. *Art News, 95*, (5) 118-121.

Creativity & Incarceration:
The Purpose of Art in a Prison Culture

Nancy Hall, A.T.R.-BC, CRC

I learned, on my first day of working in prison, that art and art making are as essential to the culture in a prison community as they are in any other community. All inhabitants of a prison, both staff and inmates, take part in assuring that the arts flourish in this most arid of places. As an art therapist, I have deeply rooted convictions regarding our species' inherent need to create and embellish. I certainly did not envision this need diminishing with incarceration. In fact, I imagined that the need must increase for individuals whose days are filled with conflict, fear, rage, and endless rumination on guilt and loss.

However, I had thought that the prison environment would be so oppressive as to stifle creativity and humanity in those who fell under its influence. I underestimated the capacity of the human spirit to find expression, even in the most adverse circumstances. I had also overestimated the power of the gray walls and gun turrets. Prisons are man-made institutions and, like most human creations, they live and breathe in a state of tension between chaos and order.

In the best of circumstances, tension may dissolve, leaving balance and harmony in its place. The need to establish harmony, if only to afford respite from tension, is as fundamental a human need as the need to create. The two are intertwined. It may be that in a prison environment, where order is imposed with such a heavy hand, an equally generous dose of chaos is needed for harmony to have a chance. This commodity is generally in good supply among prison inmates who are not, as a group, noted for self control.

Inherent in the creative process is the opportunity to seize chaos and mold its forces, often very gently, into a kind of order which is easier to bear than rules and discipline. This process may, in turn, render the inescapable trappings of a highly ordered society more easily tolerated by those of an unusually chaotic nature. The products of creativity, even those born of chaos, meet with acceptance in most cultures and the prison culture is no exception. I think that this is the key to understanding the role of the arts in prison. It serves as a middle ground in which chaos may meet order in a kind of harmony which is pleasing and satisfying to everyone.

Every state harbors a maximum security prison of legendary stature. Feared by those likely to

DRAWING TIME

find themselves in their confines, these places are harsher and less forgiving in their enforcement of prison rules and swifter in punishment than ordinary prisons. They are also more spartan, often lacking small amenities which can make incarceration tolerable.

A transfer to one of these facilities is regarded as punishment for inmates who have not adjusted well to incarceration. They are the last stop on the line for the incorrigible, the unrepentant, and the defiant. Those who find themselves in these places will face a long, upward struggle if they are to earn transfer to a more hospitable prison. There are many who never leave.

For five years, I worked in my state's most notorious maximum security prison. My appointment was with a small mental health unit providing therapeutic services to mentally ill inmates at the prison. The mental health unit was operated by the state's Office of Mental Health, with support from the Department of Corrections. It was part of a statewide system of similar programs, each housed within a maximum security prison. Administrative offices were headquartered at a secure psychiatric hospital 300 miles from the prison.

Outpatient Service

Of the several sections of this unit, the largest was an "outpatient" service which provided counseling and medication for the more stable among the inmates seeking mental health services. These included a group housed at a modern, medium security prison adjacent to the "old jail." Outpatient staff were also responsible for outreach and crisis intervention at both the maximum and medium security prisons.

The outpatient program included a small crisis unit for inmates who had become psychotic and too disruptive to remain in the general prison population. Outpatient staff were responsible for assessing inmates in the general population and arranging transfer either to the unit's dorm or to one of three cells reserved for those who had lost all control. These cells were also reserved for inmates on suicide watch and for housing of psychotic inmates transferred from nearby medium and minimum security prisons. A ten cell annex to this unit was located in the disciplinary section of the prison known as "the Box." Those inmates who did not stabilize while in the crisis unit were transferred to the secure hospital.

I was assigned to another component of the mental health unit housing the most severely mentally ill of the inmates in prison. Located in one of the prison's five cell blocks, it occupied two 39 cell galleries. The galleries were in the highest level of a three tier section of the block and our offices were located in a crossover connecting two sections. With school and workshop staff located in isolated program areas, we were the only "civilian" staff in the blocks.

I approached my new work site with a mixture of curiosity and apprehension, with no idea of what to expect. My new supervisor guided me around the galleries and introduced me to the men with whom I would be working.

The Mentally Ill in Prison

I learned, first, that serious mental illness does not necessarily protect an individual from incarceration. Most of these inmates were diagnosed with schizophrenia, endogenous depression, or bipolar disorder. Many had not taken medication in years and were floridly psychotic. The most severely ill were barely able to keep themselves clean, dressed, and adequately fed.

Most had been hospitalized for mental illness at least once. Some had spent most of their lives in psychiatric hospitals, only to be discharged when de-institutionalization became the vogue. Most had been psychotic and functioning marginally at the time of arrest. With few exceptions, their crimes were numerous but petty. Panhandling, jumping subway turnstiles, and failure to pay for cab rides or restaurant meals were common crimes. There was a small minority among this group who had committed bizarre and violent crimes, often in response to command hallucinations.

Drug-related crimes, which were also common, seemed to involve street level sale. In most cases, these people were recruited by dealers to deliver drugs to buyers on the street. They were considered desperate, vulnerable, easily manipulated, and expendable. They could generally be trusted to keep their mouths shut when arrested and they were easy to replace.

These men had been placed in a maximum security prison not because of the nature of their crimes, but because they were mentally ill. In this particular system, only the most secure prisons were equipped to accommodate people whose behavior might be erratic and unpredictable. Although preservation of order may have been the prime consideration in the enactment of this policy, it also served to protect this group of inmates from predators. Tucked away in their private cells, they were far safer in this secure environment than in the open dormitories of the medium security prisons.

Inmates were chosen for the unit through a screening process which involved review of psychiatric history and interview with a screening team composed of representatives from mental health, prison counseling, and security staff. Referrals could be made from almost any source including outpatient mental health staff, prison staff, self referral, or family request. Some of our more interesting and suitable referrals were made by inmates who had observed peculiar behavior on the part of an individual housed in a nearby cell.

Among the criteria for admission were history of psychiatric treatment or other evidence of major psychiatric disorder, inability to manage in the general prison population, and willingness to work with program staff toward developing and attaining goals. Preference was given to those who were actively but quietly psychotic, institutionalized, or victim prone. The unit also admitted individuals whose personality disorders were so severe as to interfere with day to day activities. Most often, these were men with borderline personality disorder who engaged in frequent self mutilation.

My foremost responsibility was to provide the equivalent of case management services to approximately thirty of these men. I also designed an art therapy program for the unit. All staff, regardless of professional background, functioned as primary therapists and each of us was asked to offer additional programs or groups according to our interests or expertise. Our psychologist led a bi-weekly current events discussion and a group for inmates affected by post traumatic stress disorder; a social worker supervised the unit and provided group therapy; our corrections counselor worked with an inmate peer counselor to offer counseling for sex offenders; and I had my art therapy groups.

After several years, I transferred to the "outpatient" unit where I worked with more functional inmates. They sought counseling to help with a range of issues including adjustment to incarceration, dealing with grief and loss, guilt arising from their crimes, and changing maladaptive behavior. My work also took me out into the cellblocks and "the Box" as all of the mental health staff took turns responding to calls from security staff for assistance with general population inmates who had become psychotic or suicidal. This experience gave me the opportunity to work with some of the more typical inmates. As a group, they were more emotionally damaged, self absorbed, and antisocial than the inmates in the segregated mental health program.

The Function Of Art In Prison

I began learning about the role of art in the prison culture while on that first tour of my new unit. Before I had taken my first step onto the gallery, several employees advised me to speak with a particular inmate—an artist who had been excited to hear that the unit would have an art therapist on staff. When I stopped at this man's cell, I saw that it was filled with tiny, delicate models of machines, vehicles, and jail cells. With obvious pride, he showed me his most recent piece—a helicopter constructed with strips of cardboard, wire, glue, broom straws, and toothpaste. Materials were donated by other inmates and staff who saved boxes, matchbooks, toilet paper tubes, toothpicks, writing tablets, bits of glue, and left over paint-by-number paints for him to use in his projects. His next project was to be a scale model of the U.S. Capitol.

He was not the only artist on the unit. Almost everyone had drawings or paintings posted in their cells. Some had been purchased from other inmates for cigarettes and coffee, but most had been created by the occupants of the cells in which they were displayed. Many of the drawings were stereotypical, with several distinct themes representative of a kind of prison iconography. Their common themes were oppression, rage, and defiance. One favorite image I thought of as "the double bird" consisted of two shackled hands, side by side, with both middle fingers raised in obscene salutes. The letters FTW (Fuck The World), were often inscribed somewhere in the drawing and the more elaborate renditions were wreathed in roses and thorns.

Over five years, my travels took me to virtually every corner of the prison. Wherever I went, I found evidence of people making art. The following is what I saw and learned of the purpose of art in the prison culture.

Formal Art Therapy

Only one other prison, at the time, was offering art therapy through its mental health unit. The therapist, an exhibiting artist, had been hired to work as a recreation therapist for the only women's maximum security prison in the state.

Art therapy was introduced into the prison by accident. I was not hired as an art therapist and there had been no plan to initiate an art therapy program. The service was available only to a limited number of inmates and only for as long as I was at the prison. I started three groups during my first three years with the mental health unit. Two were basic art therapy groups and the third was designed for experienced artists. Groups were held either on the gallery alongside the cells, or in a turnaround between the back ends of the galleries. Officers were not present in the area while groups were in session. This was arranged at the request of unit inmates, who felt that they would not be able to speak freely in the presence of officers. There was an intercom installed in the turnaround for emergency communication with the corrections officers desk at the head of the galleries.

Supplies were kept in locked metal cabinets in my office and in the turnaround. Most art supplies were permitted if they were not sharp or flammable. Inmates could use sharp tools and small amounts of solvents under the supervision of corrections officers, but not in programs like mine. Once in a while, gallery officers objected to a particular tool or material and I removed it from circulation.

Kneaded erasers were questioned because they could be used to mold keys or jam locks, but clay and other sculpture materials were allowed. Paints in metal tubes were considered contraband because the metal could be sharpened and used to make blades. I was asked to take precautions in discarding certain materials, particularly paintbrushes with plastic handles which could be fused or shaped to make weapons.

The basic groups were intended for inmates who were not yet ready for prison-wide educational or vocational programs. In theory, inmates moved through our system in a series of steps. Those who were too disorganized for a formal program spent their days in the cellblock, taking part in various activities offered by the mental health unit program staff. As individuals on the unit stabilized, they were referred to general population programs where they spent the bulk of their time. Those who did well in their prison programs became candidates for transfer back to general population, where they were assigned a therapist from among the mental health outpatient staff.

In working with these men, we all addressed fundamental problems which are common to most people who live in institutions. Those entering prison for the first time had no choice but to acclimate quickly to a strange and treacherous environment. Every man found a way to do this but the trick was to adjust without giving up or giving in. Those who made the adjustment and had reached the time when return to their community was imminent, were faced with the prospect of relearning skills lost through years of institutional living. In many ways, this was the greatest challenge. Failure to prepare for release into a changing world was a major factor in the high rate of recidivism among parolees.

The men assigned to work with me were generally those who felt most fearful and vulnerable. Once acclimated to the prison culture, most learned to survive by making themselves invisible, loathsome, or extremely ingratiating. This approach to life allowed little opportunity for personal growth or change. My objective was to help these men regain enough sense of competence and awareness of their own needs to begin setting goals for themselves. For most, this meant making plans for release from prison and return to family and neighborhood. In order for this to happen, they needed to find ways to examine feelings and beliefs about who they were and how they came to be in prison. They also needed to reawaken long abandoned hopes and dreams, and to adopt or restore belief in their own power to create their destinies.

The inmates in my groups responded to art therapy with guarded enthusiasm. They seemed so grateful to be out of their cells and spending time in the company of someone who was showing them kindness and respect, that they were willing to go through any motions necessary to sustain such a pleasant experience for as long as possible. At the same time, they were careful to avoid feeling real emotion and making real contact with other human beings. Most stopped short of investing any part of themselves in the work they were doing in their

DRAWING TIME

art therapy groups.

The majority were extremely constricted in verbal and graphic expression. When left to their own devices, most chose to do their artwork on small pieces of paper with pencil or black marker. Images tended to be small and sparing in detail. Stereotypical and schematic images were popular as were designs for graffiti and tattoos. Some individuals did the same drawing every week, generally featuring a person and a vehicle. I believed that the impoverished quality of their work reflected the effects of long-standing mental illness compounded by the years spent in the deadly and deadening prison environment.

Concrete Assignments Plus Basic Artmaking

Although I usually prefer to allow my clients to direct their own work in art therapy, I decided that this particular group needed guidance from me to help them give shape and color to their experiences. The members of my groups appeared unfocused and reluctant to assume the emotional or creative risks necessary for original expression. I also recognized that some needed time to get used to me and to trust me. In the prison environment, where trust can be truly dangerous, even those who are trusting by nature learn to be wary of everyone.

I began assigning themes at the beginning of each session. The most effective were those which were both concrete and broad enough to allow for interpretation. For example, I might ask group members to make a drawing inspired by the theme "growth" or I might ask them to draw the prison and include any changes that would make the place more livable. These were popular and fruitful themes. They usually resulted in interesting art and lively discussion. Still, there were many who continued to supply me with work that was superficial and empty.

My next strategy was to shift focus from the content of their work to its form, and to offer instruction in the basic principles of art making. We explored color, shape, texture, and line and talked about the use of each in the expression of feeling. I asked them to represent specific emotions using each element of design either by itself or in combination with others. In the process, I had them experiment with all of the materials available to us. I taught them to push, pull, smear, and tear. At the end of each group, we looked at each other's work and talked about the feelings evoked by what we saw.

This approach had dramatic effect. Each group, as a whole, grew increasingly busy, noisy, and interactive as the weeks passed. Their members were clearly more relaxed with me and with each other than when we first started working together. There were several reasons for this:

- They found the lessons in art making less threatening than my earlier assignments. Although they invested more of themselves in the work they did during this period, they felt less pressured.
- They saw the exercises as entertaining. Some enjoyed challenging the others to guess the meaning behind their scribbles and splashes of color.
- Our focus on instruction also enabled each man to develop his own visual language.

I had approached the groups with the assumption that their members were already familiar with basic art materials and that they each had preferences. After watching the transformation in the groups as members experimented and practiced using art materials, I understood that my assumption had been incorrect. Most of the older men had used crayons and watercolors in childhood art classes but had not made art as adults and no longer knew how to use the materials. A surprising number of the younger men, products of inadequate schools and neglectful parents, had not had any previous exposure to art materials at all.

Once group members had grown comfortable with art materials, I asked them each to begin work on an autobiographical series. I suggested themes for those who needed direction and allowed others to direct their own work, as long as it related to my original request. Group processing of the work focused on each man's image of self and on hopes and ambitions as defined through the autobiographies.

The most important effect of the art therapy experience, for the men in the group, was that it enabled them to see beyond the immediate and urgent matters related to survival in the prison environment. While survival is important, it can only guarantee a future without giving it substance. The process of contemplating both the past and the future through the images in his art allowed each man to assume responsibility for the course of his own life and to give form and substance to his future.

Another objective was to provide my clients with the means to work on their own. My third and least structured group included all the serious artists on the unit. It was open to people who considered themselves serious artists, giving them access to art supplies they could not use otherwise. We also read art history books and current art magazines, perused art supply catalogs, exchanged technical advice, discussed current art trends and the art market, and admired each other's work. It was from this group, and its members, that I learned the most about how art fits with the prison culture.

When I transferred to the outpatient unit, my groups folded. It was at this point that my role in the general prison culture expanded and I had regular contact with prison artists who were not working within a formal structure. I saw myself as a resource for these people and a witness to what they had been doing long before I got there. As I made rounds through the prison, I stopped to talk with many of the men I saw working in their cells and out on the galleries. I offered compliments, observations, and suggestions which were nearly always accepted in the spirit with which they were given. I was truly fascinated by what I saw happening and curious about why art had become so essential to prison culture.

Artmaking as a Form of Escape

The most obvious and basic function of art for prison artists is to provide one of the few means of escape from the environment. I first learned about this from a man I'd met years earlier who was an inmate assigned to a work release program in a rehabilitation hospital at which I worked. He was skilled as a craftsman and had a gentle and refined manner. It was thought he could help the occupational therapists who needed more staff to work directly with patients. He was a gifted teacher and the arrangement worked well.

One day, he brought an object to work which resembled a 20 foot wedding cake. When he unwrapped this confection, it was revealed to be a hanging table made of white yarn. At its center was a white disk nestled in a sweep of macrame knots. When suspended from the ceiling, the table top floated three feet from the floor. An elaborate arrangement of knots and fringe cascaded from the table to the floor.

DRAWING TIME

He told me that he had made it in the prison dorm, having been commissioned by one of the nurses. He had made many other pieces, including an assortment of belts, planters, handbags, and vests. He said he spent most of his free time working in macrame because it kept him sane through the long years leading to his work release assignment. Convicted of manslaughter following a barroom fight, he had spent his first years of incarceration in his state's toughest prison.

He fought through the earliest years, first to defend himself from rapes and beatings and later to defend his honor against insults and threats. Most of his fights were with inmates but he also fought with guards. Ultimately, he realized that he needed a device to serve as a buffer between himself and those who were provoking him. He decided to take up macramé.

From the beginning, he found enormous satisfaction in his work. When he talked about it with me, he said being able to escape the milieu was most critical for his self control. When he entered his world of colored yarns and knots, the rest of the world receded from his awareness and he found that taunts and insults no longer mattered. At one point, he actually had a closet in which he worked thereby isolating himself physically as well as psychologically. When each brief period of escape ended, he was able to return to the prison milieu feeling refreshed and in command.

Although he did not see this himself, I felt that his choice of medium was significant, contributing to his increasing sense of competence and control. Essentially, he began with limp and formless materials and fashioned them into objects of beauty and strength. The more unraveled he became, the more knots he tied and the stronger he felt. In the end, he was able to keep himself in sufficient control to earn transfers to less secure prisons and, finally, to work release and parole.

Avoiding Conflict by Painting

As I worked in the prison, I saw other examples of the same phenomenon. One inmate, in particular, was an extremely violent man who had committed a series of brutal crimes. Years of extreme abuse and neglect in childhood had left him irreparably damaged as an adult. He was haunted by memories of abuse, of longing for lost opportunities, and by images of his victims. Although tormented by guilt for his crimes, he was convinced that his violence would escalate once he was released from prison and he believed it would be best for all concerned if he ended his life rather than risk release from prison.

With release many years away, however, he had no compelling or immediate reason to kill himself so he decided to make the most of his prison experience while there. He worked as a prison porter and looked out for some of the weaker inmates. He worked and lived on the same gallery and had, years earlier, established certain parameters with the regular gallery officers. He would do anything custodial they asked him to do and, in return, they would let him do his time in his own way.

The officers then had a reliable worker and the inmate had his dignity and autonomy. As with many of the porters, he was permitted a few items of contraband, such as cooking oil, in exchange for his loyalty and reliability. He never asked for or expected anything unreasonable from the officers. He would not snitch, run contraband, or beat people up and these limits were respected by all on his gallery.

Every so often, a new officer or an unusually pushy inmate might show up on the gallery and disturb the equilibrium. Then, the cooking oil might be questioned or the inmate might be asked to do something against his principles and he would start to get angry.

When this happened, the only way he could keep himself under control was to paint. He surprised me the first time he told me about this as he had seemed so concrete and direct in his thinking that I found it difficult to imagine him resorting to a creative outlet of any kind to help manage stress. Nonetheless, this is what he did and it worked. Like the macramé artist, he found that he was able to create and lose himself within a new world when he painted. His ability to escape the pressures of the more immediate world enabled him to avoid conflict.

A third individual, who was a skilled artist, spent his free time making pastel and oil pastel drawings of the view from his cell. His cell faced the prison's outer wall and he was high enough to look over the wall and beyond, to a series of small thickets and fields. A city boy, he was fascinated by the seasonal changes in this microcosmic space and he made it his obsession. He drew it morning, noon, and night in every light and in every season. He learned its colors, shapes, and textures so well that he could draw it without looking at it and it became his favorite subject even when he was out of his cell and working somewhere else.

He never tired of his project. The act of studying and describing his quiet scene allowed him to travel outside the prison wall, remaining focused on each subtle change in its light and in the interplay of color and texture. He could feel that he was really there. Perhaps the opportunity to watch things come to life, bloom, wither, decay, and regenerate gave him a sense of peace and continuity. The greatest challenge for most men in prison, once the anger and defiance begin to fade, is to find some meaning in their painfully circumscribed lives. This man's perspective on life and on his place in the universe was formed, in some part, by his endless contemplation of a process both mundane and miraculous.

Transforming the Environment

For some inmates, a brief and private retreat from the world of prison was not enough. For these people, only complete transformation of the environment would do. This could be accomplished in many ways. The most common was cell decoration. While some inmates were happy to live in squalor and many were content with just the bare essentials, there were some who were compelled to create the illusion of luxury within the walls of their 10 x 10 homes. They were not allowed to have any clothing or fabric in a color used for officer's uniforms. The forbidden colors were blue, gray, black, and orange. Red, yellow, and green were permitted, however, and many inmates used colorful sheets, blankets, rugs, and towels to make their cells look like home. Burgundy sheets were especially popular. Drawings and paintings displayed on cell walls were essential to many decorating schemes. Also important were hand-crafted objects like picture frames and bookshelves which were used to display photos and gifts from home.

On a somewhat larger scale, a few inmates were permitted garden space where they brightened the austere prison landscape with pockets of color and greenery. It was my impression that this was allowed more for the benefit of staff than for inmates but the gardens appealed to everyone. The ones who seemed to benefit the most, however, were the gardeners themselves.

DRAWING TIME

The most interesting of these gardens had been constructed in a space between two cell blocks. I was told that it was created and still tended by a cranky old man who would not permit intruders to disturb its tranquil order. I passed it many times, invariably finding it empty. Its carefully placed beds of colorful petunias and impatient were always free of weeds and the surrounding grassy areas meticulously trimmed. Pathways and patches of flowers were defined with scalloped white edging made from the plastic lids of food containers. Wooden birdhouses and painted whirligigs added an element of frivolity to the otherwise dignified and highly ordered space. It was, in every respect, a triumph of a man over his environment.

While the gardeners were able to shape and transform outdoor spaces, their work had little impact on the prison interior where staff and inmates spent most of their time. It was in the interior spaces, however, where the most spectacular illusions were created. These were the murals which appeared in every block and on nearly every tier. Most were permanent fixtures, worked onto the gray metal walls by inmate artists who were long gone and long forgotten. Their themes were varied, but lifelike wilderness scenes were common as were fantastic images of dragons, castles, and well-endowed ladies in tight-fitting medieval dress.

Often, these paintings were quite large and so skillfully rendered that they appeared real. One woodland scene, in particular, was painted with such depth and dazzling realism that it evoked a brief shift in my sense of reality each time I saw it. Standing in front of it, I felt transported, though only for a moment. Corrections officers and inmates assigned to the galleries adjacent the mural were proud of this masterpiece and they worked together to insure that it was respected and well maintained.

Although I never met the men who painted most of these murals and rarely saw one in progress, I did have the privilege of watching the evolution of one of the largest and most spectacular of these monumental works. The painting was done outside my office in a hallway linking four offices and spanning the distance between two sections of the cellblock. The artist was an extraordinarily talented young man who had been placed on the mental health unit for treatment of depression. Because of his interest in art, he had been assigned to my caseload.

His mural began as a somewhat conventional outdoor scene with life-sized deer and other woodland creatures in the foreground and foliage behind. It was painted on a metal wall about 15 square feet in dimension. There was odd distortion in some of the animals and I thought that this was probably due to the fact that the paintings were faithfully copied from small magazine photographs, some of which were not easy to see. Because the photographs were from different sources, the animals had not been photographed from the same vantage point. Thus, the creatures in the painting appeared to be standing side by side but on different planes. This gave the mural a strange, disjointed quality.

When the wall was covered with painted images, we assumed that the artist was finished and that we could all sit back and enjoy this new and decorative addition to our work space. We were wrong. A few days after the painting stopped, the artist was back and hard at work making the first in an endless series of adjustments to his mural. I could not possibly recall all the changes or the order in which they occurred. I do remember that the first changes involved the destruction of several trees and the addition of some exotic animals. Most notable among these was a forlorn baby elephant, looking out of place and uneasy living in the habitat of wood ducks and white tailed deer.

CREATIVITY & INCARCERATION

Eventually, the woodland scene and its inhabitants vanished completely and was replaced by African animals standing in a swamp filled with dead trees. As the mural changed, several themes emerged and these paralleled major emotional and psychological themes in the artist's life. Severely abused as a child, he had grown to be an abuser himself and this fact caused him enormous distress. Although he was not thought to have a dissociative disorder, reports from corrections officers suggested that he entered dissociative states at times. His sense of identity appeared quite fluid and shifted almost as often as he made alterations to his mural.

While watching evidence of these themes emerge, I talked with the artist about what I was seeing and what I thought the images and changes meant. I was struck, especially, by the artist's need to keep his work in a state of flux and by the odd juxtapositions of images which gave the mural a quality of dissonance. It seemed to be the product of someone who felt unsettled and unable to find a place for himself in the world.

As long as I did not interrupt him while he was deeply involved with the mural, he welcomed my observations. These spontaneous sessions became the focus of our work together and I believe that the experience was far more useful to him than the monthly meetings we scheduled in order to meet unit requirements.

Over time, the mural extended beyond the edges of its original space, spilling out onto the surrounding walls and covering every available space in the hallway. I left the unit and transferred to another while the mural was still in progress. Each time I returned for a visit, I found it changed beyond recognition. At one point in its evolution, the animals disappeared and were replaced by people. The most startling and exuberant transformation featured a group of glamorous African women dressed in brightly patterned bathing suits, lounging in a jungle.

I did not have the privilege of seeing the mural in its finality. As the inmate artist began preparing for parole, he decided not to leave his work behind. On my last visit to the unit, before I left the prison myself, I found the walls had been restored to a pristine institutional green. Others had wanted the mural to remain, but the inmate had been adamant in his wish to remove all traces of the process which had consumed him for most of his three years on the unit.

I will never know the degree to which the artist was, himself, changed through the process of making his mural but I believe that he did experience the world differently as a result of his involvement with his painting. Whatever else it may have been, the mural was never superficial and I think it was because he put so much of himself into his work that he would not risk leaving it exposed.

The most remarkable aspect of all of these murals was the degree of staff and inmate collaboration reflected in their existence. Other prison enterprises required staff and inmates to work together toward common goals, but these murals may have been the only such venture which was not an official prison program or activity.

Cooperation between Staff and Inmates

In order for work on the murals to take place, someone had to procure paint, find a place to store it, scrounge brushes and other supplies, and arrange time for the inmate artists to do

DRAWING TIME

their work. I never knew the source of the mural paint, but I have always assumed that it was either borrowed from prison workshops, smuggled in by staff, or both. It would not have been possible for an inmate to get that much paint without help. I was asked for paint, from time to time; particularly when someone needed a color not available through ordinary channels.

Painting time could be arranged at the discretion of the gallery officers. Being permitted out on the galleries for any length of time was a privilege afforded to but a few. Among those who enjoyed this rare freedom were the gallery porters, a few odd-ball inmates who had become gallery mascots, and the muralists.

It seemed, to me, that the muralists had a special status even among those who had been favored with freedom to roam the galleries. I imagined that it must have been similar to the status of Renaissance court painters and sculptors. Because of their special skills and the nature of their contribution to gallery culture, the muralists were the objects of unparalleled respect from inmates and staff. They were allowed to pursue their work without interference and without being drawn into some of the more unsavory aspects of life on the gallery.

I believe this happened because everyone needed the murals. Art serves many purposes for members of the culture in which it finds an audience. Among them is that feelings, ideas, and beliefs may be evoked or clarified for those who contemplate the products of artistic endeavor. Art may also beautify and transform the area in which a work of art is experienced. In this particular culture, the murals seemed valued most when they made those who viewed them feel transported from the prison and into the world represented by the murals. Respite from the prison environment was necessary for everyone, including staff.

Art as Commodity

I once had a very expensive, 48 color box of Prismacolor® pencils stolen from my supply cabinet. The culprit was a young man on my caseload with whom I'd had a long and eventful therapeutic relationship. He confessed the theft when he realized he was the prime suspect of the inmates on his gallery. He told me himself rather than risk exposure through public accusation.

Discussing the incident, I asked why he wanted the pencils. He told me he had gambling debts and had been threatened with physical harm if he did not find a way to pay. Although he had access to other marketable goods, he stole the pencils because they had the greatest value in the prison black market. He exchanged them in batches of two or three for quantities of cigarettes and coffee, apparently earning enough to offset most of his debt. He warned me to be more careful with my art supplies because they were so highly prized in the prison economy. They were a means to earn goods and services for those who were skilled in their use.

One inmate on our unit sold portraits and pornographic sketches to other inmates for cigarettes, coffee, and art supplies. He accepted commissions for drawings of family members, friends, girlfriends, and celebrities, doing portraits from photographs. He also offered for sale some stock drawings of idealized African American women. The pornographic drawings were his most expressive. He let them be seen by prison staff when he was decompensating and less cautious in revealing this aspect of his imagination.

CREATIVITY & INCARCERATION

Other enterprising inmates operated thriving graphic arts studios from their cells. Among the most popular items were decorated writing paper with matching envelopes, reproductions of cartoon characters, family portraits, posters of cars or women, celebrity portraits, and decorated objects like handkerchiefs and scarves. Some items, like the scarves and cartoons, were purchased for use as gifts for sweethearts and children. Most other artwork was purchased for personal use.

One inmate on my caseload spent virtually all of his time weaving picture frames from a particular brand of potato chip bag. He cleaned the bags and then cut them into strips of blue, yellow, red, and silver. He kept some frames and sold others. This was his only source of income as he had decided not to go to a prison program.

He was locked on a special company for people who refused programs. Allowed to leave his cell for medical and mental health appointments and for limited exercise, which he generally refused, he ate all meals in his cell and was denied special activities.

He liked things this way as he never had to worry about getting into fights or being extorted by other inmates. His refusal to attend program meant that he would not be considered a good candidate for parole. He understood this and was content to stay in prison for a few months beyond his parole eligibility date as long as he was able to make his picture frames. He looked forward to eventual release because this would give him access to a greater variety of colored papers to use in making picture frames. He had exhausted all possibilities with the potato chip bags and was eager to expand his repertoire.

My favorite commercial art objects were the football helmets which proliferated in the early winter as various National Football League teams and their fans began preparing for the playoffs. The prison was located near a rust belt city famous for its brutal winter weather and its devotion to professional sports. A local graphic artist had designed a series of posters and T-shirts celebrating our "city with no illusions" which seemed to capture the character of the area. We were disdained by residents of bigger, fancier cities contributing to a collective sense of inferiority. This lifted only when one of our beloved sports teams showed signs of life around playoff time.

Of all the teams, it was our football team that inspired a passion transcending reason. For years, our boys had been so miraculous in victory and stunning in defeat that nobody was immune to the excitement and suspense of the annual playoffs, not to mention the Super Bowl. We were all rabid fans. Even so, no group of people was more impassioned over their football than the officers in the prison.

As each football season progressed, objects bearing our team's name and logo began appearing all over the prison. Most blocks had at least one area in which team logos had been painted directly onto a wall. This work was done by inmates at the request of officers. In one block, a frieze of football helmets representing all the NFL teams was painted in the block captain's office. In another, the logos for all of our city's professional sports teams were painted in the entrance to a section of the block.

Among the most popular sports accessories were full sized cutouts of football helmets. The helmets were drawn on white paper with crayon or colored pencil and then mounted on

DRAWING TIME

corrugated cardboard cut to the shape of the helmet. These objects were then finished with a protective layer of clear plastic food wrap which gave them a slick, polished appearance. The majority of these souvenirs were commissioned and purchased by corrections officers for display either near their work stations or at home. Some were also purchased by other inmates. The demand for these objects was such that an inmate could be kept busy for weeks, working to fill orders.

As was the case with the muralists, prison commercial artists were highly respected. Their contribution to prison culture could only be viewed as positive. The products of their work were valued because they enriched and beautified the environment, making it more pleasant for those who spent most or all of their time inside the prison walls.

Art for Self Expression and Emotional Release

To an art therapist, self expression and emotional release are among the most important reasons to make art. Although I found that art served a range of functions in the prison culture, I also believed that the opportunity for self expression and emotional release were critical components of the art making experience for all of those who made art in that environment, regardless of its intended purpose.

The most punishing consequence of life in prison is loss of identity. Most staff in the prison referred to inmates by their departmental identification numbers rather than by name. Corrections officers generally knew inmates by cell location. All inmates dressed in identical dark green work clothes which could not be tailored in such a way as to alter appearance. Rules regarding jewelry and other accessories were numerous and strictly enforced. Wedding bands were permitted. Hats were not allowed except during recreation time. Religious emblems, including khufis, yarmulkes, and crucifixes were permitted as long as they were not obtrusive.

For most inmates, redefining identity within the context of the prison culture became a challenge. Almost everyone started with the easiest and most obvious measures, however, and those were the ones involving alteration of physical appearance. Tattoos and unusual hairstyles were common. The most popular prison barbers were the men who could cut elaborate designs into the stubble on a closely cropped head. Skilled tattoo artists were also in demand. It seemed, to me, that facial tattoos were far more common in prison than on the street. Many men had a single teardrop tattooed in the corner of an eye. An inmate on our unit had a beautifully rendered devil baby tattooed on his neck in such a way that it appeared to be whispering into his ear. Another man had a spider's web tattooed across his face.

Many inmates defined identity through affiliation with a gang or cultural group. Wearing a group's colors was possible within the context of prison dress codes. Some groups wore bandannas in the exercise yard. Rastafarians were allowed to wear dreadlocks, as long as they were tied back, and some wore belts or hair bands decorated in Rastafarian colors of red, green, and gold. Muslims were permitted to wear khufis, which could be fashioned in a range of distinctive colors and patterns. Group membership could be more complex than the visible representations of belonging. Most groups also represented ideas and beliefs, and they offered protection for their more vulnerable members.

Among the few benefits of incarceration is the opportunity for self reflection and personal

CREATIVITY & INCARCERATION

growth. For most of us, time to think about our place in the universe is a rare commodity. Personal development may become a low priority—competing with child-rearing, work, and other human activities—unless we feel the need to make changes in the quality or direction of our lives. People in prison have nothing but time.

While many inmates spent their time in prison plotting revenge and making plans for resumption of their criminal careers, some used the time to figure out where they had been, where they were going, and how best to get to where they wanted to be. These people, who struggle to define identity, were the most successful. Their serenity and self assurance was attractive to the more confused among the other inmates and they often became jailhouse philosophers and mentors to those fortunate enough to fall under their influence.

For many of these men, making art was part of a process of self expression leading to self discovery. Whether making murals, drawing in their cells, or copying cartoon figures onto birthday cards for their children, they used art making to define their lives and to resolve conflict through the dynamics in the form and imagery in their work as well as through the manipulation of materials. They were also using art to establish identity in a more social sense. As noted previously, prison artists had a special role in the culture. They were respected, sought after, and endowed with special status and favors as a result of their contributions. Without question, this was a more constructive and satisfying way to establish identity than with tattoos and gang membership.

Emotional release within the prison culture was a more straightforward and urgent problem than that of maintaining identity. There are few human experiences more emotionally wrenching than transgressing against society, getting caught, submitting to police interrogation and community censure, losing liberty and social standing, and facing lengthy separation from friends and family. Every man in the prison endured his own variation of these events. That most were directly responsible for their own predicaments had little bearing on the intensity and turbulence of emotion or the need for emotional release. In some cases, particularly when the crime resulted in the death of a loved one, guilt was the most overwhelming emotion of all.

Direct release of emotion in a jail or prison setting is a complicated matter. Inmates were expected to maintain control over behavior at all times. The institution viewed expression of strong feeling as evidence of loss of control and responded by imposing more control. Demonstration of anger might result in disciplinary action. Tears were considered signs of weakness or instability. Displays of emotion might prompt a visit from mental health staff which could, in turn, lead to mental health observation or suicide watch. Neither option was pleasant.

The process of making art enables the artist to release emotion through the colors, lines, forms, and images in his work. The consequences of releasing emotion through making art are far more rewarding than the consequences of angry violence or emotional collapse. They are also less disruptive to the orderly progression of life in prison. For those reasons, the use of art making by individual inmates to help channel and discharge strong emotion was a positive force in that environment. As was the case for those who defined identity through the art making process, there was an element of emotional release in every mural, decorated envelope, and cardboard football helmet produced at the prison.

DRAWING TIME

Disappearing Art in Prison Programs

Any prison activity that helps inmates take command of behavior and become more self aware, beautifies the environment, and provides gratifying experiences for staff and other inmates should be encouraged. While art clearly flourished in this prison without official institutional involvement, I wondered what might have happened if art making had been supported in the same way as athletic programs. Inmates had daily access to weightlifting equipment in the gym and in the exercise yards. There were organized team sports with blocks playing against each other and there were informal basketball games played in the yards during the warm weather.

At one time, art, music, and writing programs were available at the prison. Commercial art classes were provided through the vocational training department and the writing programs were offered, for college credit, through the prison college consortium. Both the art and music programs were gone by the time I started working at the prison. The writing program was gone by the time I left.

The only remnant of the art program was a statewide exhibition held annually in the state's legislative office building. Entries were collected by the athletic staff and shipped to the state capitol. Individual inmates were responsible for preparing their work for display.

Needed: Art Studios

An art studio, scheduled in the same manner as the gym programs, could prove beneficial both to the inmates involved and to the prison as a whole. The athletic programs were valued by the prison administration because they provided inmates with outlets for aggressive energy. There was a widely held belief that they helped to make inmates more manageable. Art programs could serve a similar purpose by providing alternative outlets, perhaps reaching those individuals who were not interested in the athletic programs but whose need to release emotion was as great as those who found satisfaction through weight training or basketball.

In our prison, an art studio could be established in the vicinity of the recreational facilities with shared office space and staff. Security considerations might be similar to those for some of the prison workshops although materials and equipment required for an art studio would be far less dangerous than those used in the woodworking and metal shops. Program staff should include an art therapist skilled at guiding individuals through the process of self discovery and emotional release. An art therapist who also has clinical background would be helpful in addressing the growing problem of managing mentally ill inmates in a traditional prison milieu.

The result of such a program would be a more humane and livable prison environment for inmates as well as for staff. I also believe that providing inmates with the means for exercising their minds and developing the capacity for feeling, just as they exercise their bodies and develop muscles, might have benefits ranging far beyond the limits of the prison and those who inhabit its cramped and gloomy spaces. Most inmates leave prison, at some point. How much better it would be for the rest of the world if just a few took with them a heightened sense of self, a new respect for the feelings of others, goals and hope for a future, and a belief in their own capacity to change the direction of their lives.

CREATIVITY & INCARCERATION

This view of a prison maintenance crew, working just inside the wall, was done in oil pastel. The artist, who is described in the text, generally preferred to focus on the view just outside the wall.

References

Allen, P. (1995). *Art as a way of knowing.* Boston and London: Shambhala Publications, Inc.
Arnheim, R. (1972). *Toward a psychology of art.* Berkeley and Los Angeles: University of California Press
Chipp, H. B. (ed.) (1968). *Theories of modern art: A source book by artists and critics.* Berkeley, Los Angeles, and London: University of California Press
Dissanayake, E. (1995). *Homo aestheticus: Where art comes from and why.* Seattle and London: University of Washington Press
Janson, H.W. (1986). *History of art.* (Rev. ed.) New York: Harry N. Abrams, Inc.
Liebmann, M. (ed.) (1994). *Art therapy with offenders.* London and Bristol, Pennsylvania: Jessica Kingsley Publishers
Read, H. (1972). *The meaning of art.* (Rev. ed.) London: Faber & Faber

The Hidden Weapon: Psychodynamics of Forensic Institutions

William M. Fox, M.S.W., L.C.S.W.

The idea is not new that human institutions are the projection, extension and elaboration of the human psyche. It is, however, particularly applicable today when forensic institutions have assumed monstrous and seemingly uncontrollable proportions, taking on lives and wills of their own. Today they seem singularly inefficient at the same time that they appear clumsily powerful. We see daily intense debate over their reform or even their continued existence, the irrational over or under financing of them based on public hysteria, their growth into major oppressive industries and constituencies, and their representation of simplified and infantile ideas raised to the status of primitive ideology. Any of these events, if seen in an individual patient or family in a private practice, would immediately signal a severe and debilitating mental disorder to a clinician.

In searching for an explanatory model that would address the psychosocial pathology of these punitive institutions, the work of Melanie Klein seemed to fit quite closely. Morrison (1989) explains this well when he describes Klein's point of view as a "perspective... emphasizing the relationship of the self to a plentiful, uncontrollable, and intolerable source of power, with a consequent need to deny or protect against that object's importance" (p. 108). This is a fundamental object relationship of which prison is an elaboration and objectification.

The paranoid stage of infantile development as described by Klein was seen by Greenberg and Mitchell (1983) as "providing powerful tools for understanding the psychodynamics of older children and adults" rather than the earlier months of life of an infant (p. 148). As such, her depiction is enlightening for understanding psychodynamic object relations of all paranoid disorders, whether personality disorders, regressive states or paranoid schizophrenia. One can see that these have much in common with the institutional features of forensic establishments such as prisons, jails and state hospitals, resembling the internal object relations seen in pathological paranoid patients in clinical practice. In this paper, the attempt will be made to delineate some of these object relationships and compare them with those observed by this writer in more than twenty years of attempting to provide psychotherapeutic services within such institutional settings.

Paranoid object relations as described by Kernberg, Freud, Klein and Meissner, among others, consist primarily of developmentally primitive dynamics, including the predominance of defense mechanisms such as: projection, projective identification, primitive idealization, splitting, omnipotence, denial of a profoundly annihilative form, acting-out, clinging, and others.

Basically, all of the defense mechanisms identified by psychoanalytic writers as being characteristic of pathological characterological states prevail in these milieus. Growth, which would occur through the stage of depression, where ideals encounter reality, is not allowed. Instead, regression occurs continuously, since intense fear, hatred, anxiety and other extreme affects are the daily fare of the institutional macro-personality which is locked within its own walls. This perimeter represents the same type of a limit to growth that a personality disorder does to the self imprisoned within.

Insofar as personalities-in-development share these dynamics but naturally outgrow them, the question arises: what arrests such organic progress, either in individuals or in institutions?

Pathological characterology occurs because there is a cap on growth, a limit that is not merely solid but potentially annihilative. Plants crack concrete with growth, so this cap must be active rather than passive, or growth would triumph, and prisons would change. The paranoid consciousness equates growth with escape, hence sees the maturation of inmates as potentially threatening to the very solidity of the walls, and to the correctional mission.

Growth Means Annihilation

So, for the same reason that inmates cannot be allowed to even approach the physical boundaries of the prison, the developing ego, whether represented by inmate development, patient health, or programmatic success, cannot be allowed to approach the real containing and powerful entities within the personality or institution, since, to these objects also, growth means annihilation. "Reform," whether of a felon or of a felonious program, is only possible to a relatively developed and mature, psychosocially anchored superego. To an infantile object, which has only the primitive and infantile superego-precursor to relate to, reform threatens destruction. With little or no developmental history, such an object also has no future or continuity, hence such destruction is seen as total. Such a profound attack must be met by congruently primitive and harsh defenses, with specific behaviors, emotions, attitudes and maneuvers taken from a near-psychotic bag of tricks.

The basic paranoid dynamic is projective: one projects the undesirable parts of the psyche and then defends against their return. These disowned parts are held in a continual dyadic relationship with the projector, much like the weak force in physics. The ego and object poles of the paranoid relationship are tied together as if by a rubber cord: the greater the attempt to disown either pole, the greater its attempt to return. So, like the bungee jumper when he reaches the end of the cord, the rebound is intense.

Dynamically, the more invisible the projected objects, the more power they have. Even primitive repression is most effective when it has holes to breathe, such as dreams and fantasies, and at its most fragile (pre-psychotic) when it is the most rigid. This can be seen institutionally by the simple fact that the greater the oppression of the inmates by the correctional staff, the more danger of riot there is in a prison, jail or state hospital.

THE HIDDEN WEAPON

In turn, oppressiveness is held somewhat in check by the inmates acting powerless to the point of invisibility. This means that they must tolerate, without complaint, the continual, casual oppression that is practiced upon them, the daily infantilization and degradation, and present a continual naked vulnerability to staff, while presenting the punitive pole of the object-relation to other inmates. Submit to staff, but dominate peers. However, they cannot put the "spin" of martyrdom on their tolerance since this would invoke an overpowering increase in the threat to the punitive power of the paranoid object, hence an exponential heightening of oppression in response.

One has only to remember the great variety of historic martyrs and the influence and reaction they produced, from Joan of Arc to Nelson Mandela and George Jackson, to see this clearly. But, as was previously remarked, the level of invisibility of the inmates correlates with the level of their dynamic power.

This power is projected upon them and bears little relationship to their actual "innate" psychopathy. An inmate may possess no social or cognitive skills whatsoever, test in the level of moderate retardation, be a third grade dropout, have done significant damage to his neural pathways with drugs, alcohol and family violence, have no social support, no financial resources, have absolutely no reason to attempt an escape from the institution, and be further disabled by depression or schizophrenia, yet the staff will imagine that he is plotting on a level of criminal complexity worthy of Professor Moriarty. The paranoid "brainstorming" engaged in by staff in small groups, however, is a regressive reaction to this fantasied and projected level of criminal planning.

As we will see in Klein's system, one's best defense against envy in a closed system is splitting, so, if the inmate renews some slight level of antisocial behaviors, the level of paranoid vigilance of the staff will decline, losing its situationally hysterical quality and taking on a routine dehumanizing caretaker quality.

Routine Cycle of Boredom to Crisis

The inmate must prove that he is an inmate, just not a very competent one. But if he does not fit this stereotype, he becomes the object of a storm of projections, as the homeostatic mechanism of the paranoid institution engages, attempting to restrain the fear and rage, and return to the routine cycle of boredom to crisis.

This bored caretaker attitude is of dynamic interest. It represents the triumph of contempt over fear. It is entirely self-contradictory from a rational perspective and, so, shows the features of primitive object-relations. New staff are trained in the imminent dangerousness of the inmates, which is presented as an active, intrusive, effective, street-wise menace. This implies, at the other pole of the object relationship, a naive, childlike, hypervulnerable staff member.

The merest requests from inmates for contact, such as asking a staff member for a cigarette, are presented as the opening wedge that will, unless checked by the inclusion of the all-knowing supervisor, lead inevitably to a manipulation that will cost the staff member his job or even his life. (It should be noted, though, that little time is spent in training about what happens outside the prison walls, when the dynamics go home at night, or after the employee leaves state service.) This, of course, produces an immediate level of hypervigilance in employees that is basically unsustainable. One simply cannot function full-time in the primary-process jungle of such surreal relationships and not suffer some regression. The two things that push employees out of this are the reality principle and primitive defenses against continued terror.

The first, the reality principle, presents itself as the real personalities of the inmates, who turn out to be a heterogeneous group such as one would find in any group of men, with some very bad and dangerous types and some first-term inmates as naive as the staff themselves. If one begins to see inmates as co-equal people, the entire righteousness of the oppression in the system would be at risk.

The daily possibility of seeing the diversity of possible relationships with the inmates is the same hazard to the primitive pathology as that which accompanies the Oedipal dilemma, that of moving from dyadic, narcissistically-infused, infantile object relations to triadic and group relations. It is only in the world of the infant that one believes that, if one commits a crime, the punishment will be annihilative and permanent. (The recent severe "three-strikes" law in California is an attempt to return to this level of regressive deterrence.)

Adult reality involves a relativistic perspective on the severity of crimes, as represented by different sentences for different crimes, with each being seen as having been committed by a different person, all within a shared standard of social norms, but a standard tailored by judicial process.

It also involves the idea that it is transactionally possible to repay society for crime by permitting oneself to be incarcerated; one must be able to discharge a debt to society like any other debt. This transaction is a contract, and contracts, in order to be valid, require mutual assent, benefit and detriment to both parties, and a lack of obstacle, such as incompetence, to fruition.

The agreement on the part of society must be that someone will be left alone if they serve their time, that society must suffer the detriment of not further harassing the person when the debt is paid as well as gaining the benefit of him not committing further crimes, assuming the presence of competence in both parties. Within this contract, inmates must be considered human beings with pasts and futures, desires and rights, that are no different than those of staff, though temporarily limited by the security needs of the prison.

The second feature is that of the simple inability to live with daily terror. The reaction of the organism to terror, even in a single situation, is shock, or fight-flight. An employee cannot flee from the dynamic danger without quitting the job; one cannot fight without being fired.

So one dissociates. The individual shuts down through a process of dehumanization. The inmates are not only seen as less than human; they are annihilated. At first considered Satanic in orientation, they now become invisible.

Staff, who firmly believe that they should not become overfamiliar with inmates, freely discuss their personal lives within their hearing, or post flyers announcing the birth of their children in places where the inmates can easily see them. Rather than maintaining the professional distance recommended in training, which is no defense against the terror of their vulnerability, staff overintroduce their private lives into the inmates' milieu, treating them as if they did not exist. This gives the inmates the very power that the staff have psychically removed from them, should they choose to utilize it.

In turn, when an inmate does mention a private fact of a staff's life, it reinforces the staff's idea that the inmate is spying on them and that he is using the personal data for some criminal end. (It is, of course, quite possible that the inmate is doing just this, but the dynamic blinds the staff member in such a way that this cannot be determined and ceases to be a meaningful question. The question itself becomes suspect. Among clinicians, the chronic preoccupation with malingering is a form of this dynamic.)

This is the same phenomenon as calling the waiter by the name on the name tag and watching the paranoid "rush" as the person tries to understand how you knew a secret fact so prominently displayed. The difference in prison is that it would be equally threatening for staff members to admit that they had been so self-revelatory and they would probably be somewhat afraid of losing their jobs, hence increasing the intensity of the projection and doubling their distrust of the inmates. The waiter, though, would probably immediately see his part in it.

So the basic engine is the projective/introjective. But why cannot these contents be successfully projected or repressed? Because, according to psychoanalytic thinking, these are intensely loved and hated parts of the self and so can never be completely disowned. The more intense the affective bond between the dyadic poles, the more energized will be both the projection and the rebound.

Inmate As Person

By this definition, the great danger to the correctional staff is in seeing the inmate as being a person like themselves. This is the same dangerous opportunity for growth posed by recognizing that a demon is a projection. What would follow from this ultimately would be to permit the inmate to do anything through a morality-degrading "empathy." On the primitive level of these object relations, empathy is impossible, since it requires that there actually be two coexistent and equal objects. Empathy threatens symbiosis and annihilation, and therefore is ultimately sinister. It must be kept at a distance by projection followed by denial followed by devaluation.

"I do not want to empathize" becomes "I cannot empathize" becomes "you want to empathize" becomes "you want to empathize for secret, criminal reasons." (One should not confuse the pseudo-empathy of the staff identifying with the inmate as a paranoid object with the real, evolved empathy described above.)

Among mental health workers and medical staff, another way to reduce the annihilative to incapable is by infantilization. Melanie Klein (1957/1975) described this phenomenon when she wrote:

> Gratitude is closely bound up with generosity. Inner wealth derives from having assimilated the good object so that the individual becomes able to share its gifts with others... By contrast, with people in whom this feeling of inner wealth and strength is not sufficiently established, bouts of generosity are often followed by an exaggerated need for appreciation and gratitude, and consequently by persecutory anxieties of having been impoverished and robbed, (p. 189).

When staff members truly believe that someone cannot help himself, e.g., an acutely manic or paraplegic inmate, they can frequently reduce the threat by treating these men as if they were infants, reacting to psychotic rage with a knowing and grandparental smile. They can also over-attend to physical problems, even those that are chronic and not life-threatening, so that they can see the inmate as a "case" and not a threat.

A Fluctuating Yardstick

It is interesting to see Bud Allen's (1989) definition of professionalism in correctional employees:

> The accomplishment of professionalism in law enforcement differs from that in most other organizations because employee demands and expectations are unique. In most large organizations or professions, competence is acquired by a constant process of doing, and professionalism is achieved by predetermined modes of behavior. But in law enforcement, a new set of standards can be required for each situation—those rules must very often be made up by the individual officer at the time an incident occurs.
>
> Another demand that requires quick emotional changes is the switch from sternness to pacification and involves sets of professional standards that are extremely difficult to achieve, (pp. 25-26).

Clearly, from the above citation, one cannot call these "standards" at all. A standard is a gauge or criterion against which other things are measured. One cannot measure professional behavior against a constantly fluctuating yardstick. In such chaos, a law enforcement officer could logically defend him or herself on the witness stand by saying "I behaved in a professional manner by making up a rule on the spur of the moment." We have seen recently what such ad-hoc, adrenaline-generated "professionalism" has cost in various police practices that have started riots or resulted in the acquittal of guilty defendants. Neither the law nor medicine could function in this manner.

Overall, the truest thing that Allen says here is that such professional standards are difficult to achieve. Substitute the word "impossible" and you have the truth.

But what he implies is profound. He suggests working within a paranoid system, in which laxity is dangerous, rules continually change, life or death issues are decided on no fixed system of response, and a code of professionalism is impossible to establish or achieve for any period of time, or to teach to others. He depicts the same sociodynamic reality that is further elaborated in this article, but he asserts that one must work in it, and simultaneously demonstrates the impossibility of this task.

In psychiatric nursing, particularly in forensic settings, the criminal background and behavior are central to an understanding of and treatment of psychiatric illness. However, the fact that this "solution" to the daily fear is not effective may be seen by the rapidity with which it disappears when the infantilized inmate is proven to be a liar, or becomes insufficiently grateful for the "Big Nurse" ministrations, and is replaced by a retaliatory, vengeful rage that re-establishes the split, and reinforces the paranoid "truths" of the environment.

"You cannot trust them; they never get enough" and "how dare they ask for anything when they have nothing coming in the first place?" As Klein pointed out, the lack of gratitude is converted into fear, in those who have not assimilated the good object, and prison does not tolerate such assimilation.

In a paranoid context, the stranger is always threatening and any reassuring moves are even more so. An inmate who dares to behave as if he were a "free person" is an equal and so, a threat to injure, kill, steal from, or otherwise antisocially molest, and that inmate will most probably become the subject of an immediate move to oppress. The free person who does not practice dominance of the inmate is also suspect.

The projected punitive id-fragment is always the worst kind of menace to the very existence of the dyadically coupled object, but it is so primitive that it threatens literal universal annihilation, in this case, of the entire institution.

"Overfamiliarity"

With the paranoid genius for condensation and oversimplification, an inmate smiling at you and looking you in the eye is regarded as an actual assault or as the precursor to some antisocial manipulation. This must be stopped immediately, because the dynamic implication is that one loses one's power to resist as the process continues: this increasing weakness and loss of identity is institutionally promoted as the inevitable price of any behavior except preemptive paranoid assault. The process of this failure is referred to as "overfamiliarity," and there is mandatory annual training provided in how to avoid it.

Adaptation to reality and its changes requires all organisms to be constantly self-correcting and to strive for homeostatic relief, no matter how temporary. Since reality is change and not structure, the supposedly static paranoid framework is continually threatened by the smallest new data, natural changes or new inmates or personnel. The new is generally understood through a priority-making function that is based on learned probabilities.

A stranger who approaches you on the streets is regarded with quite differing responses depending on a variety of factors, both internal and external. Though in the current climate of generalized fear of crime, one's possible responses are probably narrowed, there is still a wide range: if the person is dressed in a certain way, moves in a certain way, smiles in a certain way, has a credible reason for violating your bubble of personal space, and if you are in a mood to be receptive to such signals and contexts, you will most probably relax and accept the person as an equal.

"Positive" Invisibility

But in a paranoid society, even the hint of equality in an inmate is a threat. To not be seen as a threat, inmates must achieve invisibility. Therefore, inmates who really do have some high level criminal abilities merely have to remain invisible and they can achieve great things in prison. The staff will permit and encourage such invisibility. This "positive" invisibility consists of following all rules and orders without any reaction, no matter how abusive or provocative, and of never coming to the negative attention of staff. But also, an inmate must remain somewhat neutrally polite and friendly with staff, like a good-enough servant. Yet this requires a much higher level of self-containedness than prison, paradoxically, permits.

The "well-behaved" inmate is very likely to be an example of Klein's (1960/1975) "excessively good and submissive" child (p. 273). In this formulation, the developing person experiences sporadic depression based on the developing repugnance with his aggressive and destructive impulses towards the loved object.

In infants, Klein sees this as productive of sleep disorders, difficulties with eating, a continual demand for attention and the inability to be content by themselves. All of these are seen in prison in psychiatric patients to an excessive degree.

Frequently, the treated inmate is one who is excessively good and submissive. But in Klein's view, this behavior is a splitting mechanism that truly prevents the realization of creative potential, such as the ability to make reparation (refrain from criminal behavior). Such integration requires pain and the experience of internal conflict, and the whole nature of the prison environment is designed to prevent this, frequently substituting projected and acted-out pain for the necessary internalized depressive and sober pain.

Continually reinventing enemies and the pain this causes is a projective, splitting defense, that contains a good amount of idealization. Klein indicated that idealization is a "corollary of persecutory anxiety" (1960/1975, p. 274).

In prison, overladen with persecutory anxiety, the idealization must function within the splitting. Frequently, the supercriminal status is the idealized form for the bad guys, and the "supercop" is the idealized form for the good guys. (Note: the primitive form of the splitting is suggested strongly by the use of the cartoon level terms "good guys and bad guys" by correctional staff themselves.) Hence, fundamental to the system is an eternally primitive form of idealization, but one that cannot grow into an active ego ideal without taking, along with it, the split.

One can become a supercop or a supercriminal without ever integrating one's good or bad objects. Klein says that "the need for integration... derives from the unconscious knowledge that hate can only be mitigated by love, and, if the two are kept apart, this mitigation cannot succeed" (1960/1975, p. 274).

The split-off hatred, aggression and pain not only remain unintegrated in the individuals but in the institution. The hatred of inmates by staff and the hatred of staff by inmates is the highest that can be achieved, a primitive and unyielding form of splitting that will prevent growth, encourage violence and ensure, for generations to come, the presence and power of crime.

In a climate filled with a condensation of Oedipal gossip and primitive fear, the withholding of personal data becomes a necessity for survival, i.e. resistance to regression. In the absence of real data, the environment is replete with floating primitive fantasies and bizarre behaviors. Many of these images and behaviors are concerned with Kleinian and Freudian objects: feces, food, babies, suddenly revealed penises, and ambivalent sexuality infused with aggression. (The range of "drag queen" to transsexual is as remarkable in the inmates as the steroid body sculptures in the male and female guards.)

One pervasive environmental characteristic is a tremendous desire to know, which Klein (1928/1975) called the "epistemophilic impulse" (p. 188) but which is here coupled with a severe devaluation of knowledge gained. The truth of events is always deeper, always more hidden, always more sinister. Looking for Truth In a Climate of Lies is the paranoid script at its most fundamental, and this is the motivating epistemology in prison. Like the Gnostic heresies in Christianity, the evident truth is sophia prunikos, wisdom the whore, and the hidden revelatory truth constantly retreats from the intense, clutching fingers of the hungry seeker. According to Hans Jonas, this is the "...orgiastic feast prepared by the world for the seduction of man, [in which] ignorance is not a neutral state but is itself a positive counter-condition to that of knowledge, actively induced and maintained to prevent it," (1963, p .71).

So Everyone is intensely interested in Everyone, but only as a potential devaluative or exploitable prey. Growth, wisdom, love, and real knowledge lie elsewhere and are "alien" to this environment which, in Gnosticism, as in prison, is the entire world.

The Hidden Weapon

A favorite fantasy that demonstrates this aspect of the psychodynamic environment is the hidden weapon. This can be experienced by the reader who may not have worked in a forensic setting by simply doing the following exercises:

- Select any three small portable objects from the environment around you.
- Imagine the first object.
- Imagine a way that you could use it to hurt someone.
- Having imagined this, imagine being hurt by it.
- Imagine yourself both in pain and being angrily criticized by your peers and your supervisor for being so stupid as to be hurt by it.
- Convert these fearful scenarios into security procedures that prohibit the object of class of objects.
- Imagine the second object.
- Imagine that it was made by someone with a sexual secret.
- Imagine that somewhere within the object, there is a symbol or representation of that sexual secret.
- Imagine that this person was trying to sexually dominate you by keeping it a secret, and was also ridiculing you by presenting it to you in the symbolized form.
- Imagine being blamed by your peers and supervisor for bringing this on yourself with your naivete.
- Convert this repulsive/attractive scenario into a security procedure that prohibits the class of objects and forbids the behaviors that created the object.
- Imagine the third object.
- Imagine a way in which it could be used to escape from prison.
- Imagine that everyone else sees it except you.
- Imagine that the person has escaped and that you are now being told that you should have known and that you inadvertently provided the means.
- Imagine a policy that would prevent such stupidity as yours.
- Take the three objects and combine the implied behaviors into one person, an inmate, who is assaultive, sexually predatory and hyper-opportunistically looking for a means to escape.
- Try to imagine working as this person's therapist, while obeying all of the security procedures that you have devised, and in the milieu in which people blame you for these things.

The discovery of secret aggression, secret sexuality and secret growth is only the next layer of the quest for the Ultimate Secret. This can never be seen or found, because it is a projection in a paranoid system. It can, however, be projected onto an object.

Klein (1930/1975) saw the object of knowledge as the control of the destruction of the mother:

"The dominant aim is to possess himself of the contents of the mother's body and to destroy her by means of every weapon which sadism can command" (p. 219). This is an excellent description of the dynamic mentioned above, but it is projected by the staff onto the inmates and does not originate with them, though they, like everyone else in the milieu, partake of these object relations.

If Klein is to be believed, the defense in early Oedipal stages (for her, the first year of life) is against destructive impulses. Klein sees as central paranoid anxiety, which is a fear of massive and deadly retaliation by the mother and father's penis (which is inside the mother) avenging the destruction fantasized by the child. Fantasized or (to use Klein's technically specific spelling) "phantasied" destruction leads to the fear of annihilative retaliation, and the next stage, the depressive, cannot occur.

The Dynamic of Envy

The other Kleinian dynamic that is pervasive in prison is that of envy. If an inmate looks too "good" or unaffected by his status, if he acts too equal, the dynamic of envy is empowered. Klein (1957/1975) defines envy as "the angry feeling that another person possesses and enjoys something desirable—the envious impulse being to take it away or to spoil it" (p. 181). The inmate who possesses a good core, particularly if it is any form of the depressive position, must be robbed or spoiled.

The continual spoilage can be easily seen in the routine statement made by staff about paroling inmates: "He'll be back." This may or may not be true, but within the paranoid structure described herein, a tremendous effort is devoted to making it true. The daily deprivation of all good objects through this envious dynamic is profound and has the unconsciously desired results.

Envy is defended against by splitting, the division of the world into good objects and bad objects. But envy continually undermines its own effectiveness by producing more hatred and projection, and the fear of persecution and attack is greatly increased. By the production of fear of all kinds, the prison itself reinforces envy, and sabotages splitting. Envy works to pull down into the paranoid soup any persons, staff or inmates, who represent good objects; the better the object, the stronger the envy.

Nurturant therapy, as a good object, is productive of malice and scorn. It is seen either as naive, therefore dangerous, or as ineffective, therefore not good enough. So the options are envy or splitting, coupled with primitive idealization and otherwise paranoid saturation of both sides of the split that subtly ruins it as a defense mechanism. The goal of splitting developmentally is to reconstitute an ego, i.e. an adult persona that can be more effectively moral, because he or she sees clearly that the totally good and the totally bad are more conceptual than actual.

But envy, hatred and projective mechanisms pull regressively towards disintegration even of the prison itself as they also drag the individual psyche into psychosis. This is the homeostasis that gives the illusion of a "stabilized" paranoid system: envy, devaluation, and annihilation claw down the edifice of splitting, which, as it reacts and regains lost ground, re-empowers envy, devaluation and splitting. It is the circular stability of developmental arrest, by nature unstable and temporary, the enraged dog chasing his tail.

This envy, it must be emphasized, is of good objects, which includes any object in which paranoid egos invest, whether inmates or staff members. Envy spreads to projections of projections in a generalizing search-and-destroy mission. These can be anything: an artistic creation or a pack of cigarettes or friends or an attorney's address or a daily schedule or, even, a first name. They can be animate or inanimate, human or nonhuman. But wherever there is an investment of libido or aggression, there is a systematic envious destruction of these objects, and whatever threatens growth (escape) is the most quickly eliminated.

Envious Destruction

One recent example of this was an inmate who spent months making a model Spanish galleon out of tongue depressors, a creative feat, only to have it confiscated as a misuse of state property. This is an excellent instance of pure envy, since the tongue depressors were no longer usable as anything, presented no risk to security (they had been broken into small segments), and were not expensive items. Yet the ship was confiscated.

Another example is the recent elimination of exercise equipment and the extreme limitations placed on the amount of weight that can be used by inmates on the remaining equipment. The argument is given that inmates are more dangerous as they become more muscular, yet there is no identifiable correlation between greater muscularity and greater assaultiveness.

The main motive for the inmates is the prevention of assaults by other inmates, and a narcissistic investment in one's own body as a defense against the paranoid system of the prison as well as a territorial investment in the weight pile areas. However, driven by the legislature and the public, the tide of envious deprivation has reached a new high water mark, and even the physical potentiality of one's own body, a truly primitive object, is controlled and another good object is spoiled.

Whereas regularly housed, non-mentally ill inmates are permitted only a modicum of neutralized objects, those identified as mentally ill or excessively violent are deprived even of these objects to an excessive degree. In acute psychiatric units, one must use the liquid soap, for example, in a group shower and there is resistance to inmates having their own toiletries. The active paranoid imagination of the staff will, of course, produce the "security excuse" for this, but the reality is psychodynamic: it is the envious, whittling-away of one's possessions, the routine, uncaring, pseudodemocratic ("if we allow you to have it, we will have to allow all of the inmates to have it") destruction of one's good objects.

Reparation

All losses, in Kleinian thinking, and the depressive stage thus produced are the results of one's own destructiveness, and "our strongest hatred is directed against the hatred in ourselves" (Klein, 1937/1975, p. 340). Reparation occurs as a result of this depressive stage, and the paranoid environment, whether intrapsychic or projected and reintrojected as a universe of menace, prevents this from occurring for everyone within it. The inmates must defend themselves against the prison itself and the staff must defend themselves against identifying with this annihilative, primitive, punitive object. Without reparation, there can be only recidivism, since the inmate cannot escape from these object relations even when he leaves the prison. These relations are reinforced by the parole agent and the disapproval and contempt of society in general. Without reparation, the regressive pull of the paranoid position represented by the prison is truly irresistible; inmates will return to avoid retaliation. Without reparation, loss becomes chronic and chronically defended against. One is chronically desolate and empty, and one's world is correspondingly desolate and empty.

Creativity and love are the products of reparation and developmentally complete (relatively) depression, which then permit the acceptance of hatred in oneself and in others and create positive expectations for the future, and therefore, reinforces hope and possibility. The prison, by continually converting depression into paranoia, murders hope and flattens all possibility. As inmates are told "You'll be back," the world is reinforced as a paranoid object, and the hopeful possibility, of "paying your debt to society" is canceled. The pressure from an increasingly fearful and ignorant society for longer and less determinate sentences further reinforces the prison as such a paranoid system, as a juggernaut of hopelessness and desperation, of pervasive fear and true intrapsychic and societal imprisonment.

One healthy response to the rigidity of the paranoid system is humor. Insofar as humor threatens structure, the joke is seen as the phenomenological equivalent of a planned escape, and humor must be managed. If the humor is at the expense of the inmates, it is permitted and even encouraged: finding the threatening ridiculous permits and reinforces the idea of the superiority of the guards to the inmates and so functions like the S.S. laughing at their helpless prisoners. Yet humor used like this is never self-referential and therefore cannot be growth-inducing. Indeed, this type of humor reinforces the paranoia.

But humor used to make fun of the system or its keepers rapidly produces a punitive response from the system, because it threatens the structure and is therefore equated with secret criminality. This is mirrored in the society at large, which has decided that its problems can only be solved if "taken seriously," which means being approached with a paranoid level of angry intensity that denies the relief of the entire systemic collapse afforded by humor.

In terms of real power, even without the paranoid dynamic of the system, even without the characterologic baggage that staff bring to the job, it is still true that power without love corrupts the person who possesses it. The power that parents have over children would be oppressive without love. Slave owners in antebellum United States claimed that they loved their slaves like parents, but this did not prevent the abuses and dehumanization that slavery routinely produced. If anything, it functioned as a parental justification for all of the evils of slavery, such as whipping and, ironically, the actual splitting-up of real families. At this point, someone will, of course, raise the objection that the difference was profound. The slaves were innocent victims. Yet the dynamics of dehumanizing oppressive systems are the same. The reality of someone committing a crime, no matter of what seriousness, and someone being treated as if they had, are dynamically identical and produce the same results. The reality of personal responsibility for crime is immediately subsumed to role, and the oppressive and paranoid dynamics follow logically. Of course, making the innocent guilty as a justification for punishing them is a truism of history, but the guilty require only slightly less justification.

What prison as a paranoid system cannot produce, like the individual personality disorder, is the creative spiral of healthy behaviors that generate other healthy behaviors. In the absence of predominantly pathological dynamics, and when free from the double-bind of developmental arrests, institutions or persons have, in their psychosocial foregrounds, object-states that could lead to a more evolved development. Some of these are an integrated and tolerant conscience that recognizes the variability of ethical situations; a genuinely mature belief in the efficacy of obeying the law and an acceptance of the limits of law-abidance as well; an ability to tolerate the frustration of long-term social planning and goals, as required by the gradual reduction of crime; an abhorrence of the futility of wasted human and economic resources; a genuine, good-natured love for people, their creativity, their objects, and potential for growth; and, last but not least, a real, indefatigable, self-deprecating, and positively iconoclastic sense of humor.

References
Allen, B. & Bosta, D. (1993). *Games criminals play: How you can profit by knowing them*. Sacramento: Rae John Publishers.
Greenberg, J. R. & Mitchell, S. A. (1983). *Object relations in psychoanalytic theory*. Cambridge: Harvard University Press.
Jonas, H. (1963). *The gnostic religion*. Boston: Beacon Hill Press.
Klein, M. (1975). A contribution to the psychogenesis of manic-depressive states. In R.E. Money-Kyrlie (Ed.), *Melanie Klein—Love, guilt and reparation and other works— 1921-1945*. (pp.262-289). New York: Delacorte Press\Seymour Lawrence. (Original work published 1935)
Klein, M. (1975). Early stages of the Oedipus conflict. In R.E. Money-Kyrlie (Ed.), *Melanie Klein—Love, guilt and reparation and other works—1921-1945*. (pp.186-198). New York: Delacorte Press\Seymour Lawrence. (Original work published 1928)
Klein, M. (1975). Envy and gratitude. In R.E. Money-Kyrlie (Ed.), *Melanie Klein—Envy and gratitude and other works—1946-1963*. (pp.176-235). New York: Delacorte Press\Seymour Lawrence. (Original work published 1957)
Klein, M. (1975). Love, guilt and reparation. In R.E. Money-Kyrlie (Ed.), *Melanie Klein—Love, guilt, and reparation and other works—1921-1945*. (pp. 306-343). New York: Delacorte Press\Seymour Lawrence. (Original work published 1937)
Klein, M. (1975). On mental health . In R.E. Money-Kyrlie (Ed.), *Melanie Klein—Envy and gratitude and other works—1946-1963*. (pp.268-274). New York: Delacorte Press\Seymour Lawrence. (Original work published 1960)
Morrison, A. P. (1989). *Shame, the underside of narcissism*. Hillsdale, New Jersey: The Analytic Press

Part 2

SOME SOLUTIONS

The Ultimate Hidden Weapon:
Art Therapy and the Compromise Option

David Gussak, MA, A.T.R.-BC

Prison is described as a paranoid system by Fox in his chapter *The Hidden Weapon*, using an object-relations model. He defines this primitive relationship as made up of two poles, the ego and the object. As this primitive relationship only consists of these two poles, what happens if a third entity, a clinician, is introduced into this system?

This article will explore the work of a therapist, specifically an art therapist in this setting, delineating the difficulties, the advantages and some of the results.

The Compromise Option

Fox says "nurturant therapy...is productive of malice and scorn," a product of the paranoia inherent in the system. Given the projected invasive quality of the third agent, the clinician must choose among three options:

- The clinician can be pulled toward either the ego or the object.

Commonly, a clinician after a period of working in this setting can become part of the paranoid system, and become overly punitive, or overly empathic and solicitous. For example, some clinicians quit their jobs as therapists, and become correctional officers, while others behave illegally and break the rules of the facility by doing favors for the inmates. Eventually, these latter clinicians are caught, and "walked-out." (The person who breaks the rules is literally "walked out" of the institution. Accompanied by two correctional officers, the offending staff person is told to leave everything, and is escorted to the front gate where he or she must turn in their identification card. He or she may or may not have legal charges filed, depending on the seriousness of the infraction.)

- The clinician can remain neutral and try to maintain his or her own integrity, only to be ridiculed by both sides, making his services valueless.

Neither side will accept the clinician's services, as this primitive environment cannot support a third entity. Although some correctional staff do not adhere closely to these primitive principles, and do see the value of therapy and actually are concerned about their charges, the system itself will not, and cannot, progress beyond a primitive dyadic stage.

DRAWING TIME

- The clinician can compromise.

He or she can follow the rules, accept scorn from the correctional staff and resentment from the inmates, but at the same time be strong enough to work within these limitations by compromise. The complication of this option arises because compromise requires a perspective and an understanding of both poles, which those in a primitive relationship would suspect. So the clinician must compromise while not appearing to, meeting the expectations of the establishment and the inmates, without either side suspecting that there is a compromise with the other pole. This is difficult but possible.

The compromise option is by far the most productive and desirable. Only with this method can a third entity remain separate, avoiding the magnetic draw of either pole. Through compromise, the clinician can function, and therapy, despite its reputation, can occur.

When art therapy is used, a whole new dimension of paranoia is created. Fox takes the reader through the phenomenon of the "hidden weapon" explaining that anything in a paranoid system can be altered for the expression of aggression, sexuality and escape. Consequently, the creativity evoked by the process of art therapy is inherently suspect.

The Act of Creating Art

The act of creating art has been directly linked to the instinctual, primitive impulses that are most feared; aggression and sexuality. Ellen Dissanayake (1992) states that art and sex, rather than substitutes for each other, are "each primal behaviors that have become elaborated in the essential service of affiliation and bonding" (p. 193). She also indicates (1988) that "...the impulses that drive some people to violence are the same impulses that drive the artist to create. Art and violence are perhaps alike primarily in the fact that both can be considered expressions and agents of feelings" (p. 140). Kramer (1971) and Rank (1932) talk of creativity as a by-product of the sublimation of these instinctual, libidinal impulses.

The act of creating has also long been associated with the act of "escape." It allows an inmate/patient to retreat into a fantasy world that he has created. For a little while, creating allows a healthy diversion from bleak surroundings. This, of course, contradicts the purpose of the correctional system, which is to remind an inmate, every waking moment, that he is in prison to be punished.

In an illustration of paranoid reaction to art, a correctional nurse became upset over an inmate/patient's nicely rendered portrait of a woman (please refer to the chapter *Breaking Through Barriers* for the structure of the facility and how art therapy is accomplished). The nurse believed the inmate deliberately drew the indentation in the neck to look like a penis, and wanted the inmate to be given a disciplinary write-up that could result in the loss of parole time, lengthening his sentence. In the opinion of many staff members, arriving at that conclusion required much over-interpretation. Whether or not there was an "actual" penis hidden in the throat of the drawn woman, the institutional fear of the object's primitive sexuality was enough to create this strong paranoid reaction.

Another paranoid response was to a delusional inmate/patient's drawing, consisting of simple doodles of floating skulls and half naked female warriors drawn with a golf pencil on a piece of notebook paper. The correctional staff brought this drawing to the attention of the unit

THE ULTIMATE HIDDEN WEAPON

treatment team, voicing concern over the "aggressive, violent, delusional nature" of the images. They had removed the drawing from the inmate/patient's cell without his knowledge.

During the treatment team conference, I was asked to "interpret" the drawing. I informed the team that we would not discuss the drawings until after the patient left. When the inmate/patient became visibly upset, he was assured that his artwork would be returned to him. The drawing was "interpreted" later as stereotypical, representative of drawings frequently done by rebellious and talented adolescents.

The staff chose to make impotent the imaginary aggression of the images by exercising their control over the object. To the obvious dismay of the inmate/patient, the staff had taken the work he had created, reminding him that as "property of the state," he had no right to invest even in his own artwork.

Ironically, there was one drawing by this patient to which the staff could have reacted with appropriate concern. On the back of one of his drawings, he drew a map with labeled landmarks, streets and banks. Next to the map was a list of objects that could be used to make an escape attempt, or rob a bank.

Maps are contraband in prison, and the drawing of a map could have resulted in punishment. The staff chose to become concerned about doodles, and never noticed an obvious, and potentially dangerous, infraction of rules. The correctional staff was more concerned about their imaginary projection of aggression than something real. The treatment team was made aware of the map, and during an informal one-to-one session, the improprieties of possessing a map in prison and why the staff might be concerned if the map was seen was explained carefully.

The Ultimate Hidden Weapon

In most cases, however, the art created during art therapy becomes the ultimate hidden weapon since art has the ability to hide the therapeutic process. The act of making art allows therapy to happen, allows the expression of the instinctual impulses, while the "environment" remains unaware. In this sense, the hidden process becomes the core of the art therapy. It allows the inmate/patient to express himself in most situations without fear of retaliation from the environment.

During an art therapy session, correctional people come into the group and see the inmates participating in what they perceive as childish activities. They comment on it, talking down to the inmate/patient, belittling them for "coloring." To infantilize someone is to make them impotent, harmless. It is a way for the ego to take power away from the projected object. Fox describes infantilization as a means of annihilation.

An art therapist in any other setting might want to protect the integrity of the group process and tell the staff privately what the process is actually eliciting. In prison, that could be self-defeating. Although the tasks are quite powerful for the participants in the group, they appear benign and simplistic to the correctional staff. The art therapist should allow the staff to continue to think that way and ignore their infantilizing behavior so that the staff, in turn, do not become wary and fearful of the process. Only when the results of the tasks become obviously meaningful to the correctional staff do they react strongly.

DRAWING TIME

Sometimes correctional staff can be drawn into the group with a little prompting. While participating, the staff person will make fun of his or her own art piece, and develop what appears on the surface to be a sense of camaraderie and empathy with others in the group. The staff person's sense of distrust and hostility seems momentarily suspended, almost absorbed. However, it is not a response to any sort of bond with the inmates, nor is it empathy. Once the process is over, he or she will return to the same distant relationship and resume prior suspicions.

The Compromise Option in Action

In the name of security, stringent institutional rules have developed concerning what art tools and materials can and cannot be used. Here the fantasy of the hidden weapon becomes real and so produces a veritable obstacle course for the art therapist. Some examples follow:

- At the time of this writing, scissors have been completely banned, despite the fact that several months earlier, safety scissors were considered appropriate. Safety scissors obtained long ago can still be used, but new ones will not come through the gate.

- Long pencils have become dangerous, since one was used in a recent hostage-taking. (In a later chapter, an art therapist will describe what it was like being held hostage by an inmate wielding sharp pencils.)

- Clay, the material of choice for three-dimensional exercises, is considered contraband.

Three-dimensional techniques are important for the prison environment because they foster "growth" and expansion beyond two-dimensional parameters and limitations. However, clay can be used to jam locks, to make impressions of keys, to hide things, or it can be shaped into 'shivs.' Therefore, the Compromise Option found new, nonthreatening materials for the construction of three-dimensional objects.

Paper

One compromise was paper sculptures, as seen in figures 1 and 2. The inmate/patients construct three-dimensional forms with limited supplies (white paper, safety scissors and glue), creating a familiar challenge in this environment; making the most from the least.

Figure 1 was a paper sculpture constructed by Mr. C, anxious because he was being paroled in four days. His anxiety was exacerbated by a long history of alcohol abuse and barely stabilized delusional and persecutory symptoms. When allowed to draw freely, he drew a rigid, tightly controlled image of a three-dimensional cross. In his three-dimensional piece, he clearly demonstrated a looser, less controlled style. The three-dimensional format encouraged the expression of his anxiety, otherwise repressed.

Figure 2 was constructed by Mr. R who had already served 12 years of a life sentence for first-degree murder. With this exercise, he formed a hollow, closed, geometric form, with an inaccessible core. This was a startling metaphor for this inmate/patient, who learned through experience that for his survival, it was necessary to present a structured solid exterior, while concealing what was inside.

Plaster of Paris

Another means of three-dimensional expression, as seen in figures 3 through 6, is plaster. Although plaster dries into a rocklike substance, which could be used as a weapon, it is

THE ULTIMATE HIDDEN WEAPON

Figure 1: Mr. C—white paper sculpture

Figure 2: Mr. R—white paper sculpture

nevertheless permitted because it dries before the end of each session, making it easy to be accounted for. Additionally, plaster is not a new material to the institution since the hospital staff uses it for casts.

Mixed plaster is poured into cupped hands to set. The plaster is wet and soggy and heats up dramatically as it hardens. The inmate/patients must stay in the same position for at least 15 to 20 minutes for the piece to harden enough to move their fingers without cracking it. (It is important to tell the inmate/patients to wriggle their fingers slightly as the plaster dries to give their fingers enough room to be removed easily.) Once dried, the plaster can be painted.

Tactile senses are called into play because of the variable range of texture, temperature and solidity of the drying plaster. Trust issues are addressed because the inmate/patients are helpless with their hands bound by the plaster. Generally there are no feelings of competition or inadequacy as there are no expectations for creating a recognizable form.

Figure 3 was created by Mr. N, in prison for second degree robbery. Admitted for psychotic depression, he heard voices and attempted to swallow razor blades. While on the unit, he selectively interacted with a few people. He knew the importance of not drawing attention to himself. During this art therapy session he maintained a flat, depressive affect and had little difficulty as the piece dried in his hand. However, he appeared somewhat wary of the other patients and remained quiet.

The darkness and the monochromatic quality of the piece suggested depression. However, he used a lot of energy in choosing the colors and mixing them to a shade that was finally satisfactory. He displayed the new blue-green color with quiet pride, showing it to select members of the group. The lack of bright colors demonstrated Mr. N's tendency to avoid drawing attention to himself. Painting his piece in this fashion might have been his way to

63

DRAWING TIME

Figure 3: Mr. N—plaster hand sculpture with acrylic paint

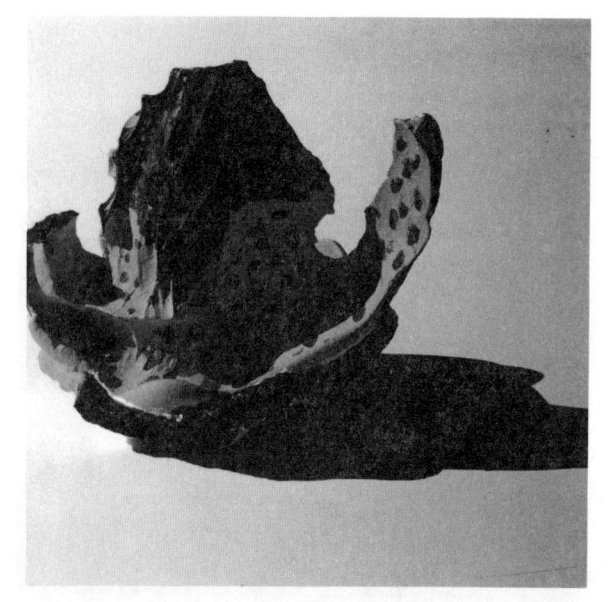

Figure 4: Mr. F—plaster hand sculpture with acrylic paint

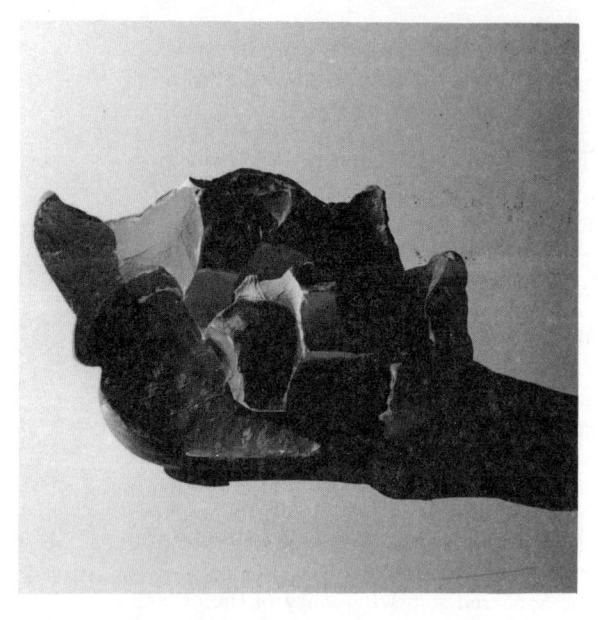

Figure 5: Mr. Y—plaster hand sculpture with acrylic paint

Figure 6: Mr. C— plaster hand sculpture unpainted

"blend into the background," and remain inconspicuous. Mr. N was a tall man, reflective in the large size of the piece. He deliberately and painstakingly became "monochromatic," both in his behavior, and in his art piece.

Figure 4 was completed by Mr. F, a 29 year old man, in prison for first degree burglary, and due for parole in 2002. When he was admitted to the unit for several suicide attempts he was resistant and withdrawn. By the time he was discharged six months later, he had improved a great deal. He participated more in groups, interacted better with his peers, and was much brighter in mood. His artwork was completed about two months into his stay on the unit, when he was still basically quiet. He had no difficulty waiting for it to dry, indicating he was more comfortable around his peers. He took great care in removing his hands, exhibiting a sense of pride for his piece.

The piece is quite large, and brightly painted. It seems to grow upwards, as he appeared to do, out of his depression. Although still generally quiet during this process, he smiled a great deal, and expressed his enjoyment of the project, which apparently gave him a feeling of fulfillment and satisfaction.

Figure 5 was created by Mr. Y, who was in prison after attempting to use his automobile as a "deadly weapon," and resisting a peace officer. He was admitted to the unit for being socially withdrawn, yelling, and talking about hanging himself. A psychologist who interviewed Mr. Y prior to his trial said his aggressive act was a result of his bipolar disorder. Since he began taking medication, he was free of his manic symptoms, was quiet and interacted well with his peers.

The art process was important for Mr. Y because he demonstrated an increase in frustration tolerance, patience and control. The task gauged how well the treatment had worked for his symptoms. Neither mania or restlessness was present in Mr. Y throughout the art process. He painted his piece using blue and yellow, deliberately leaving some spaces bare. Leaving bare spaces may well have been reflective of the scattered energy evident with controlled, hypomanic behavior. I found it interesting that someone with a bipolar diagnosis should also be bipolar with his color use (as seen with the complementary colors).

Figure 6 was created by Mr. C (the artist of figure 1), who chose not to paint his piece. This may have been a reflection of his earlier tendency to avoid taking chances or try anything new, as seen with his inclination to rigidly stick with his schema of the three-dimensional cross.

Paper Making
Papermaking was another means of creating three-dimensional form, as seen in figures 7 through 10. The pulp must be mixed in the blender before the group meeting for security reasons. Colored pulp, grass, leaves, used paper and torn blue denim fabric were added to the pulp to create interesting designs and colors in the paper, ensuring that no two pieces of paper came out the same. The latter material, the denim fabric, was particularly symbolic for the group, since their uniforms were blue denim shirts, slacks and jackets.

The inmate/patients shaped the paper before it dried to create three-dimensional forms. Similar to the other projects, there was no standard form for the papermaking products. The possibilities for feelings of competition and inadequacy were again reduced as there were no expectations of creating a recognizable image. Again the inmate/patients developed some ability to delay gratification because of the time between creating the wet piece of paper, waiting until everyone had made a piece, and then waiting for the paper to dry.

Figure 7 was created by Mr. N (the artist of figure 4). He allowed his first piece of paper dry into a wrinkled, three-dimensional form, gluing it to a second flat piece of handmade paper. In

DRAWING TIME

Figure 7: Mr. N—handmade paper and ink markers

Figure 8: Mr. Y—handmade paper and ink markers

Figure 10a: Mr. V—handmade paper and ink markers

Figure 10b: Mr. V—handmade paper and ink markers

contrast to his previous monochromatic plaster hand sculpture, he incorporated more color, taking the chance of drawing attention to himself. However, he expressed some anxiety by scribbling lines and tearing the corners of the paper.

In a dramatic example of how art therapy can allow the expression of dangerous feelings safely, without jeopardy, Mr. N was able to demonstrate his anxiety nonverbally and innocuously in front of both the group and the staff, who would not know to "read anxiety" in his scribblings and paper tearing.

Figure 8 was completed by Mr. Y (the artist of figure 5). After making two pieces of handmade paper, similar to one another, he cut one into smaller pieces and glued them to the other. If seen from an angle, the top pieces seemed to grow from the bottom piece. If seen from the front, the top pieces blended into the background. Unlike Mr. N, who was more expressive with this project than his plaster sculpture, Mr. Y's style became more subdued and "hidden." He began to "disappear" on the unit as he drew very little attention to himself. Unless looked at from a different angle, Mr. Y became lost.

In the correctional setting, an inmate who asks for attention is seen as weak by his peers, and as bothersome by the staff. Mr. Y was a slightly-built man, and to call attention to himself would have been dangerous. Consequently, he learned to become quiet and unobtrusive on the unit. His art clearly communicated what Mr. Y dared not say out loud.

Figure 9 (see color plate 7) was completed by Mr. L, a 22 year old kidnapper, not scheduled for parole until 2013. Admitted to the acute psychiatric unit for severe depression, suicide attempts and refusing his medication, he was constantly preoccupied by voices in his head which he could not understand. He believed it was the voice of Hitler speaking in German and he knew the voices were angry at him for leaving his "skinhead" gang.

He also complained of shocks in his head, possibly a residual effect of his long history of methamphetamine abuse. All this made Mr. L anxious, resulting in poor impulse and anger control. This, coupled with angry voices he could not understand, made him feel alienated. The clearest way he communicated his sense of isolation was when he plaintively suggested that he study German so that he could understand and communicate with the voices in his head.

Art therapy was the logical choice of treatment since he was unable to express himself verbally, was quiet and brooding and rarely interacted with others. During the papermaking project, Mr. L, like Mr. N, allowed the first piece of paper to dry in a three-dimensional, wrinkled form. He glued this to the top of the second sheet, and drew the design in ink markers after the papers had dried.

He drew the background in a controlled fashion, taking great care in its construction. He seemed to underline his sense of isolation in this piece. The top was shaped like a barren mountain. At the corners of the bottom piece of paper he drew black, squiggly lines radiating towards the mountain, possibly reminiscent of the shocks he felt in his head. The lines might also be indicative of the frightening background "noise" in his head in a language he did not understand. His artwork seemed expressive of how he felt about the situation that he endured.

During this art therapy session, Mr. L demonstrated more self-control and comfort in the group because he did not have to talk about his issues. As no one had expectations of him, he did not feel judged by the group.

Figure 10 (a and b) was created by Mr. V, who was imprisoned for an intricately-planned bank robbery aborted by a silent alarm. He and his partner shot at the police with military assault weapons while trying to escape. Not only did he shoot an officer in the leg, but he killed a tied-up kidnap victim, shooting him in the back of the head. He was convicted of robbery, kidnap, assault with a deadly weapon, assault with intent to kill and first degree murder. He was given a life sentence.

Shortly before his admission to the hospital, Mr. V cut his arm, causing tendon damage, and made several other suicide attempts. In one attempt, after a deliberate medication overdose, he was comatose for three weeks. Mr. V believed himself to be smarter than everyone on the unit, and enjoyed showing people up with his trivial knowledge. Mr. V also made it clear that he wanted to kill himself, and that staff was too stupid and inadequate to stop him.

Mr. V's bank robbery failed because of poor planning for which he blamed others. He believed those hurt because of his stupidity and inadequacy deserved what they got. For example, he killed his tied-up victim, believing that someone so inadequate that he allowed himself to be kidnapped deserved to die. His sense that the inadequate and stupid deserve to die eventually came full circle, and he believed he himself should die. The only way he could prove others were more stupid than he was for others to be unable to stop him from killing himself, thus confirming his sense of superiority and projected inadequacy. The reality ultimately was not that staff was too inadequate to stop him from killing himself, but that Mr. V was too inadequate to refrain from hurting himself. He continually mocked me. Rather than be drawn in and respond to his taunts, I used the Compromise Option and allowed his provocative behavior to continue, if only to involve him in art therapy.

His particular art therapy project displayed the forensic dynamics that actually led to the crime. The product (figure 10) developed into a clear message. On the top piece of handmade paper was a warning not to lift the piece of paper. Once lifted, the "victim" read the message, "Bite Me." When Mr. V described the piece of work, he stated, "Whoever disregards the warning gets what they deserve." The order to not lift the paper is the equivalent to "don't rob the bank." When he robbed the bank, and bungled the job so well, "bite me" was the appropriate result. Therefore, the victims he speaks of, the ones who "get what they deserve" are not only those he hurt and killed, but himself as well.

Mr. V's art piece was actually considered humorous by some of the other group members. However, if this message had been directed towards staff, the results would have been drastically different, resulting in a punitive action. Through art therapy, Mr. V was presented a safe arena in which to express himself and his convoluted thinking.

Mask-Making

Mask-making, another valuable tool, has been a dilemma in the prison. As a rule, creating masks is forbidden because it is seen as part of escape attempts. However, possibly unbeknownst to the correctional staff, the inmates in the prison have already "escaped by putting on masks." In order to hide themselves from others in the dangerous environment, the inmates wear other faces, putting up walls and defenses to hide themselves. Therefore, the creating of masks in a group can be seen as a naturally evolving art task, concretizing what they do all the time.

In the book, *The Mystic Imagination*, Stephen Larsen (1990) stressed the importance of mask-making:

THE ULTIMATE HIDDEN WEAPON

> When one enters 'concealment' behind the mask, there is a paradoxical freeing of behavior. A transformation of character may take place, as hidden or suppressed parts of the self come to the fore. Ultimately the transformation is revealing rather than concealing. There is a glimpse of the inner cast of characters that inhabits each one of us, (p. 236).

Therefore, two events occur at once; the inmate/patients create masks to hide behind, yet the masks become truer forms of expression, ones that can be verbally denied if necessary.

However, since creating masks is illegal in prison, in order to use such an important art therapy task, the Compromise Option had to be used (as seen in figures 11 through 15). Since the main security concern was to prevent the inmate/patients from disguising themselves, the trick was to create a mask that could not possibly resemble a face. Paper plates were used simply because there was no way they could be made to look like actual faces.

Figure 11 was created by Mr. W, a gregarious and talkative inmate, in prison serving his most recent parole violation for drug use. He was admitted to the unit because he was preoccupied with religious delusions. He stabilized quickly after taking medication, and was scheduled for parole within two months. He voiced fears of getting into trouble that would interfere with his parole.

During previous parole revocations, Mr. W did not invest himself in art tasks, remaining superficial in his approach. However, since mask-making is, by definition, superficial in the sense of creating a surface with the intent to cover, Mr. W actually found the task comfortable enough to express his true feelings; anxiety over his upcoming parole and fear that he might once again fail. The black piece of tissue paper over the mouth was to "gag" himself to avoid further trouble, showing awareness that he could create problems with his parole if he talked too much. In addition, no evidence in this piece suggested religious preoccupation.

Among the many advantages and power of art therapy with this population is the ability to compare artwork of recidivists from previous prison time and parole revocations to predict the possibility of recidivism, and deal with it. (While this book was going into publication, Mr. W called the unit to let the staff know that he was able to get his parole relocated to where he was closer to his family, was holding down a steady job, and was getting married.)

Figure 12 was created by Mr. N, (described earlier), four months after his admission to the acute unit. The mask is completed with tissue paper, black and pink felt, silver-shiny paper, and sparkles. The beard, mustache and hair on the mask look like his own, but the mask reveals a more colorful and flamboyant character, with the pink hair style reminiscent of Dennis Rodman. By the time he completed his mask, he seemed more comfortable on the unit. Compared to his hand sculpture in figure 3 and his papermaking project in figure 7, Mr. N was willing to take even more creative risks. For the first time, he made a piece that was more expressive and outgoing. However, the emphasis around the eyes and the exaggerated ears amplified his need to be aware continually of what was going on around him.

Figure 13 was completed by Mr. S, in prison with a life sentence for two counts of first degree murder and three counts of attempted murder. After he was laid off from his job at an engineering firm, he returned and planted a bomb which injured three people. Then he shot and killed two more.

DRAWING TIME

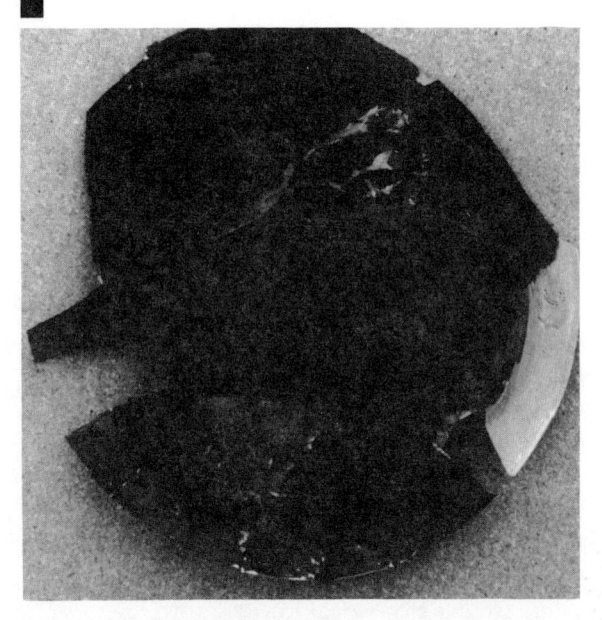

Figure 11: Mr. W—paper plate mask

Figure 12: Mr. N—paper plate mask

Mr. S had been insisting forcefully that his co-workers listen to his bizarre interpretations of the Bible, such as justifying murder, by insisting that Ezekiel really meant "easy kill". He believed that in being laid off, he had been persecuted for his beliefs, and that those responsible were preventing him from spreading the "True Gospel." Therefore, afterwards, he felt no remorse. Mr. S was in a maximum security prison when he became angry and hostile after his religious beliefs were confronted by the correctional staff. He was then transferred for acute psychiatric care, where, although he seemed meek and quiet, he would become angry when his beliefs were questioned by the clinical staff. Whenever he interacted verbally in sessions, his lengthy religious preaching dominated the conversations. Fortunately, art therapy with its nonverbal aspects made it unnecessary for Mr. S to preach to his peers.

Figure 13: Mr. S—paper plate mask

Mr. S used markers and pink and black felt to design a mask of a cat (figure 13) presumably a representation of himself. On another level, the mask seemed to be what he believed he was. The image of a cat was the last image that could be associated with this large, ungraceful older man who lacked any prowess. On the second level, possibly, this mask was how he saw

THE ULTIMATE HIDDEN WEAPON

himself, a competent, powerful messenger of God who should destroy all nonbelievers. At the same time, the image of a cat, always wary of those around it, revealed Mr. S's paranoid nature and fear of nonbelievers. Creating a mask allowed Mr. S to express himself without fear of retribution or persecution by the staff and fellow inmate/patients.

The next mask, figure 14 (a and b), was created by Mr. J, a 27 year old man, in prison because he violated his parole. He was scheduled to be paroled within a month of his admission to the unit.

Mr. J presented himself as a cheerful and affable person. However, within Mr. J, there was a clear split. Despite his happy and problem-free facade, he was actually suffering from lupus, an autoimmune disease which affects the connective tissues of joints and muscles. He had many physical problems including a scarred face, swollen finger joints and high blood pressure. Despite repeated warnings, Mr. J, denying any real illness, rarely complied with his strict salt-free diet so he retained water, and gained weight rapidly.

Denial also showed up in a form of "focused dementia" about his future. He was unable, or unwilling, to discuss his future beyond a couple of days, including any plans for a successful parole. However, in order to treat the lupus, Mr. J had to participate in continual ongoing care. For there to be a semblance of success in treatment, his denial had to be counteracted on a daily basis.

The strength of the split and denial that Mr. J experienced was seen in the split of the mask he created in art therapy (figure 14). Mr. J wanted the mask to look like Charlie Chaplin. He put sparkles on the cheeks, black felt for the nose and mustache, used blue and pink markers to outline the eyes and black construction paper for the hat. Despite his intention to make a

Figure 14a: Mr. J— paper plate mask (front)   *Figure 14b: Mr. J—paper plate mask (back)*

comedic mask, the face is rather somber. Mr. J then turned the plate over and added black and blue tissue paper, and sparkles. He labeled these as "worms on the brain". The mask displayed his duality. The outside of the mask, although somber looking, was intended to be Charlie Chaplin, who made others laugh. The "worms" on the "inside" represented his illness, Lupus, burrowing into his brain. The presence of the two ideas on different sides of the same work of art generally is indicative of denial.

After he completed the mask, he was able to talk briefly about his illness in the group. He said, despite what he was told by the doctors, he still knew very little about the disease. The cheerful facade was momentarily broken and he was able to discuss how he felt about being sick and how uncertain he was about his future. By the time he was paroled, he was in compliance with dietary orders and lost some of the excess weight he had gained. He also listened more attentively to the doctors and clinical staff when given feedback about how to take care of himself. When he finally left, he had a more solid plan for his immediate future.

The mask in figure 15 (see color plate 6), was created by Mr. V (described earlier) using color markers. With no eyeholes, the wearer could not see out (and no one could see in). Under the face of the devil, was the message, "Trust me." Mr. V's mask further elaborated the dynamics seen in figure 10: "If you are stupid and inadequate enough to trust the devil, you deserve what you get," in essence, a continuation of the "Do Not Lift Me, Bite Me" dichotomy— "Trust Me, but watch out if you do. I'm the devil."

He may also have created this mask to show what he had stirred up around him. In attempts to cause friction between his peers and the staff, he would forever proclaim the staff's inadequacies despite appeals by them to be trusted. For Mr. V, untrustworthiness equaled powerlessness. Although his partner trusted him to plan a successful robbery, he was powerless to do so, and proved himself inadequate. Again, Mr. V attempted to demonstrate his belief that the staff were powerless to stop him from killing himself. Essentially, the mask and the message "trust me" were incongruous, as were Mr. V's perceptions of himself.

As demonstrated by the above illustrations, the Compromise Option can be incorporated, art projects assigned, and therapy achieved, despite the institutional limits on support, materials and tasks.

Conclusion

The primitive relationship that comprises the correctional system does not easily allow for a third factor, a clinician. Therefore, in order to maintain an identity, and perform the job required, the art therapist must adopt the Compromise Option: one must compromise without appearing to do so.

In this respect, art therapy has both advantages and disadvantages in the prison setting. By its nature alone, art exposes and explores the three components that are most feared; aggression, sexuality and escape. By tolerating infantilization, and using the "hidden" qualities of art, art therapy explores the individual therapeutic issues of the inmate/patients. Consequently, the process of art therapy becomes the ultimate hidden weapon.

References

Dissanayake, E. (1992). *Homoaestheticus: Where art comes from and why*. New York: The Free Press

Dissanayake, E. (1988). *What is art for?* Seattle: University of Washington Press

Kramer, E. (1993, second edition). *Art as therapy with children*. Chicago: Magnolia Street Publishers

Rank, O. (1932). *Art and artist*. New York: W.W. Norton and Company

Larsen, S. (1990). *The mystic imagination: Your quest for meaning through personal mythology*. New York: Bantam Books

No Artist Rants and Raves When He Creates
Creative Art Therapies and Psychiatry in Forensic Settings

Stephen Rojcewicz, MD

> *Sic forensibus ministeriis exercitati frequenter ad carminis tranquillitatem tanquam ad portum feliciorem refugerunt.*
> —*Petronii Arbitri Satyricon, 118.*

The above quotation comes from Titus Petronius, commonly identified as an important Roman official and arbiter of high fashion under the Emperor Nero. It occurs in his picaresque novel, the *Satyricon* (c. AD 60/1939), where it was originally meant satirically. However, it well exemplifies both the inherent difficulty of psychiatric treatment in a forensic setting, and the unique opportunity provided by the creative arts therapies. My rough translation of this quotation reads:

> "In this way, those who are exhausted by forensic matters often find refuge in the tranquillity of poetry as in a more fortunate haven."

As a forensic psychiatrist, I have found that this statement contains much therapeutic wisdom.

The subject of the sentence, *exercitati*, refers to those who are exhausted, tired out, exercised in the extreme. While it may also refer to administrators and therapists, it applies fundamentally to inmates and patients, exhausted by their mental health, social and legal problems, and often exhausted by the institutional system. This paper will detail, from the perspective of a forensic psychiatrist, how they find refuge *ad carminis tranquillitatem*, in the tranquillity of poetry. The Latin word *carmen, carminis* can mean song as well as poetry. In the broadest sense, this paper also applies to therapeutic breakthroughs accomplished through art therapy and all the creative arts therapies in forensic settings, although it will concentrate primarily on poetry therapy.

The psychiatric problems inherent in forensic settings are formidable, easily leading therapists to be "exhausted by forensic matters," as Petronius wrote. Prisons and forensic psychiatric hospitals are filled with the most difficult-to-treat patient populations. These individuals present themselves as:

- severe schizophrenics with incredibly impoverished backgrounds

- chronic substance abusers with organic brain damage
- anti-social personality disorders lacking any empathy for others
- impulse disorders with long histories of violent acting-out, and
- victims of child physical and sexual abuse who appear condemned to perpetuate the abuse pattern.

Rather than suffering from one such disorder, a great many forensic patients suffer from co-morbid conditions, one disorder worsening the others, in a synergy and an almost geometric progression of misery and pathology.

It is not solely the difficult-to-treat diagnoses that frustrate our therapeutic efforts in forensic settings. The underlying traditions of institutions can be intensely anti-therapeutic, prisons ruled by a subculture of violence, with pervasive hopelessness and inhumanity. The institutional attitude may itself emphasize punitiveness and minimize rehabilitation, sometimes even abandoning virtual control of the worst cellblocks to the most violent among the inmates.

State and local governmental down-sizing has lead to funding shortages and staff vacancies in mental health programs in jails, prisons, and state psychiatric hospitals. Even in the most ideal forensic mental health environment, built-in roadblocks to therapeutic change still exist. So many difficult-to-treat psychiatric disorders and a pervasive anti-therapeutic tradition combine to create a therapeutic challenge that can only be described as epic and heroic, if not downright quixotic.

"Refuge in the Tranquillity of Poetry"

But violent machismo, excessive punitiveness and therapeutic nihilism are not the only traditions of forensic settings. To quote from the Satyricon, "Those who are exhausted by forensic matters often find refuge in the tranquillity of poetry." This is not merely a poetic figure of speech. Great works of literature and creativity have also been nurtured in prisons. The list of prison-inspired fiction, poetry, philosophy and memoirs is quite substantial, including many that have become fundamental documents of civilization.

Perhaps the greatest work of Western philosophy is Plato's *Apology of Socrates*. This profound philosophic dialogue is an account of Socrates' trial in Athens in 399 BC. on charges of corrupting the minds of the young. The dialogue consists of Socrates' defense speech, the apology for his life; an examination of what Socrates considers to be appropriate penalties; and finally the speech of Socrates after he is condemned to death, reflecting on death. Two more Platonic dialogues, Crito and Phaedo, examine the experiences of Socrates while awaiting death, and on the day of his execution.

Incarceration has inspired other philosophers in addition to Socrates and Plato. Boethius wrote *The Consolation of Philosophy*, a work with enormous influence on medieval intellectual life, while imprisoned. In more modern times, Dietrich Bonhoeffer composed *The Cost of Discipleship* while in a Nazi prison.

Gruesome Siberian prisons have given rise to Fyodor Dostoevsky's *Notes from Underground* and Alexander Solzhenitsin's *One Day in the Life of Ivan Denisovich*. *The Adventures of Marco Polo* joins *The Adventures of Don Quixote* by Miguel Cervantes as major books reported to be written, at least in part, while the author was incarcerated. François Villon, André Chénier,

Oscar Wilde, Paul Verlaine and Guillaume Apollinaire are a few of the poets who have created works while in prison, or used their prison experience as the basis for major writings.

While great painting and music might seem more difficult to create in forensic settings, the English artist Benjamin Robert Haydon did produce admired works while incarcerated, and the best-selling *Symphony Number 3* (the Symphony of Sorrowful Songs) by the Polish composer Henryk Górecki, sets to music, among other sorrowful songs, writings found inscribed on the wall of a cell in Gestapo headquarters in Zakopane, Poland.

Our focus, for purposes of this paper, is on a particular literary form—poetry written in prison or inspired by the author's experience of incarceration, with particular reference to the value of poetry therapy and other creative arts therapies in forensic mental health settings.

Oscar Wilde transformed his experience of incarceration into the moving prose of *De Profundis* and the haunting poetry of *The Ballad of Reading Gaol* (Wilde 1897/1981). François Villon composed moving poems about his prison experience. His *Ballad of the Hanged Men* or *L'Épitaphe Villon en Forme de Ballade* is great poetry about the issue of his death sentence, later commuted to banishment (Villon 1463/1970). Nineteenth century American folk poetry, in the multiple popular versions of *The Cowboy's Lament* (Hollander, 1993), emphasized the similar theme of a deathbed confession and exhortation to others not to follow the same life of crime and dissipation.

Writers-in-the-Prisons

In late 20th century America, there has been a resurgence of interest in correctional and forensic poetry, with alternative-to-prison programs that emphasize literature seminars. ABC News has broadcast a feature on Cornelius Cunningham, currently a mentor in the Across Ages project at Temple University, who has credited poetry and creative literature as saving his life after many years in prison. Anthologies have been published containing poetry written in prisons. The National Endowment for the Arts has sponsored Writers-in-the-Prisons, similar to the successful Writers-in-the-Schools program, often resulting in the creation of stunning poems (Denberg, 1990). There is even a site on the Internet, *Voice of the Prisoner*, showcasing art and poetry of men and women in jails and prisons.

Poetry Therapy

Poetry therapy (sometimes called bibliotherapy) is the intentional use of poetry and other forms of literature for healing and for personal growth. Poetry therapists provide individual assessments of clients, leadership in poetry therapy groups, and individual psychotherapy services using poetry therapy techniques. As typically practiced, group therapy forms the bulk of poetry therapy experience.

In a poetry therapy session, an existing poem may be chosen by the therapist or by group members, a collaborative poem may be created by the group members as a whole, or a new poem may be created by an individual client or the therapist. A basic principle in choosing a poem for use is that the poem's emotional tone should match the clinical situation or the mood of the individual client, but not be excessively negative or depressing, or glorify suicide or anti-social behavior. The poem is chosen not primarily for its literary merit, but for its usefulness as a tool for awareness, self-discovery and therapeutic change.

The published accounts of poetry therapy in correctional and forensic settings are quite moving. Barkley (1985) describes therapeutic writing of poetry in individual psychotherapy with prison inmates. If faced with a therapeutic impasse, the therapist himself tries to write a poem that he considers applicable to the individual, then requests the individual to express in poetry what he cannot otherwise say. According to Barkley, discussion of the resulting poetry:
- enhances the individual's awareness of his emotional life
- allows the non-verbal to become verbal
- clarifies highly confused feelings, and
- eventually provides a lasting, positive impact on the process of therapeutic communication.

Berger and Giovan (1990) have detailed the use of poetry, music and creative writing in a therapeutic group setting in a forensic psychiatric unit, noting:
- a decrease in the patients' sociopathic attitudes
- an increased ability to tolerate frustration and
- an increased ability to disclose feelings of pain, guilt and sadness.

At its most effective, poetry therapy was significant in helping the patients recognize and accept responsibility for what led to their incarceration.

Cellini and Young (1976) have also detailed the therapeutic use of poetry therapy or bibliotherapy among prison inmates, and Rubin (1974) has written about the therapeutic value of prison libraries.

Stino (1995) has described how the process of the creative writing of poetry and a rap song, through an adult literary classroom in a county jail, not only increased literary skills, but led to therapeutic change in the incarcerated youth involved. The writing process itself, with its stages of brainstorming, drafting, revising, and ultimate dissemination of the final creative work, helped the individuals think through their values, improve their self-esteem, and made them more interested and empathic of others in the community.

In addition to the above papers, there is much current innovative work using poetry, narrative stories and creative writing in prisons and forensic settings, not yet fully documented in the professional literature.

The following sections explore the use of poetry therapy (and other creative arts therapies) and the selection of individual poems to address critical aspects in the treatment of the mentally ill forensic population. This exploration will lead to understanding some ways in which the creative arts therapies contribute to therapeutic change in individuals in correctional and forensic mental health settings.

Culture Shock for First Time Entrants

For first time entrants into the correctional or forensic mental health system, the intake process is shattering. The first few days in jail for a newly arrested person is a time of high risk for suicide and for psychotic decompensation. The individual is isolated, confused, frightened, disoriented, and in massive culture shock.

A poetic masterpiece helpful in therapy at such a time is *À La Santé*, written in 1911 by Guillaume Apollinaire. The poem was written at la Santé prison, where the poet was incarcerated for suspected complicity in the theft of the Mona Lisa from the Louvre. The poem captures the sense of desolation, impending doom and loss of identity that comes with incarceration. The work is most moving in the original French, with its haunting rhymes and phonetic effects. However, although many individuals who are not criminally responsible for major crimes, both wrote poetry and spoke fluent French, most forensic patients will require an English translation. I give the beginning of the poem in the original (Apollinaire 1911/1965, p. 140), then the English translation by William Meredith which best captures the spirit of the poem (Apollinaire 1964, p. 199):

À La Santé
Avant d'entrer dans ma cellule
Il a fallu me mettre nu
Et quelle voix sinistre ulule
Guillaume, qu'es-tu devenu?
Le Lazare entrant dans la tombe
Au lieu d'en sortit comme il fit
A dieu, adieu, chantante ronde
O mes années ô jeunes filles

At La Santé Prison
Before going into my cell
I had to strip nude.
And what dire voice howls
Guillaume, what have you become?
This Lazarus enters the tomb,
Not comes out, as he should.
Farewell, farewell, singing round
Of my years, of my girls.

In the next stanza, Apollinaire depicts the loss of identity; instead of a person with a name, he is now merely the number of a cell in a numbered cellblock:

Non, je ne me sens plus là
Moi-même
Je suis le quinze de la
Onzième

No, I no longer feel that I'm
Myself,
I am number fifteen of the
Eleventh.

The poem goes on to describe the sense of isolation, aloneness, boredom, frustration and pain that accompany the onset of incarceration, but in beautiful language, rhyme and a highly structured stanza form. This poem can be quite therapeutic for individuals disoriented by their entry into a forensic setting, who can benefit from the realization that their experience is empathically understood, and can even be potentially transformed into something moving and meaningful.

Many wonderful poems, not written specifically for a prison or forensic setting, address the sense of identity and issues of self-esteem in ways that are highly applicable to forensic psychiatric patients. One such work found very helpful with this population is *I'm Nobody! Who are you?* by Emily Dickinson (1861/1960, p. 133):

I'm Nobody! Who are you?
I'm Nobody! Who are you?
Are you - Nobody - Too?
Then there's a pair of us?
Don't tell! they'd advertise - you know!
How dreary - to be - Somebody!
How public - like a Frog -
To tell one's name - the livelong June -
To an admiring Bog.

A powerful poem that addresses the false sense of identity that can come from destructive and anti-social behavior, and from the phoniness of a machismo life style is *We Real Cool* by Gwendolyn Brooks (1960/1987, p. 331). Although originally written over 35 years ago, the poem still speaks eloquently about the waste of lives inherent in the glorification of being "cool" and being a member of a gang:

We Real Cool
We real cool. We
Left school. We
Lurk late. We
Strike straight. We
Sing sin. We
Think gin. We
Jazz June. We
Die soon.

Long-standing personality patterns are highly resistant to change. Forensic patients with personality disorders not only repeat self-defeating behavior, but often blame others for the negative consequences of their behavior. The following poem, *Autobiography in Five Short Chapters*, by Portia Nelson (1993), was used successfully to help decrease self-destructive acting out behavior in a female forensic psychiatric patient suffering from borderline personality disorder.

Autobiography in Five Short Chapters
I. I walk down the street.
   There is a deep hole in the sidewalk.
   I fall in
   I am lost ... I am helpless
   It isn't my fault.
   It takes forever to find a way out.

II. I walk down the same street.
    There is a deep hole in the sidewalk.
    I pretend I don't see it.

    I fall in again.
    I can't believe I am in the same place.
    But it isn't my fault.
    It still takes a long time to get out.

III. I walk down the same street
    There is a deep hole in the sidewalk.
    I see it is there.
    I still fall in ...it's a habit.
    My eyes are open.
    I know where I am.
    It is my fault.
    I get out immediately.

IV. I walk down the same street.
    There is a deep hole in the sidewalk.
    I walk around it.

V. I walk down another street.

With good humor, the poem depicts the repetition compulsion inherent in much self-destructive behavior, and substitutes a sense of being responsible for an earlier sense of helplessness and blame of others. The five stanzas needed for resolution are a gentle reminder to the patient that it will take much time and trial-and-error in order to change long-standing attitudes and behavior, but that change is possible. Often patients can laugh at themselves after reading this poem for the first time, beginning to obtain some insight and motivation for change.

Useful poems for changing long-standing behavior patterns stress respect for others and for authority, and help the individual find ways to express anger and frustration appropriately (Hynes and Hynes-Berry, 1994). Many persons in forensic settings have never been able to express their feelings directly, honestly or accurately. Poetry and the creative arts may enable them to express for the first time what they have been unable to say in any constructive manner.

For those individuals who act out violently, a superb poem is the first stanza of *A Poison Tree* by William Blake (1794/1977, p. 129):

    I was angry with my friend:
    I told my wrath, my wrath did end.
    I was angry with my foe:
    I told it not, my wrath did grow.

In an alternative to violent acting out, this poem emphasizes talking about the anger, as well as expressing feelings in general through writing and the creative arts.

Identification With Literary Characters

Nina Diana (1996) has described her therapeutic success in using simple stories and fairy tales with forensic inpatients, including those found "not criminally responsible" for major crimes, and those who have been found "incompetent to stand trial." The use of simple, but not childish stories, such as *The Emperor's New Clothes, The Boy Who Cried Wolf, The Ugly Duckling,* etc., often capture the imagination of forensic inpatients, and allow them to identify with specific characters.

Patients can then role play, testing out different behaviors that they would not attempt purely on their own. The character in some sense becomes a powerful guide to the possibility of new behavior. Significant insight into their mental illness has occurred.

For example, patients with paranoid delusions or paranoid personality disorder and aggressive behavior have been able to identify with the character in *Porky the Porcupine* (Wallas, 1985). This character is abrasive and excessively assertive, but the story shows that his personality style is a defense against overwhelming insecurity. The patient's ability to see this connection in a literary character can be the first important step in gaining the insight that his or her own paranoid or aggressive style is not their fundamental personality, but a reaction to insecurity and feelings of inadequacy.

Young black females often can identify with, and gain strength from, the characters in the poems of black female writers. Nikki Giovanni's poem, *Housecleaning* (1975) has provided such inspiration for several female patients at a forensic psychiatric hospital, especially from the standpoint of making decisions to change certain behavior patterns or to end destructive relationships:

> **Housecleaning**
> i always liked housecleaning
> even as a child
> and unfortunately this habit has
> carried over and i find
> i must remove you
> from my life.

Other forensic patients may show strong identification with more malignant characters, such as legendary gangsters or Darth Vader from the *Star Wars* movies (Rojcewicz, 1987). Identification with these characters may not lead to any positive change, but the therapist can focus on the redeeming features of the characters or on any positive side to their biographies.

Sublimation

With specific patients, the production of creative art can direct sublimation of otherwise pathological impulses. A poem as an invective or satire can take the place of physical assault, for example.

One dramatic example comes from the work of Anne Corson, ATR, an art therapist at Saint Luke Institute, Silver Spring, MD. A patient with exhibitionism created a painting with three-dimensional shutters. The shutters open to reveal a beautiful art object inside. The impulse to drop his pants and expose himself was thus changed into the more socially acceptable and fully legal experience of artistic expression.

A remarkable thing occurs in the writing of poetry. Using structure, whether it be a stanzaic form, a rhyme scheme, a meter, or the use of simple poetic techniques and figures of speech, somehow results in more freedom and allows fuller expression. This benefit of structure is even more pronounced in the therapeutic writing of poetry. Even semi-literate individuals can stick to some fundamental structure. The structure can be self-imposed or a pre-existed structure can be used or modified. Forensic psychiatric patients have used the exact meter and rhyme scheme of famous poems, including schoolroom classics such as *Trees* by Joyce Kilmer, and *The Raven* by Edgar Allan Poe, to express their own work in poetry.

Poetry, art therapy and the creative arts therapies tap into intense, fundamental human emotions, powerful, indeed often overpowering. Instead of being expressed helter-skelter, raw emotions can be channeled through the overall artistic structure.

The inherent interplay between freedom of expression, raw emotions and a highly organized structure accounts for much of the therapeutic benefit of the creative arts therapies in prisons and forensic settings. The therapist works indirectly, choosing some appropriate material, helping with expression, but not directly attacking fragile defenses or immediately challenging personality patterns.

Indirect versus Direct Confrontation

The direct confrontation of self-defeating personality patterns and behavior does have some therapeutic role, especially in issues of substance abuse. For many forensic patients, however, direct confrontation is often counter-productive, leading to power struggles and narcissistic conflicts, and the sense of being disrespected or humiliated. The indirect approach of the creative arts therapist allows the forensic patient to proceed at an appropriate pace, without experiencing a severe, undue assault on self-esteem.

It is often striking and highly therapeutic when a forensic patient creates an original work of art. Many times, especially in the early stages of a therapeutic alliance, using a pre-existing poem, or collaborating rather than working alone on a poem or work of art, is less threatening to the emotional equilibrium of the patient. Less anxiety and defensiveness helps with the therapeutic process. If the already existing poem, for example, is well chosen, the patient can delineate more clearly critical personal issues and conflicts, allowing him or her to feel less isolated and alone.

However, if the patient creates an original work of art, there will be even more ventilation and sublimation, and he will begin learning healthy identification and increased empathy for others.

If the patient stays working with pre-existing poems or with collaborative efforts to create a poem or work of art, he or she still benefits greatly. The interplay between raw emotional material and the organized structure in which such emotions are expressed constitutes a tool of the very highest therapeutic value.

Conclusion

Creative arts therapies promote an integration of basic raw emotions with a highly organized structure, allowing primitive feelings and impulses to be placed in perspective, mastered and expressed in a more constructive manner. The therapist does not directly assault defenses and masks, but uses them creatively. Through the creative arts therapies, the client develops self-worth, handles some critical conflicts non-verbally and symbolically, and increases overall functioning.

Let us return to the quotation from the Roman author Petronius:

> "In this way, those who are exhausted by forensic matters often find refuge in the tranquillity of poetry as in a more fortunate haven (ad portum feliciorem)."

The Latin word portus, portum (haven, refuge, harbor) is almost linguistically identical to the Latin porta (gate). Indeed, the creative arts therapies are such a more fortunate haven, a gateway opening into therapeutic possibilities that might otherwise be blocked for forensic patients.

I would like to end with a paraphrase of the last line from the poem, *The Prophet Jeremiah* by Barry Ivker (1994). Ivker wrote, in iambic pentameter:

> "No poet rants and raves when he can write,"

...capturing the essence of the therapeutic value of poetry and the creative arts therapies in prisons and forensic settings.

If someone is channeling raw emotions and critical conflicts into the structure of creative art, he or she is not acting out, regressing or even standing still, but is constructively working on underlying problems, a major contribution to the overall treatment plan. I will slightly modify this quote, so that it fully applies to the therapeutic benefit of artistic structure for the incarcerated. We conclude, "No artist rants and raves when he creates."

References

Apollinaire, G. (1965). *Oeuvres poétiques*. Paris: Bibliothèque de la Pléiade. (Original work written 1911).

Apollinaire, G. (1964). *Alcools: Poems 1898-1913*. (W. Meredith, Trans.). Garden City, New York: Doubleday

Barkley, B.J. (1985). Poetry in a cage: Therapy in a correctional setting. In *Poetry as healer*. (J.J. Leedy, Ed.). New York: The Vanguard Press, 135-149.

Berger A., Giovan M. (1990). Poetic interventions with forensic patients. *Journal of Poetry Therapy (4)* 83-92.

Blake, W. (1977). A poison tree, In *the complete poems*. London: Penguin Books. (Original work published 1794)

Brooks, G. (1987). We real cool, In *Blacks*. Chicago: David Company. p. 331 (Original work published 1960)

Cellini, H.R. and Young, O. (1976). Bibliotherapy in institutions. *Transaction Analysis Journal* 6, 407-409.

Denberg, K. (1990). Poetry in the prisons: Coming back up with light. *Journal of Poetry Therapy (4)*, 21-26.

Diana, N. (1996). Happily ever after...Using fairy tales with the chronically mentally ill. Workshop presented at the *16th Annual Conference, National Association for Poetry Therapy*, Columbia, MD, May 4, 1996.

Dickinson, E. (1960). I'm Nobody! Who are you?, In *The complete poems of Emily Dickinson*. (T.H. Johnson, Ed.) Boston: Little, Brown and Co. (Original work written 1861)

Giovanni, N. (1996). Housecleaning, In *The selected poems of Nikki Giovanni*. New York: William Morrow and Company, p.74 (Original work published 1975)

Hollander, J., Ed. (1993). *American poetry: The nineteenth century. Volume 2*. New York: Library of America.

Hynes, A.M. & Hynes-Berry, M. (1994). *Biblio/poetry therapy. The interactive process: A handbook.* St. Cloud, MN: North Star Press

Ivker, B. (1994). The prophet Jeremiah, in Poetry/Art therapy: the message and the medium. *Journal of Poetry Therapy 7,* 197-201.

Nelson, P. (1993). *There's a hole in my sidewalk: The romance of self-discovery.* Hillsboro, OR: Beyond Words Publishers

Petronius (1939). *Petronii arbitri satyricon reliquiae.* (K. Mueller, Ed.). Stuttgart: B.G. Teubner (Original work published c. AD 60)

Rojcewicz, S. (1987). Darth Vader: Masks, power, and meaning. *Journal of Poetry Therapy 1,* 23-30.

Rubin, R. (1974). Prison libraries: Focus on service to the ex-advantaged. *Catholic Library World 45,* 438-440.

Stino, Z. (1995). Writing as therapy in a county jail. *Journal of Poetry Therapy 9,* 13-23.

Villon, F. (1970). L'Épitaphe Villon en forme de ballade, In *Oeuvres.* Paris: Garnier Fréres, 152-154. (Original work written 1463)

Wallas, L. (1985). *Stories for the third ear.* New York: Norton

Wilde, O. (1981). The ballad of Reading Gaol, In *The portable Oscar Wilde.* London: Penguin Books (Original work published 1897)

Suspending Normal Prison Taboos Through the Arts
in a Prison Psychiatric Setting

Jack Cheney, MA, A.T.R.

Imprisonment for many proves unbearable. Inmates, for many reasons and with an arsenal of devices, attempt to end their lives in prison. Correctional officers intervene regularly, cutting down would-be hangings, applying first-aid to those who self-inflict slashes, and seek immediate medical attention for those who overdose. Many survivors are brought to our acute-care psychiatric hospital administered through the mental health department in a prison in Northern California.

As an art therapist and member of an interdisciplinary treatment team, I help these people stabilize through the use of the arts. In the singing of songs, playing of instruments, drawing, imagining, sculpting and talking, normal prison taboos against sharing information and showing emotions can be suspended for a while, helping these prisoners not only outlive their sentences but, while on our unit, develop coping skills and insights to find direction and meaning in their lives.

Change of Direction
Following the closure of Camarillo State Hospital and Developmental Center, where for ten years I co-directed the Art Therapy/Fine Arts Discovery Program serving approximately 300 disabled individuals per week (Cheney, 1993), I am one of many who have opted to work in a correctional setting. More and more of the mentally ill are finding their way into the prison system as well.

Working with assaultive and self-abusive individuals at Camarillo, I developed intervention strategies using the arts which engaged the most disturbed individuals. I challenged my clientele to explore many forms of expression in search of the ones they most naturally possessed and enjoyed. I used songs, stories, two and three-dimensional arts, rhythms, creative writing and musical instruments to encourage a feeling of safety and acceptance.

Case Study—Randy
The following is the case study of one prison inmate/patient, Randy, who came to us on Halloween after he severely cut into his right arm with a razor and was found bleeding and nearly unconscious in his cell on the mainline.

DRAWING TIME

When Randy was first admitted to our unit, he spoke with a halting and stuttered speech pattern, and appeared depressed. When asked by our admitting psychiatrist if he was still thinking of harming himself, his answer was a vague "I don't know, I don't think so." As he answered, his eyes were fixed on the floor. He appeared like a child caged in a man's body. Persuaded more by his body language than his words, the treatment team decided to keep a close eye on him. Determined to frustrate his self-destructive momentum, we placed him in five-point restraints in a stripped cell. A rotating shift of R.N.'s and Medical Technical Assistants (MTAs) continually monitored him for the first 48 hours. By the time Randy was ready to come out of his cell for in-depth assessments, he had spent 10 days gradually being allowed more freedom of movement.

I first met Randy on a one-to-one basis when he was more stable yet still on low suicide watch. Escorted by two MTAs, Randy entered my office, a converted 6 by 9 foot, one-man cell which I share with a colleague. Appearing still somewhat guarded and depressed, Randy took a seat at the desk furthest from the door. I gave him a sheet of construction paper and a set of oil pastels. I placed the same materials in front of me and began to draw a few lines across the page. I invited Randy to draw whatever he liked. He opened his box of pastels and began.

As we talked and drew, Randy explained that the reason he had attempted suicide was because he was sick of life locked up with other inmates. He talked about life on the mainline where he felt that he was "caged with animals, you can't sleep, you can't shower. Those guys will fuck with you any way they can." He talked a little about previous suicide attempts by cutting and overdosing.

He set down the pastel and looked straight at me. "I really need some help. I convinced them at the other prison that I was losing it. They brought me to this prison for treatment but I ended up back on mainline. I just couldn't take it." It appeared that Randy's suicide attempt was a cry for help that almost went too far. Randy talked about his 23 year history of substance abuse and dependence. His arms were covered with tattoos. A life of self-destructive and antisocial behavior behind him, his eyes looked teary as he talked about what he had put his mother through.

I finished the interview by asking the standard questions. Randy expressed willingness to participate in substance abuse treatment groups and other planned scheduled treatment groups including expressive art therapy. Before Randy was rehoused, we briefly showed one another our drawings. Randy's first drawing was a stylized sun and rose, stereotypical prison tattoo art, (figure 1).

Randy's files provided more clues about him as a victim of physical abuse at the hands of his substance-dependent father. His mother had also been in and out of trouble with the courts.

Randy began drinking by the age of 9, and was sniffing glue in junior high school. By the time he was 16, Randy was seriously drug-dependent using heroin, alcohol, marijuana, and methamphetamines. As an adult, Randy had been incarcerated, paroled and returned to prison for a number of crimes including prostitution, weapons possession, and several drug-related charges. Most recently, he had been incarcerated on a parole violation after two months of freedom where he was living on the streets, eating from garbage cans. He was charged with

SUSPENDING NORMAL PRISON TABOOS

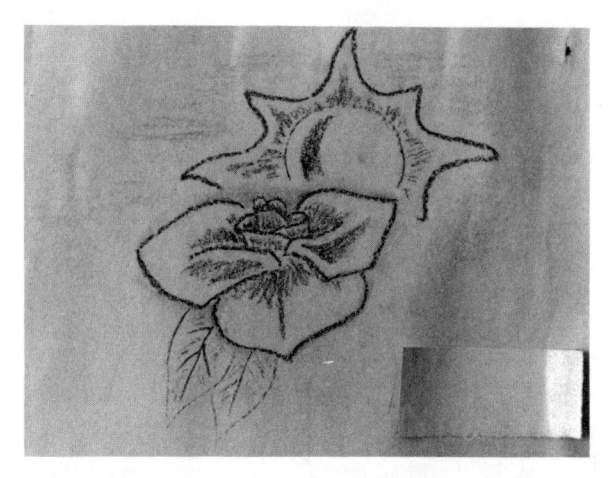

Figure 1: Randy—oil pastel on paper

trespassing and absconding. Being returned to "three hots and a cot" in prison seemed better than his life on the street.

Randy needed to develop ways to cope. He needed to learn how to understand and express his feelings appropriately, to relate constructively with others, and to face his dependence on drugs. Critically, he needed to experience life without drugs. So incarcerated by his fears, attitudes and limited choices, Randy had no clue that life, even life in prison, could hold positive learning experiences.

The first group that Randy participated in was a one hour, weekly music exploration and stress reduction group. On their way to attend our first session each inmate left their individual cells as custody staff cried out "coming down!" Randy and the eight other participants were ushered single file into our treatment room where they sat in chairs in front of me. With my guitar in hand, I welcomed them and told them that this group was going to be about the language of music. Eighteen eyes were fixed on me, their faces revealing nothing. I offered them a box filled with rhythm instruments and each man chose one without comment. Prisoners don't express feelings, equating displays of emotion with weakness.

Placing my hopes in the music itself, I began to play. I chose not to confront, redirect, council, or in any way cajole participation from the inmate/patients. I started playing "Day-o," a popular Harry Belafonte song. I let go of my role as therapist and tried to enjoy simply playing and singing. I relaxed. One verse, one refrain, one rhythm instrument almost imperceptibly began to keep the beat. Enjoyment of the music became easier, and I made some brief eye contact. The group as a whole seemed to relax their guard. Other men joined in and the rhythms became louder. After a few more verses, all of the men were adding their particular rhythms to the whole. Postures were changing. Stiff bodies which appeared distrustful at first, slowly, as the music attained momentum, gave way to rocking, and open postures. The maracas which Randy had chosen rattled along with the rest.

Several more songs followed. They began to make requests. Setting aside accepted "big house" protocol, they began to sing softly. All together, we explored "Twist and Shout," "If I Had A

DRAWING TIME

Hammer" and "Blowing In The Wind." At one point, Carlos, one of the Hispanic participants requested "La Bamba." We played and sang this old Mexican standard by Richie Valens. The intensity, which had been building, reached a crescendo. The entire unit could easily hear the sounds as they echoed down the unit corridor and through the cells.

At the end of the song, I asked whether anyone knew the translation of the words in "La Bamba." No one spoke, so I told them about the romantic intentions around which "La Bamba" was composed. All eyes were on me, as they listened intently. I told them about the man who was in love with a beautiful woman. He wished to dance the Bamba with her. His life would not be complete without her grace. He would do anything, even become the captain of a ship if that was what it would take to win her love. Not allowing their faces to reveal the memories, thoughts, and emotions stirring within them, their eyes had softened and they hung on every word.

I asked if any of the men had ever felt so strongly about the love of another. Each man, including Randy, indicated through subtle nods, that they had. With time enough for one more song, Randy asked for John Lennon's "Imagine." Much can happen within the span of a one-hour group. Inmates, emotionally encapsulated by their prison setting and survival protocols fifty minutes earlier, softly played their rhythm instruments and sang "You may think I'm a dreamer, but I'm not the only one, I hope someday you will join us, and the world will live as one."

Moving Between Musical and Verbal Forms

These music/relaxation groups were the first groups I conducted in my new work setting. We met once a week, on Mondays. Every week the participants would prison march into the room to the sound of the gruff announcement of "coming down." As they began to trust the group structure we had established, initial hyper-vigilance gave way to enjoyment more rapidly each week. Moving between musical and verbal forms the group explored feelings, stories, communication and cooperation. Randy became adept at the playing of the maracas. We discussed how the making of rhythm is the same as having another voice to use. We explored how each voice added something special to the whole. We also explored the critical role of listening. The quality of listening and the quality of expression improved each week. As Ray, one 28-year-old participant said, "This feels like life."

As communication and adaptive behavior increased in the group I was able to explore an expanding affective field with the music. I was able to introduce some children's classic songs into the repertoire. Therapeutic discussions about memories of childhood attended the heartfelt singing of "Puff the Magic Dragon" "John Jacob Jingleheimer Schmidt" and "Froggy Went 'a Courting.'" Following the singing of "Froggy," spontaneously Randy talked of the "one good thing about when I was a kid. My dad sometimes took us camping and fishing at Lake Casitas, in Southern California." We talked about how such a pleasant memory can be chosen as an internal refuge and help us keep centered when going through crises.

Randy's life to this point had been characterized by poor focus and poorer choices. His parents, for the most part, had modeled maladaptive responses to stress. By the time Randy had barely reached the age of reason, as a nine-year-old he sought solace in alcohol.

Randy's progress in the music/relaxation group mirrored the rest of the members. After a few

SUSPENDING NORMAL PRISON TABOOS

weeks, his mistrustful expressions gave way. He made song requests, talked about some of the memories triggered by the songs, and, importantly, learned to play an instrument known as a "snake" with many modulations and nuances. Though not a good listener at first, Randy's ensemble skills improved every week. In the teaching of breathing as part of singing, I introduced relaxation breathing as taught by Thich Nhat Hanh, a Zen Buddhist master. Randy appeared to pay special attention to this technique. "As you breathe in, think only, 'I am breathing in'." I said, and "As you breathe out, think only, 'I am breathing out'." He sat relaxed but erect, newly focused.

Randy threw himself into the therapeutic milieu. He came out for everything from yard group to substance abuse prevention. In his cell, he would read continually. Given the appropriate way that he interacted with staff and other inmate/patients, Randy was considered a model prisoner.

String and Ink Art

In the meantime, art supplies had arrived, protocols approved and I began conducting a weekly two-hour expressive art therapy group. In this format, I integrate art and music. Each session begins with a period of creative expression through music where negative transference dissolves and participants are primed for the visually creative activity which follows.

For the first group, I introduced them to the string art technique. By dragging the ink-soaked string around a white sheet of drawing paper, abstract patterns are created, requiring no drawing ability whatsoever, (Virshup, 1978). The high-contrast images made by the random ink marks are dramatic. Then the participants use their imagination and "see" forms in the patterns of blacks and whites, just like we identify images in clouds or in cracks on walls. With chalk pastels, everyone develops the forms they see. The whole group seemed to respond well to this gestalt drawing adventure.

In his turn, Randy shared his composition with the rest of the group (figure 2). "Here are palm trees on a tropical island. The sun is shining and it looks like the wind is blowing."

I had spent a few moments introducing the notion that drawing from our imagination is like dreaming with our eyes open. The images we create are open to interpretation on a very personal level.

"What is the feeling you get from looking at the picture?" I asked. "It feels like freedom," Randy replied, looking directly at me. I inquired, "Is there a part of the picture that you feel the most like?" Randy responded, "Yeah, the trees, I think." I asked, "What about the trees?" Quickly again he stated, "They live on an island, free from everything, but there's beauty all around."

Figure 2: Randy—ink and chalk on paper

DRAWING TIME

An inmate's tropical dreamland, Randy's drawing struck a chord with the other participants. Heads nodded agreement.

Experience has taught me that underneath such uncorrupted ideation deep conflicts often lurk; the isolation of the island, the unpredictable force of the wind, the lush landscape suggest deep anxiety and discomfort. I left his tendencies to seek escape and isolation in their subliminal form, allowing him to feel the reinforcement of the group and the joy of creation as he took these first steps toward self awareness.

Following the processing of everyone's imaginative forms, we ended with a song. "Dust in the Wind" closed our experience. "Don't hang on. Nothing lasts forever but the earth and sky." As we sang, smiles appeared on their faces. The theme of the song seemed to evoke contrasting feelings about the mystery of life and our own anonymity.

Signs of Distress

Shortly thereafter, Randy's condition took a downward turn. We were getting used to seeing Randy come out for almost everything the unit had to offer. In general he appeared intelligent, flexible, friendly and on respectful terms with the other men. However, over the course of about two weeks Randy began showing signs of distress. He appeared more sluggish in the morning, starting to decline when asked to early groups. His interactions with others became shorter and his walk became more of a shuffle. Randy had already been referred to the Day Treatment Program, but recent signs were troubling. When asked how he was feeling, he would only say that he wasn't sleeping "too good" lately. Unit records confirmed that his food intake had decreased as well. Sleeping medications were prescribed by our psychiatrist but his overall presentation didn't improve much over the next week.

During this period Randy drew figure 3. The directive I chose for this group session was based on first tracing the outline of their hands. Participants then draw a representation of their feelings inside the hand. Colors and shapes put outside the hand represent the feelings about the world-at-large. In this way, they explore the possible relationship between color and feelings in a simple format.

Appearing somewhat distracted, Randy in his turn showed his drawing to the group. He said, "First I drew the eye. On the end of the fingers are all my feelings. I've been a little sensitive lately. I've been waking up with a lot of bad dreams."

Asked about the patterns of lines Randy said, "I think it's about being strong and surviving." To me, the eye and the overall composition suggested hyper-vigilance and defensiveness. Allowing art therapy to be mostly subliminal at this point, I did no interpreting.

At his next Treatment Team Conference that week Randy revealed more about his current condition. He appeared very depressed, looking very much as he had when he was first admitted. His eyes were averted and

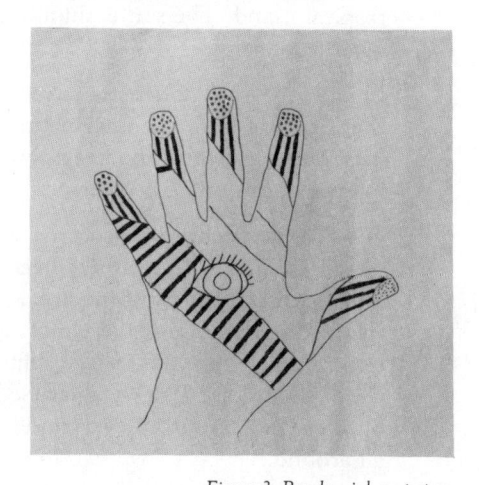

Figure 3: Randy—ink on paper

SUSPENDING NORMAL PRISON TABOOS

he appeared anxious. He had not cut on himself for the two months he had been on the unit and his behavior otherwise had been good. As discussed, Randy had already been referred to the Day Treatment Program for in-depth stabilization. Showing signs of lack of sleep, he told the treatment team that he didn't think he was ready for the transfer.

"I'm waking up with a lot of nightmares. I don't think I can make it yet in a dorm."

Asked what the nightmares were like, Randy answered, "I don't know. A lot of screaming, I guess. They wake me up and I can't get back to sleep."

In the course of the discussion Randy was asked if he had any thoughts of hurting himself lately. Randy replied that he sometimes thinks about cutting on himself, again. The treatment team decided to go ahead with the referral process but asked Randy to contract to tell staff when he thought he might hurt himself.

When the treatment team met again on Randy's behalf, I offered to do a focused intervention. It was agreed that a one-on-one weekly expressive art therapy hour would help Randy cope with the anxieties currently frustrating his successful transfer to the Day Treatment Program. Randy was willing to see me alone.

The next day I asked him to draw a picture showing what it was like living in his dorm cell on the mainline when he last cut on himself. In figure 4, Randy placed himself on the bottom bunk bed surrounded by the other men. The man on the top bunk is the only figure with any features, two little swipes of the pen for eyes and a mouth. This man's feet intersect the bottom of Randy's torso. The four figures on the floor appear to be leaning in on Randy, crowding his space. The figures on the floor have only stubs for arms while his arms appear bound. The only figure with arms is, again, the one on the top bunk. The entire drawing was done smoothly and economically.

Randy talked about how the other men would "fuck" with him, intimidate him and torment him. I asked about the figures and Randy said "Every dorm has some jerk like this guy," pointing to the one on the top bunk. "He gets these other guys going." Randy talked about how he hated to be called names, but had no way of preventing it.

When asked if this situation reminded him of anything from any other time, maybe when he felt bullied and harassed, not too surprisingly, Randy answered that his childhood was "a lot like that." I asked him about the feelings he used to have when he was a kid. He started to explain: "When I was a kid I used to try to get out of the house before my Dad came home. Sometimes he would get drunk. We'd get stuck there with him if he started getting drunk. He'd beat on my Mom and us....there was a lot of screaming."

When I asked if the screaming in his night-

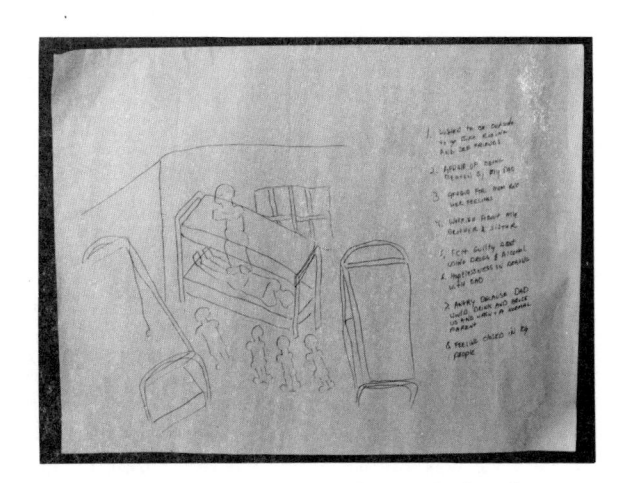

Figure 4: Randy—ink on paper

93

DRAWING TIME

mares was like the screaming he remembered from home, he said the nightmares he has had for years were often scenes from the many years his father held his family hostage. At one time, Randy said his father cut himself deeply and just sat and bled in front of the three children. By the time he was nine he said he had begun drinking.

I asked Randy to make a list of some of the thoughts and feelings he could remember from this part of his childhood. He numbered eight along the right outside border of the page:

1. Wished to go bike riding and see friends.
2. Afraid of being beaten by my Dad.
3. Afraid for Mom and her feelings.
4. Worried about my brother and sister.
5. Felt guilty about using drugs and alcohol.
6. Felt hopeless dealing with Dad.
7. Angry because Dad would drink and abuse us and wasn't a normal parent.
8. Feeling closed in by people.

At this point in the session Randy became as animated as I had ever seen him. We discussed how with incarceration Randy had found a reenactment of the torments of his childhood. We began to talk in general terms about how one's past trauma can affect us; how it affects how we live and restricts the choices we make. The time to wind up the session had come. During closure we discussed coping with these troubling memories through relaxation and breathing. I played some soft guitar. Randy leaned back and relaxed in his chair.

Over the next couple of days Randy's vitality seemed to increase. He started coming out for the morning groups again. He was talkative and reported that he was sleeping better at night. His walking pace, however, was still slow.

Dealing with Stimulus and Movement Deprivation

For the next one-on-one session we did a three-dimensional project exploring coping options, and engage more of his body in the creative process through the use of tactile materials. During their stay on our acute unit, inmate/patients spend most of their time locked in their individual cells. They must all adapt to stimulus and movement deprivation. If their behavior warrants, they are allowed less than one hour of exercise per day outside on a cement court yard.

Inmates, it is well known, can and will make weapons from anything and everything. Because of such security concerns, materials which can be used in therapy is carefully restricted and monitored. The control of materials is serious business in this world.

"With a little newspaper, tape and wheat paste, sculptures can be created," I explained to Randy. "Think of an animal to build from nature or from your imagination." Randy seemed to know immediately what form he was after. With great concentration he threw himself into crinkling the paper, taping it into solid forms then joining the separate elements together with more tape.

Randy reminisced as he worked, explaining he had done paper mache with his mother when he was young, which was one happy memory with her from his childhood. Randy created the body as a cylinder, a cone-shaped head and four tightly-wound, spindly legs. Soon these elements were all connected, and a dog-like creature stood before us. Randy then connected a tail and two pointed ears.

All the time, Randy spontaneously recited pleasant recollections from his childhood. He talked again about camping and fishing with his father, about riding bikes with friends, and small events that happened with his brother and sister and the few friends he had. Randy continued to inventory his life, talking about how he had become seriously drug dependent by age 16.

His brother had suffered for years with drug dependency but had "got his life together" and become a drug and alcohol counselor. Randy talked about his own road which lead him through eight separate suicide attempts mostly when in jail or prison. As we closed, I asked Randy, how he was doing with his nightmares. He said. "Before I go to sleep I quiet down and start by relaxing my feet. I move up my leg, and the rest of my body until I reach the top of my head. I've been sleeping a lot better. That's something my Mom taught me. I use the breathing thing you taught me, too."

Back Up To Speed

In the mornings, Randy again came out for groups. There was a new bounce in his step. All shifts reported that his appetite was very good. Third watch reported that he was sleeping through the night.

The next time we met for individual therapy, it was time to apply the gooey wheat paste and water soaked paper on the rolled and taped form. Randy gave every appearance of a five-year-old making mud pies as he dove his hands into the mixture and worked the dry paste into the liquid. He ripped and dipped the paper into the wheat paste and carefully smoothed each section on his dog. After he had covered the whole sculpture and washed his hands, he made a list of adjectives that he would use to describe the dog, which he referred to as Spuds after "Spuds McKenzie," figure 5a. As he came up with adjectives, he painted "Spuds" with a white undercoat. I wrote down:

1. Friendly
2. Outgoing
3. Playful
4. Flexible
5. Intelligent
6. Patient
7. Instinctual
8. Reacts to Survive
9. Toughness as needed

Together we looked at the list. Did "Spuds" have what it takes to make it in a dorm setting in prison. Randy thought he probably could. Did any of the words he used describe the artist who created "Spuds." Randy could see that. We discussed "Spuds" as representative of Randy's own coping powers; powers that he had but undervalued all along. We discussed each attribute on the list in turn and how it could be understood as survival strengths, as abilities to be used to avoid conflict and increase the possibility of his survival in a dorm setting.

DRAWING TIME

Figure 5a: Randy—"Spuds", wheat paste, tape and paper

Figure 5b: Randy

"You can't be friends with everyone but if you have one or two, it really helps. Sometimes you just have to tough it out. That's where my patience helps out, too." Randy continued up and down the list and displayed insight about the appropriate times and places to use each ability. Randy said that he really wanted to "get his shit together" so that sometime after his release he could find a girlfriend. Future talk.

"Spuds" was already creating a little excitement on the unit. Not used to the inmate/patients making three-dimensional objects, the staff complimented Randy on his creativity. Watching the proud, smiling look on Randy's face, one could see that he enjoyed the reinforcing attention and recognition. As we ended the session we playfully sang "You Ain't Nothing But A Hound Dog."

During the next treatment team meeting Randy showed considerably more poise than the last time. He said he was ready for the Day Treatment Program and the drug counseling program there. Given that his release date was only eight months away, it was likely that he would parole out of this transitional program.

For the next couple of weeks, Randy attended programming waiting for his referral to be processed. At our last one-on-one session, we went over all of his artwork and discussed the many memories, feelings and thoughts elicited by each. Randy painted the eyes, nose and mouth on "Spuds" and we played some blues and folk songs. He appeared relaxed, his beard neatly trimmed. Smiling easily, he said a few words about our work together. "The art and music helped a lot" he said. "I think I see things clearer that I did before. This is the best therapy I've ever had."

The next day, officers escorted Randy in belly-chains to the Day Treatment Program. Randy had been on our unit 115 days. Truly, he had made important gains, but what lay ahead for him? The guarded, severely depressed man who had shuffled into our treatment cell block was now leaving with as an energetic gait as chains will allow, head raised, face friendly and pleasant, seemingly ready for what lay ahead.

During treatment he had talked clearly about many of the difficult forces at work in his life and had explored the dynamics of his life in many creative forms. He had worked with his painful and tragic history, but the most difficult days of his personal recovery certainly lay ahead.

Fears Subliminally Expressed

Reviewing my assessment of "Spuds," the dog presented himself much as Randy had just moments earlier. He was alert, oriented, engaging, playful and available on one hand. But when viewing the dog's right side (figure 5b) a closer look at this hound reveals a number of characteristics consistent with Randy's chronic anxiety. Vigilance reminiscent of Randy's hand drawing can be read in "Spuds," darkly-circled right eye. Might fully-erect ears also be scanning for threatening sounds? When viewed from the rear (figure 5c), subconscious fears and a struggle for balance on thin legs is the effect. Spuds had provided a symbol through which Randy could conceptualize, verbalize and appreciate his own strengths as well as express a number of deeply-rooted fears subliminally.

It is said that the most important thing in life is not where you are but in what direction you are heading. Continued healing for Randy will not be simple. In acute care we can only hope that the sum of a patient's recovery is sufficient to prepare him for the next level of care.

Conclusion

In the larger view, Randy's case asks more questions that it answers. Abusive treatment had trained him in maladaptive behavior to this point. No effective interventions had helped him recover fully from what he endured as a child.

However, what Randy had recaptured of his life in this brief time through the applied use of creative art therapeutics is notable. Moving first with other men to explore and regain his personal rhythms, Randy discovered the power of his voice in the singing of familiar songs. Self knowledge and social awareness developed hand-in-hand with the growth of Randy's ability to listen critically together with others.

Randy's expressive range expanded rapidly until it included two and three-dimensional imagery as well as music. Finally Randy was able to hear, draw and begin to understand his own inner world. Fortunately, Randy's subconscious mind seemed to present horrible

Figure 5c: Randy

visions of his deep conflicts at a time when he had the language and support necessary to begin dealing with these images.

That this story took place within prison walls is remarkable for two reasons. First, the prison environment itself dictates that all semblance of personal expression be suppressed. A prison is known for its oppressive, confining architecture and strict role-defined dress codes. It is literally the last place anyone would naturally look for spontaneity and joy. Security concerns dictate that only the most benign expressive materials be used in an environment based on sensory and movement deprivation. Second, mirroring their physical environment, inmates themselves adhere to rigid codes of conduct. As mentioned, displays of emotion are viewed by inmates and staff alike as signs of weakness. Creative art therapy, however, offers a portal through which individuals may temporarily escape the suffocating prison existence. Entering an expressive realm where primary forms of language and sophisticated forms of awareness coexist, inmate/patients suspend their fears and taboos. Though they daily return to the world of chains and locks, they gain and retain meaningful healing experiences that they have during their creative self-expressive therapies.

References

Cheney, J. (1993). Development of Camarillo State Hospital's art therapy/fine arts discovery studio. In E. Virshup (Ed.), *California art therapy trends* (p. 231-262). Chicago, Il.: Magnolia Street Publishers.

Virshup, E. (1978). *Right brain people in a left brain world.* Los Angeles: The Guild of Tutors Press

Plate 1: chalk pastels on paper

Plate 2: chalk pastels on paper

*Plate 3: Albert W.—"The Man in the Wall...it is I", 1994,
toilet paper, ivory soap, found radio antennae, jute, acrylic
—courtesy Ironhouse Inspirations, Clearfield, PA*

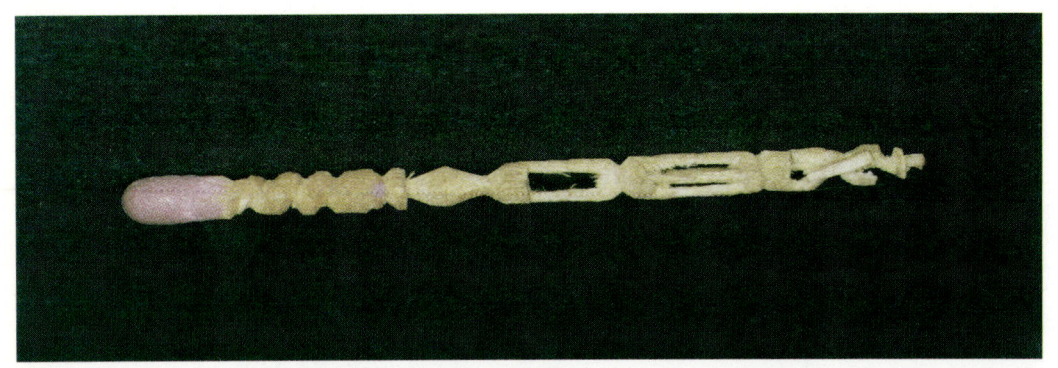

Plate 4: artist unknown—"William Penn atop City Hall, Philadelphia", carved matchstick, circa 1965 courtesy Eastern State Penitentiary, from the collection of A.D. Boxer, M.D.

Plate 5: Albert W.—parody on "Don't Drop the Soap" myth, 1994, toilet paper, ivory soap, jute, acrylic courtesy Ironhouse Inspirations, Clearfield, PA

Plate 6: chalk pastels on paper

Plate 7: Mr. L, *handmade paper with ink markers*

Plate 8: *"Landscape—a nice place to be"*, Primo

Plate 9: Primo—"Daughter on Her Death Bed"

Plate 10: Primo—"American Gothisd"

Art Therapy in a Managed Care Environment at John T. Montford Psychiatric Medical Prison

Janis Woodall, MS, A.T.R., L.M.S.W.-A.C.P.
Pamela M. Diamond, Ph.D.
Ann Hanson Howe, M.S.W., L.M.S.W.-A.C.P.

In January 1993, the Texas Legislature established a managed health care advisory committee and charged it with developing a managed health care delivery system to provide services to Texas Department of Criminal Justice (TDCJ) inmates. Texas Tech University Health Sciences Center (TTUHSC) was awarded the managed health care contract for the TDCJ western region of Texas. There are 22 prisons in the region and approximately 30,000 inmates. The region covers an area of approximately 120,000 square miles (this is twice the size of New England!) that is primarily rural. Under the agreement, TDCJ contracts with TTUHSC to provide health and psychiatric services at the prison sites on a capitated basis. This is a relatively new term in health care—*capitation* simply fixes costs by charging by the inmate/patient rather than by the amount of services rendered.

The John T. Montford Psychiatric Medical Unit, located in Lubbock, Texas, opened in July of 1995, and was the first in-patient psychiatric facility to provide services under the new managed care contract. TDCJ and TTUHSC established an intensive and bold new model for treatment at this facility. The new model relies on the use of multidisciplinary teams to plan and provide treatment to the diverse psychiatric inmate population housed at this unit. An Art Therapy Program was an integral part of the initial planning, along with other habilitation therapies such as music therapy, occupational therapy, and recreation therapy, psychology, psychiatry, social work, nursing, and corrections are also represented on the treatment teams at the facility. The Department of Program Evaluation and Outcome Studies coordinates psychological assessments, designs outcome and process evaluations, performs unit-wide needs assessments, and oversees the comprehensive data base that linked information from the various teams together electronically.

Program Development

The Montford program is designed to provide several levels of care. Inmate/patients who are referred for psychiatric assessment from general population prison units are initially received at the crisis management ward. At this point a team will assess the patient for admission to the unit. Each inmate/patient is given an initial battery of psychological tests which includes Morey's *Personality Assessment Inventory* (PAI), (1991) and the *Millon Clinical Multiaxial Inventory, third edition* (MCMI-3), (Millon, 1994). Inmate/patients are assessed very carefully for malingering using clinical interviews, behavioral observations, and structured assessments such as the *Structured Interview for Reported Symptoms* (SIRS), (Rogers, 1992). Inmate/patients found to be malingering are returned to a general population unit. Patients found to be in need of psychiatric services are officially admitted to the acute care ward. There they receive an even more extensive battery of psychological tests[1] to determine the nature of their psychological disturbance and allow staff to better determine their treatment needs. When inmate/patients are stable, they are transferred to the intermediate or extended care unit where they receive a combination of psycho-pharmacological, psychotherapeutic, and psycho-social treatments.

Ongoing care for each inmate/patient is provided by a multidisciplinary treatment team that generally consists of a psychiatrist, psychologist, social worker, nurse, correctional officer captain, correctional officer, art therapist, music therapist, recreational therapist, occupational therapist, substance abuse counselors, school counselor consultants and clerical support staff. Based on the treatment team's observations and the results of the psychological testing, individual treatment plans are developed. These plans include very specific goals, and designate specific treatments to help the inmate/patient achieve these goals. Each treatment plan is reviewed on a regular basis throughout the inmate's stay on the unit, and is adjusted according to need.

Time-Limited Psychotherapy Groups

Ethical managed health care tries to re-engineer treatment to achieve clinical objectives in the least costly manner. Psychotherapy group programs, including art therapy, set clear and specific goals of treatment. These goals are the link to the treatment plan developed by the treatment team.

A population-based approach to developing time-limited psychotherapy groups has been very effective in our psychiatric medical prison unit. Data collected during the first six months of operation were analyzed to determine the dominant symptom clusters that characterized the inmate/patients who were coming to the Montford Unit. A cluster analysis of the clinical scales of the MCMI-3 (Diamond, Wang, and Giles, 1996) revealed the patients coming to Montford suffered from a variety of severe depressive and anxiety based disorders. Although some suffered from thought disorders, these were not as common as had been expected. Analyses of the neuropsychological test data revealed that many of the men also were experiencing cognitive disorders that were seriously disabling. Many of the men had extensive histories of substance abuse, head injury and trauma and their lifestyle had apparently taken its toll on their ability to plan, follow through and generally function as a person with a normal brain.

These findings formed the basis for the development of the group therapy program. Anxiety and depression were primary targets for intervention. Individual needs, in terms of cognitive function, were considered and groups were developed providing a range of cognitive chal-

---

[1] Inmate/patients are given the Structured Clinical Interview for Diagnosis, Clinical Version (SCID-CV), (First, Gibbon, Spizer & Williams, 1996), the Buss Perry Aggression Questionnaire (BPAQ), (Buss & Perry, 1992), the Brief Psychiatric Rating Scale (BPRS), (Overall, 1988), and a neuropsychological screen consisting the the Executive interview (EXIT), (Royall, Mahurin & Gray, 1992), the Folstein Mini-Mental Status Exam (MMSE), (Folstein, Folstein & McHugh, 1975), and the Qualitative Evaluation of Dementia (QED), (Royall, Mahurin, Cornell & Gray, 1993).

lenges. One entire ward (50 men) was devoted to providing care to the more seriously demented patients in the unit. This allowed for the development of specific groups that were designed to address their special needs and limitations.

Outcome Measures and Studies

Program evaluation is an integral component of treatment at the Montford Unit. Its initial contribution was to assist treatment and administrative staff in defining the population that was to be served. As specific programs have been designed and implemented, the role of program evaluation has expanded into the development of outcome measures and outcome studies in order to assess the utility of individual programs as well as the "program" as a whole. For each group that is designed, there are pre and post measures that link directly to the stated objectives of the group.

These measures capture knowledge, attitude, and/or level of symptomology, depending on the stated goals of the group. Standard instruments may be used, however, many of these measures have been developed specifically for the Montford Unit. In addition to the pre and post measures, process measures are developed to monitor inmate/patient progress on very concrete, observable behaviors during each group session. These measures are all developed collaboratively with clinical input from the therapist and technical assistance from the program evaluation staff. The process of developing these measures has, in and of itself, contributed to the refinement of group goals and objectives.

By using data to guide the development of programs and then linking inmates to specific treatments based upon a match between their individual psychiatric needs (determined through a structured assessment process) and the stated goals and objective of the program, and by further monitoring the individual's progress while receiving this treatment, we have developed an effective, accountable, and responsive set of programs to assist the inmates who come to Montford for psychiatric care.

Art Therapy at the Unit

The Team:

The multidisciplinary treatment team is a part of the managed care system at the Montford Psychiatric Medical Unit. The art therapist along with the music therapist, recreational therapist, occupational therapist and social workers provide a broad but focused program of group psychotherapy.

As described above, each inmate/patient is prescribed a group therapy program on the basis of therapeutic needs identified in the inmate/patient's treatment plan. Each inmate/patient who has been referred to group therapy is expected to attend three to six groups a week. They are also expected to participate in a substance abuse treatment program and to attend the Windham School if they have not yet completed their high school education. Most inmate/patients also work at the prison during part of their day.

The Art Therapy department works with the Social Work, Music Therapy, Occupational Therapy, and Recreation Therapy departments, as well as the chemical dependency counselor to provide psychotherapy and psychoeducational groups. Together, this team provides around five hundred hours of group therapy per week.

DRAWING TIME

The Mission:
The mission of art therapy at the Montford Unit is to provide a creative and safe environment that fosters and encourages the growth of self-respect, respect for others, and the determination to make constructive changes in one's life. Other important goals of the Art Therapy Program are to teach new skills through the effective use of art and art therapy, and to help each inmate use art as a tool for healing.

The program was developed with the belief that art therapy can provide an experience which may enable inmate/patients of many different functional levels to develop constructive outlets for their feelings, and provide them with some insight into their problems and experiences. With these insights, it is hoped that inmate/patients will gain knowledge into the dysfunctional and criminal behaviors that have been a part of their past in order to make real changes in their lives.

The program was also designed to help inmate/patients develop coping skills to assist them in their day-to day life in the prison, as well as when they return to either the general population prison or the community. The hope is that these skills will help prevent recidivism by supporting substance abstinence, compliance with psychiatric treatment, and the development of healthy lifestyles and social ties when they return to society.

The Structure:
The Art Therapy Program offers both art therapy and art studio groups. Both are designed to assist the inmate/patient in the development of self-esteem and new coping and social skills through the positive use of expressive media. Goals for both types of art therapy groups focus on improving social skills and developing self-respect and respect for the rights of others. Both also are designed to help inmate/patients to reduce physical and emotional tension and to develop constructive leisure.

Individuals are referred to art therapy or art studio groups based upon certain inclusion and exclusion criteria that are clearly defined and based upon both diagnostic indicators and behavioral criteria. The treatment team objectives, inmate/patient objectives, section anchor points for measuring process, pre and post tests and treatment goals are also clearly stated in the group outlines. These criteria assist the treatment team in making referral decisions.

Appendix A provides the criteria for the Art Studio Group and Appendix B shows the group criteria and outline for the Art Therapy Group. In both the Art Therapy and Art Studio groups, the first session is devoted to the administration of pre-tests, and explaining and discussing the group's structure, process, goals and objectives. Post tests are administered during the last group session and inmate/patients who successfully complete either Art Therapy or Art Studio receive a certificate.

The Art Studio program includes the following groups: drawing, sculpture, painting, ceramics and multi-media.

These groups focus on developing art skills and are educational and task oriented. These groups are appropriate for low, medium and high functioning inmate/patients. While conversation is not discouraged, the focus of the group is on the making of art. The therapist's role is one of teacher and facilitator, and one of the primary goals is to develop the inmate/patient's creative and expressive abilities through encouragement and exposure to multiple media. Positive social skills are encouraged and reinforced through the sharing of ideas, media, and the group appreciation of the finished art products.

The Art Therapy Program offers two types of groups: art therapy and art and music therapy combination group. Both groups focus on creating artwork that is related to an assigned subject. Every session has a segment of time devoted to making the art product and a discussion phase in which inmate/patients relate thoughts and feelings about their artwork. Inmate/patients must be moderate to high functioning to participate in these groups.

At the initial art therapy session, each inmate/patient is asked to sign "The Art Therapy Full Value Contract" (Appendix C). This contract, adapted from an instrument developed by Gilliland (1985), spells out the nature of the patient/therapist relationship within this setting and discusses concepts of confidentiality and the expectations of the therapist regarding disclosure and/or privacy within the prison setting. The group process and art tasks are focused on allowing inmate/patients to express themselves non-verbally.

While inmate/patients are encouraged to discuss their history and symptoms in the groups, the primary goal is to get them to go forward and develop positive coping skills. The art is helpful in that it provides an outlet for both positive and negative feelings while the group discussion can be used to help re-direct energy into concrete ways of making change.

Artwork completed in either art studio or art therapy may either be mailed to someone on the inmate/patient's visitation list, picked up by an authorized visitor or donated for display and charitable contributions. Artwork is also displayed in the habilitation therapy area of the unit with the inmate/patient's permission. These completed projects give the inmate/patient a sense of accomplishment and aid in improving self-esteem.

The following case studies were produced by these inmate/patients in art therapy groups. We will give a brief history of each individual, describe his involvement in art therapy, and discuss the artwork that was produced. By providing this as context, the artwork will provide insight into the inmate/patient's history and treatment issues as well as into his process and progress in therapy.

Mr. Andrews: History

Mr. Andrews[2], a 23-year-old, white, single, male was admitted to the John T. Montford Psychiatric Medical Prison in August of 1995 as a transfer patient[3] from another Psychiatric Prison facility. He first received psychiatric treatment in prison in September of 1992. At that time his major symptoms were suicidal ideation and hearing "voices."

Mr. Andrews is from a family in which physical, sexual, and psychological abuse was common. He attempted to hang himself at age eight and has attempted suicide several times since

---

2 All names used in this paper are pseudonyms that in no way resemble the actual name of the inmate/patient being described.

3 When the Montford Unit first opened in July of 1995, approximately 400 psychiatric inmates from other TDCJ facilities were transferred in to Montford over a six week period. After the initial group arrived, when inmates were received, the Montford Unit began the intake and screening procedures described in the paper. Transferred inmates were initially screened using a subset of the psychological test battery referred to in the text.

DRAWING TIME

then. At age 16, he joined a satanic cult and participated in sexual rituals. By the time he was 18, he had made three more suicide attempts by overdosing on medication. He began using inhalants when he was seven and has used and abused most common street drugs as well as alcohol. He has received treatment in the free world for both drug dependency and depression on numerous occasions. Mr. Andrews has a very poor work history and a history of homosexual behavior. Prior to this incarceration, he was arrested twice for theft and spent time in jail for both. His current conviction is for the murder of a homosexual male acquaintance. This event occurred when he and some friends were attempting to rob this acquaintance. He has served 5 years of the 30 year sentence he received for this murder. Mr. Andrews reports both auditory and visual hallucinations of the murder victim telling him that he has a choice of suicide or letting him (the murder victim) take over.

Mr. Andrews was given a primary DSM-IV, Axis I diagnosis of major depression, severe, recurrent with psychotic features. His secondary Axis I diagnosis is polysubstance dependence in remission. In addition to these Axis I disorders, Mr. Andrews was given an Axis II diagnosis of borderline personality disorder. Initial testing on the MCMI-3 revealed a schizotypal, avoidant and depressive personality type who was experiencing a major depression and serious anxiety. Subsequent testing on the Center for Epidemiological Studies Depression Scale (CES-D) (Radloff, 1977), and the Penn State Worry Questionnaire (PSWQ) (Meyer, Miller, Metzger & Borkovec, 1990), concur with these findings. His scores on the PSWQ reflect the most severe, ruminative type of anxiety and his scores on that instrument have been consistently high across multiple administrations. The CES-D scores were also initially quite high, indicating severe depression. However, Mr. Andrews did show some improvement on this instrument, concurrent with his participation in art therapy.

In addition to art therapy, Mr. Andrews has participated in the stretching group, relaxation group, music therapy, occupational therapy, Windham School, and vocational office support. The stretching and relaxation groups are part of the standard program offered to all inmates showing evidence of anxiety prior to their being referred to any other group treatment.

The goal of these groups is to provide the inmate/patient with some strategic anxiety reducing skills that they can use whenever needed. Mr. Andrews has been generally cooperative in all of his group treatments, and he has not had any disciplinary problems in the past year. His family support is minimal though there is a strong link between the patient and his grandmother as they write each other monthly. He also has begun to correspond to a friend in the free world.

The treatment team has recently placed Mr. Andrews on discharge status which means that he will soon be ready to return to the general prison population. He has been stabilized on his medication and the hallucinatory experiences seem to be well controlled.

Art Therapy

Mr. Andrews was referred to the Art Therapy Program by his treatment team to address the following objectives:

- develop positive expressive skills both verbal and non-verbal
- improve social skills including respect for self and the rights of others
- develop skills to reduce the symptoms of depression and anxiety

- establish constructive leisure skills that will prevent future substance abuse and recidivism.

Mr. Andrews attended eight one-hour art therapy sessions with seven other men. The groups were held twice a week in the Art therapy room, which is a large open room with work tables, a kiln, sink, and projects from both art and occupational therapy projects on display. This room is away from the inmate/patient cells and the ward dayroom areas and is seen as a warm and creative area. Inmates must meet certain behavioral criteria in order to attend groups off their wards and it is considered a privilege to be able to do so. For security reasons, although a correctional officer must be in the room at all times, the officer does not interact with the group while it is in session.

During the first session, pre-tests using the CES-D for depression and PSWQ for anxiety were administered. Scores were made available to the therapist prior to the next scheduled meeting of the group. For Mr. Andrews, as mentioned earlier, these assessments confirmed that he was indeed suffering from high levels of anxiety and depression. In addition to the testing and general introductions to the group, the Art Therapy Full Value Contract (see Appendix C) was discussed and signed at this time.

The Artwork

Drawing #1: Task: Where am I going?, Title: *Highway to Hell*, Media: 12 x18, marker on paper.

Mr. Andrews was quite talkative during the discussion phase of the activity and said that he thought his drawing in many ways represented his future and choices he must make. When he first heard the topic, "Where am I going?," his first thought was that he was going to a bar to get a drink. He said that although he now realizes that his addiction to drugs and alcohol contributed to his past crimes and incarceration, he is still not sure if he wants to change paths.

The other members of the group listened to his explanation of his drawing and discussed constructive leisure activities and choices a person could make instead of using drugs and alcohol. They suggested AA support groups, sports, and family/church activities as alternatives to drugs, alcohol, and crime. Mr. Andrews responded that he enjoyed art and music, however he admitted being drawn to drugs, alcohol and other illegal activities.

In many ways, *Highway to Hell* appears to reflect Mr. Andrews's addictions and his interest in the occult. The heavily shadowed cactus may represent his expressed anxiety regarding his destiny if he continues down this path. The Satanic figure holding the sign suggests aggression (sharp teeth) and may represent auditory (large unusual ears) and visual (eyes with no pupils) hallucinations as well as possible homosexual conflict (ears unusually drawn).

The center figure of the serpent or snake could represent himself. If this were true, the fact that the figure has no arms or legs might suggest guilt feelings and general feelings of depression. It could also suggest a lack of independence and autonomy, which would certainly fit in with his current situation.

Since this was an initial group, there was little probing for associations or symbols. However, the characteristics in the art mentioned above are consistent with what is known about Mr. Andrews and with his stated ambivalence about changing his lifestyle. His willingness to draw

DRAWING TIME

Figure 1: Mr. Andrews—"Highway to Hell"

Figure 2: Mr. Andrews—"The Hanging"

and discuss some of these feelings with the group were seen as a good beginning.

Drawing #2: Task: Free drawing, Title: *The Hanging*, Media: 18 x 24, pastel on paper.

This free drawing was done during time available after the regular art therapy session. Mr. Andrews did not share anything about this drawing with the group, and this choice was respected as per the Art Therapy Full Value Contract. In response to the content of the

106

picture, after the group was adjourned, the therapist asked if he was having any suicidal thoughts. Although he stated that he always has suicidal thoughts, he denied having a current plan. The treatment team was notified and he was further assessed for suicidal risk. Although he was not placed on overt suicide precautions, he was closely observed by staff for several days for any signs of decompensation.

During this session, Mr. Andrews' affect was blunted and he did not interact with the group. The drawing of the hanging is quite suggestive of suicidal ideation, depressive thoughts, and self-destructive tendencies and attempts. The head is considered the site of intellectual and fantasy activity and is associated with the control of impulses and emotions. It is also often considered to be the center for socializing needs, communication, and other interpersonal abilities. It is interesting to note that in his drawing the head is cut off visually not only by the rope but also by the lack of color on the neck area. This may be a link to his own ability to communicate, socialize appropriately, and control his impulsive behaviors that have been affected by his traumatic childhood and his substance abuse.

In the drawing, Mr. Andrews also omitted the ears and the nose on the figure. The omission of the ears suggests that he may still be experiencing auditory hallucinations. The omission of the nose may represent continued sexual identity conflict. This again is consistent with the patient's own history of hallucinations and his difficulty with sexual identity.

The frown on the mouth could illustrate his sadness and may reflect his own affect in this group. The sun figure may portray authority figures in his life, ranging from his father who deserted him when he was a child to the authorities in the prison who now control his life.

It is significant to observe that the person drawn looks childlike—he was eight when he first tried to hang himself. His father had left home and he had been sexually abused by his stepfather. Mr. Andrews was also experimenting with drugs, including inhalants, during this time. The drawing may well represent a memory of a very traumatic event in his life, as well as a representation of continued depression and suicidal ideation.

Drawings # 3 and # 4: Task: Feelings—Positive and Negative

During one session, inmate/patients were asked to draw two pictures: one was to reflect positive feelings, and the other negative feelings. Both were to be in colors representing the feelings expressed.

Drawing #3 Title: *Freedom*, Media: 18 x 24, pastel on paper.

Mr. Andrews drew a picture of a bird and a heart representing a positive feeling. During the discussion phase of the session he stated that this picture represented his desire for freedom. He stated that "hope" was his positive feeling. His affect was appropriate during this group. He was focused and appeared to enjoy working with the pastels. The bird in the picture looks like he is struggling to lift the bleeding heart.

The heart has long been viewed as the psychological and physical center of a human being. The bleeding heart may represent losses he has suffered in his lifetime. These losses may include his father's desertion and the break up of his home, the loss of childhood innocence as a result of sexual abuse and drug addiction, the loss of his health because of mental illness, and the loss of his freedom as a result of incarceration.

DRAWING TIME

Figure 3: Mr. Andrews —"Freedam"

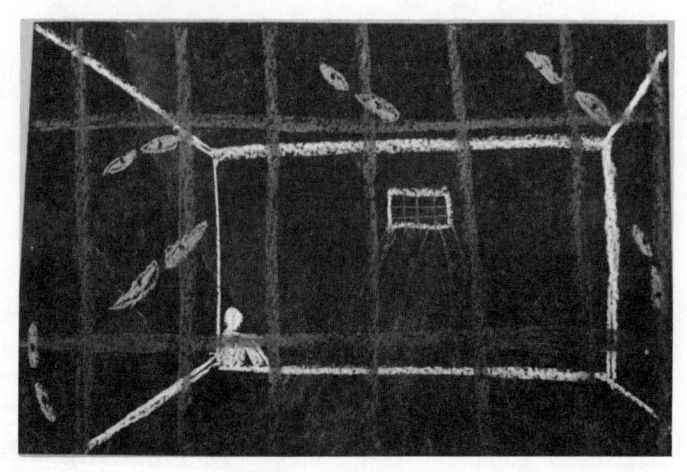

Figure 4: Mr. Andrews—"Prison Eyes"

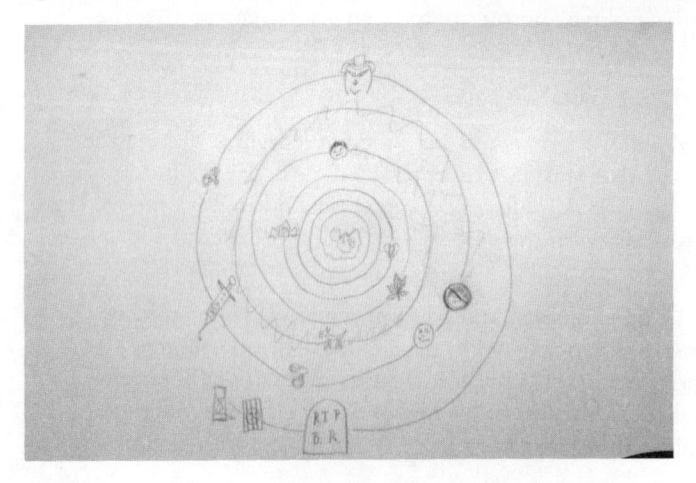

Figure 5: Mr. Andrews— "Lifeline"

108

The bird may also represent freedom as a hope for a better life in spite of being burdened by the suffering of the past.

Drawing #4: Title: *Prison Eyes*, Media: 18 x 24, pastel on paper.

Mr. Andrews described his negative feeling drawing as how it felt to be frightened and alone in his cell. He said he felt like he was being watched and he was hearing voices. This drawing describes his negative feelings of paranoia and fear. Mr. Andrews also said that the drawing represents how he feels when he is not on medication.

Mr. Andrews had good eye contact and his voice was calm as he described the drawing. He appeared to have insight into how medication has helped ameliorate his hallucinations and paranoia. The prison cell and bars appear to keep the tiny human figure captive and render him incapable of autonomy. The yellow eyes characterize the inmate/patient's visual hallucinations and paranoia.

This drawing illustrates his history of hallucinations and incarceration. The overall feeling is one of isolation and depression, and of how frightening mental illness can be. The group identified with his feelings of depression, isolation, and fear.

Drawing #5: Task: Lifeline, Media: 12 x 18, pencil on paper

The group was asked to draw their lifelines. They were asked to include significant events in their life such as: earliest memory, happiest moment, saddest moment, first alcohol use, first incarceration, and family events.

When describing his lifeline, Mr. Andrews said that one of most painful events in his life was when his father left home. He felt his heart broke when his parents divorced. He went on to describe his first experimentation with marijuana and pointed out the place on the lifeline where this had occurred.

As he talked about the lifeline, he described how sad and alone he felt when his dog was run over and died. Apparently it was around this time that he tried to hang himself and was placed in a psychiatric hospital. He followed the lifeline around to where he began to use intravenous drugs. It was during this time that he was arrested several times and had some serious relationship problems that he now feels were because of his need to finance his drug habit.

He then followed the lifeline around to the crime of murder for which he is currently incarcerated. He added that the last figure on the lifeline was a broken hour glass and that time was running out.

The Lifeline task is very sensitive and is used only after some measure of trust and cohesiveness has developed in a group. Mr. Andrews was sad as he described his lifeline, but he maintained appropriate eye contact and affect. It was interesting that he chose to use what appears to be a true lifeline, his own umbilical cord, for the drawing. It is also significant that he used a mandala-like effect to represent the circle of his life. At other times, Mr. Andrews has said that he believes that his life has been predestined and will end in suicide. This statement is consistent with the broken hour glass at the end of the lifeline.

Mr. Andrews appears to have some insight into how devastating the losses of his father, a

DRAWING TIME

secure home, his pet, and his freedom have been in his life. He also appears to recognize that drugs and alcohol have significantly affected his behavior and contributed to negative events in his life. The group was very supportive as he described his life. Many of the group members identified with the same issues of dysfunctional family and substance abuse.

Summary

Mr. Andrews began the group in at the beginning of April, 1996, and completed it by the end of that month. He participated in a total of eight sessions and received a certificate for his successful completion. His mood and affect fluctuated somewhat over the four-week period, however, he was always appropriate and respectful of the therapist, officer, and other group members. Mr. Andrews was able to communicate well in the groups and he was able to develop positive expressive skills to somewhat reduce the symptoms of depression. During this time, he attended all groups and school and did not isolate himself or make any suicidal gestures.

He stated that he would draw in his cell when he felt stressed or upset. This was encouraged as a positive coping mechanism and good use of leisure time. His post test measures on depression and anxiety indicated that while his depression had lessened somewhat, his anxiety was still quite high.

Mr. Andrews's artwork clearly reflects his history. The group provided him with a place where he could express his feelings both verbally and non-verbally in a constructive way. After the group ended, Mr. Andrews continued to attend school and other psychotherapy groups. The treatment team recently placed him on discharge status as it is now felt that he has stabilized and will be able to function in a general population unit.

Mr. Brown: History

Mr. Brown is 28-year-old, white, single, male who was transferred to the John T. Montford Psychiatric Medical Prison in August of 1995 from another psychiatric prison hospital. He was referred to Montford for continuing treatment for serious depression accompanied by suicidal ideation.

Mr. Brown has a sister, two years older, and a brother, three years younger. He had one other younger brother who was accidentally shot with an arrow and bled to death at the age of 17. Mr. Brown grew up very active in the Baptist church and participated in youth activities during his teens. Mr. Brown's parents divorced when he was about 10 years old, and he lived with his mother after the divorce. His mother did not remarry until he was 20 years old. Although Mr. Brown lived with a friend when he first left home, he moved back home again after a short time. He was living on his own again for about a year and a half prior to his incarceration. Both of his parents and his stepfather have been his primary support while he has been in prison.

Mr. Brown did not have any disciplinary problems in school until he reached high school. There he got into trouble for cutting up and disrupting class. Although he has average intelligence, he took special education classes for math and science. He did have a positive experience in English, however, and developed a friendship with his teacher. Mr. Brown made primarily C's in school but dropped out half way through his senior year. He has since earned his GED.

Mr. Brown was sexually abused in his early adolescence by an older male neighbor, a doctor, and a youth minister. He also has a history of chemical abuse beginning at age 15. He has used alcohol, marijuana, and ecstasy, although he reports that he stopped using drugs in 1991. There is a strong family history of alcoholism on the paternal side of his family. Both his father and his grandfather are alcoholics. His father has received treatment and is currently in recovery. Mr. Brown has also attended Alcoholics Anonymous and Substance Abuse Treatment programs while in prison.

In addition to substance abuse, Mr. Brown has a history of both auditory and visual hallucinations which are currently controlled with medication. He first experienced problems with depression, paranoid ideation, anxiety, and obsessive thoughts at the age of seven and was treated in the free world for depression following a suicide attempt at age 20. Since his arrival at the Montford Unit, he has continued to suffer from these symptoms. In addition to problems with anxiety, depression, and polysubstance dependence, Mr. Brown has difficulty dealing with people and isolates himself.

Mr. Brown is currently serving a five-year sentence for aggravated sexual assault of a child under 14. He has a history of two prior arrests and he has not received major disciplinary cases while in prison. It is especially significant that Mr. Brown is due for release from prison in January of 1997. He has served "flat time" and will be released to full freedom without any connection with parole or the criminal justice system.

At Montford, Mr. Brown was given a primary Axis I diagnosis of Pedophillia and a secondary Axis I diagnosis of Polysubstance Dependence, in remission. He also has a primary Axis II diagnosis of Antisocial Personality Disorder with Borderline and Narcissistic Traits. Preliminary testing using the MCMI-3 revealed a depressive, dependent personality type with passive-aggressive tendencies and borderline features. He also showed elevations on anxiety. This high anxiety was also reflected in his scores on the PSWQ. The CES-D administered at the beginning of his time in art therapy also indicated severe depression. In addition to these assessments, more recent testing on the PAI have supported a diagnosis of schizophrenia—undifferentiated type. This would be consistent with his self-reports of hallucinatory experiences, his difficulty relating to people, and his occasional paranoia.

In addition to art therapy, Mr. Brown has been referred to the following groups: occupational therapy, substance abuse treatment, school, music therapy, anger management, stress management, and art and music therapy combination group.

Art Therapy

Mr. Brown was referred to art therapy by his treatment team to address the following objectives:

- develop positive expressive skills both verbal and non-verbal
- improve social skills including respect for self and the rights of others
- develop skills to reduce physical and emotional tension, and
- establish constructive leisure skills that will prevent future substance abuse and recidivism.

Mr. Brown has participated in both art therapy and the art and music therapy combination group. Although he completed seven sessions in art therapy, he missed the last session

DRAWING TIME

because of a disciplinary case related to his oppositional behavior. He was later referred to art and music therapy to work on reducing his anxiety and depression. This time he was able to complete all eight sessions successfully.

The artwork selected for this case reflects his obsessive compulsive disorder, depression, anxiety, and isolative behavior. He states that drawing and music are constructive outlets for his feelings. The artwork selected also presents an overall theme of self-protection and anxiety about returning to the free world.

The Artwork

Drawing #6: Task: The Tree That Represents Me, Title: *Weeping Willow*, Media: 12 x 18, colored marker on paper.

When Mr. Brown was asked to draw a tree that would represent himself, he drew a weeping willow tree. He said little about it except that it represented sadness in his life. This drawing is the only selection from the art therapy group in which Mr. Brown participated. He was verbal and cooperative during this session. He contributed actively to the discussion, although he shared little beyond the surface about his drawing. During the group, his affect was appropriate and the other group members were supportive of him and he, in return, was considerate of them as they shared their drawings.

The weeping willow tree that he drew is suggestive of depression. The tree has a transparency that often indicates poor reality contact, poor judgment, anxiety, and sexual disturbance. The overall look of the tree gives the impression of an umbrella providing protection and safety.

Flying birds like the ones seen in the picture are often found in drawings of people with anxiety.

Drawing #7: Task: free drawing, Title: *The Body*, Media: 12 x 18, colored marker on paper.

Mr. Brown drew this picture during one of his first sessions in the art and music combination group. During the discussion phase of the group, he stated that he had watched a television program about the FBI and related it to the body that he had drawn. He smiled inappropriately when he said he had not been able to get it off his mind. He denied that the drawing represented himself, but his smile indicated that he knew that the drawing would be seen as disturbing. The therapist took the drawing to the treatment team and documented the session.

The body he drew is certainly isolated under the ground. The tree suggests low energy level and avoidance of reality. The knot in the picture could relate to trauma experienced during his adolescent years. This drawing is indeed very disturbing and indicates that Mr. Brown may feel extremely hopeless about returning to society, although it is unclear if the body it represents is himself or someone else.

Drawing #8: Task: free drawing, Title: *The Forest*, Media: 12 x 18, colored marker on paper.

Mr. Brown drew the forest while listening to soothing recorded music. During the discussion phase of the group, he described the figure as being in a forest. The therapist commented on the red sky and Mr. Brown replied that he did not realize he had painted the sky red. Mr. Brown was verbal and cooperative during the group and he worked very quickly on this

ART THERAPY IN A MANAGED CARE ENVIRONMENT

Figure 6: Mr. Brown— "Weeping Willow"

Figure 8: Mr. Brown— "The Forest"

Figure 7: Mr. Brown—"The Body"

DRAWING TIME

drawing—taking only minutes to complete it. His own comment about not realizing he had painted the sky red had a dissociative feel to it, however, there is no reported dissociation in his history.

The theme of protection again arises in this session, as the figure in the drawing appears to be protected by the trees from the threatening red sky. The chaotic crowns on the trees are also suggestive of inner tension and confusion. One might speculate that Mr. Brown is experiencing considerable anxiety about returning to the free world.

Drawing #9: Task: free drawing, Title: *The Train*, Media: 12 x 18, colored marker on paper.

Drawn while listening to relaxing pre-recorded music, *The Train* was the second drawing completed during this session. It was completed in just a few minutes and Mr. Brown did not wish to talk about it at all. Since this was part of the full value contract, his wishes were respected. Mr. Brown is generally quite reserved in this group.

The figure in the drawing appears to be in considerable danger. If he stays on the track, the train will crush him. If he jumps off the track he may die from the fall or drown in the water below. The trees in the drawing have chaotic crowns that are suggestive of inner tension and confusion. However, the figure falling from the bridge does have a protective enclosure around him.

Drawing #10: Task: free drawing, Title: *Colorful Cathedral*, Media: 12 x 18, colored marker on paper.

Mr. Brown took less than 10 minutes to complete this detailed drawing which was based on a photograph. Again, as in the previous session, Mr. Brown was unwilling to say much about his drawing. In spite of not talking, he was cooperative in other ways and completed the assigned task.

The building that he drew again appears to be a protective structure and the overall theme of this drawing appears to be his need for protection from the outside world. The windows drawn without panes suggest hostility and oppositional tendencies as well as possible oral and anal eroticism. This would be consistent with his diagnosis and his homosexual lifestyle.

Drawing #11: Task: Free drawing, Title: *Raining Hearts*, Media: 12 x 18, colored marker on paper.

Mr. Brown completed this drawing while listening to music in the art and music combination group. He was very focused on the drawing and worked quickly. He again chose not to comment on the drawing.

The clouds in the drawing appear very chaotic and threatening as the lightning strikes. The rain is mixed with hearts in a very heavy downpour. As the figure is walking away from the dock on the lake, he is not only protected from the rain by the umbrella but also by the tree foliage. The figure is enclosed and protected from a dangerous environment. The crowns of the trees have a transparent look and the treatment of the limbs is a confused jumble of lines. This suggests confusion, impulsivity, and emotional lability.

Summary

Mr. Brown, a 28-year-old, white male suffers from anxiety and depression. He has a diagnosis

Figure 9: Mr. Brown—"The Train"

Figure 10: Mr. Brown—"Colorful Cathedral"

Figure 11: Mr. Brown—"Raining Hearts"

of Pedophillia and Polysubstance Dependence. He does have the benefit of average intelligence and the ability to express himself through art in a constructive way. The overall theme of the drawings selected from his work seems to indicate a great deal of anxiety about returning to the free world. Protective enclosures of many types permeate his productions.

The treatment focus of his remaining sentence will be to help him set goals for himself for when he returns to society. He will be encouraged to participate in groups that focus on re-entry into the free world, including substance abuse education and the development of leisure and recreation skills. In addition to art therapy, he is currently receiving individual therapy that focuses on the treatment of sexual offenders.

Conclusions

As we have stated, managed care concepts such as the use of program evaluation, multidisciplinary treatment teams, and goal directed group therapy have added to the effectiveness of the delivery of art therapy in our setting. This intensive and bold new model has allowed us to provide treatment that achieves clinical objectives in a cost effective manner. Most importantly, managed care has provided an environment in which the provision of art therapy has helped inmate/patients develop constructive outlets for emotions, build self esteem, self respect and the respect for others, learn insight into their problems, and learn improved life skills. This will help inmate/patients to cope with the psychiatric prison setting and prepare them to make choices that will improve their lives in prison and in the free world.

The case studies chosen for this chapter illustrate the importance of allowing inmate/patients the privacy to express themselves non-verbally through art. These powerful drawings provide constructive outlets for tension, anxiety, and fear. Having constructive outlets in art therapy and other psychotherapy groups have been helpful in reducing depressive symptoms. In both of the cases described, depressive scales decreased from pre-test to post-test administrations. The anxiety scales, however, did not show similar improvement.

One might theorize that in prison it is necessary to have a certain amount of anxiety to survive. In this case, we might do well to help the inmate/patient decrease his anxiety enough that he can function without being in a constant state of panic, while allowing him to retain enough anxiety that he can continue to function safely in this environment.

The cases described in this chapter are also good examples of how the interface between program evaluation and program design has allowed specific groups to be organized and implemented. Art therapy is used to target depression and anxiety while other groups have been designed to deal with dementia, borderline symptoms, anger management, and so forth. Treatment teams therefore have a variety of groups to which they can refer the inmate/patients. The development of the different types of programs offered at Montford was based upon empirical data.

The process described is an example of how to design and implement programs which meet the specific needs of the clients, rather than only providing services that are based upon therapist or administrative preference. In the prison system, we do not have the luxury of turning away patients when they are in need because we don't have the right "program." We must, in some way, develop services that are appropriate, efficient, and effective to meet the changing, and sometimes unexpected, needs of our clients—the inmates.

References

Buss, A. H., & Perry, M. (1992). The aggression questionnaire. *Journal of Personality and Social Psychology, 63* (3), 452-459.

Diamond, P. M., Wang, E. W. & Giles, C. L. (1996). Empirically derived MCMI-III profiles of psychiatric prisoners facilitate program development. Presented at the *104th annual convention of the American Psychological Association* in Toronto, Canada.

First, M. B., Gibbon, M., Spitzer, R. L. & Williams, J. B. (1996). *Users' guide for the Structured Clinical Interview for DSM-IV Axis I disorders - clinician version.* New York: Biometrics Research

Folstein, M. F., Folstein, S. E. & McHugh, P. R. (1975). Mini-Mental State: A practical method for grading the cognitive state of patients for the clinician. *Journal of Psychiatric Research, 12,* 188-198.

Gilliland, I. (1985). *A foundational guide to art therapy.* Napa, CA: Women in Process Seminars

Liebmann, M. (1994). *Art therapy with offenders.* London, Jessica Kingley, Ltd.

Liebmann, M. (1996). *Art therapy for groups.* Cambridge, MA: Brookline Books

Meyer, T. J., Miller, M. L., Metzger, R. L. & Borkovec, T. D. (1990). Development and validation of the Penn State Worry Questionnaire. *Behavioral Research Therapy, 28* (6), 487-495.

Millon, T. (1994). *MCMI-III manual.* Minneapolis, MN: National Computer Systems

Morey, L. (1991). *Personality assessment inventory: Professional manual.* Odessa, FL: Psychological Assessment Resources, Inc.

Ogden, D. P. (1986). *Psychodiagnostics and personality assessment: A handbook.* Second edition. Los Angeles, CA: Western Psychological Services

Overall, J. E. (1988). The brief psychiatric rating scale (BPRS): Recent developments in ascertainment and scaling. *Psychopharmacology Bulletin, 24,* 97-99.

Radloff, L. S. (1977). The CES-D Scale: A new self-report depression scale for research in the general population. *Applied Psychological Measurement, 1,* 385-401.

Rogers, R. (1992). *Structured interview of reported symptoms: Professional manual.* Odessa, FL: Psychological Assessment Resources, Inc.

Royall, D. R., Mahurin, R. K., & Gray, K. F. (1992). Bedside assessment of executive cognitive impairment: The executive interview. *Journal of the American Geriatric Society, 40,* 1221-1226.

Royall, D. R., Mahurin, R. K., Cornell, J & Gray, K. F. (1993). Bedside assessment of dementia type using the Qualitative Evaluation of Dementia. *Neuropsychiatry, Neuropsychology, and Behavioral Neurology, 6* (4), 235-244.

The authors would like to acknowledge the assistance of several individuals who contributed to this manuscript: Tsyvia Akavya, R.N., R.M.T, Eugene Wang, M.S., Patricia Grabowski and Leticia Galarza.

APPENDIX A
Patient Criteria For Art Studio

AXIS I Inclusion: All diagnoses
    Exclusion: None
AXIS II Inclusion: All diagnoses
    Exclusion: None
AXIS III Inclusion: All diagnoses
    Exclusion: None
AXIS IV Inclusion: Level 3 and up. Mild to moderate stressors
    Exclusion: Assault precautions
AXIS V Inclusion: All
    Exclusion: None

Treatment Team Objectives:
1. increase social interaction
2. decrease isolation
3. decrease stress
4. improve self esteem
5. develop constructive outlets for feelings/self-expression
6. develop creativity and basic art skills

Treatment Goals:
1. improve social skills including the respect for self and others
2. complete all sessions
3. use art to reduce stress
4. improve self esteem through successful completion of projects
5. use new skills for constructive leisure activities and outlets for feelings
6. develop new art skills and creativity

Session Anchors:
Inmates are rated on the following items each time they attend a group:
    Participation (none to active—5 point scale)
    Stays on Task (never to almost always—5 point scale)
    Frustration Tolerance (none to excellent—5 point scale)
    Follows Instructions (never to almost always—5 point scale)

Inmate Objectives:
1. complete four or six week program
2. stress management
3. learn new techniques in art media
4. increase self esteem

Inmate Attention Span: one to two hours
Inmate Ability to Follow Instructions: needs to be capable of following simple instructions
Inmate Motivation: minimum to maximum

ART THERAPY IN A MANAGED CARE ENVIRONMENT

APPENDIX B
Patient Criteria For Art Therapy Group

AXIS I Inclusion: All except as noted below
    Exclusion: Any disorder with uncontrolled hallucinations or psychotic features
AXIS II Inclusion: All
    Exclusion: None
AXIS III Inclusion: All except as noted below
    Exclusion: Active tuberculosis
AXIS IV Inclusion: Appropriate level
    Exclusion: Those on assault precautions and individuals displaying disruptive behavior
AXIS V Inclusion: All
    Exclusion: None

Treatment Team Objectives:
1. development of self esteem and new skills through positive expression, both verbal and nonverbal
2. improvement in social skills
3. development of respect for self and the rights of others
4. development of skills in reducing physical and emotional tension
5. establishment of constructive leisure activity skills to prevent substanceabuse and recidivism

Treatment Goals:
1. Inmate/patient will improve social skills and develop positive expressive skills through engaging in appropriate conversation, discussing thoughts and feelings about artwork and listening to others.
2. Inmate/patient will develop or improve the ability to respect the rights of others through listening to others' experiences in a supportive manner.
3. Inmate/patient will be able to utilize various art modalities as a constructive way of reducing stress rather than substance abuse or other illegal activities.

Session Anchors / Pre and Post Tests
Participation: none, slight, moderate, good, active
Verbal Expression: very little, slight, moderate, good, high disclosure
Artistic Expression: very little, slight, moderate, very creative
Ability to Listen: very little, slight, moderate, good, excellent

CES-D (depression scale)

PSWQ (anxiety scale)

Inmate Objectives:
1. The inmate/patient will produce artwork pertaining to particular subject assigned at each session.
2. During the discussion phase of each session, the inmate/patient will verbalize thoughts or

DRAWING TIME

3. The inmate/patient will give evidence of listening to other group members during the discussion such as a visual contact, supportive comments, or looking at the artwork.

Inmate Attention Span:
Needs to be capable of listening, observing, and interacting with others for a period of one hour.

Inmate Ability to Follow Instructions:
Moderate, with no more than a moderate need for clarification or repetition.

Inmate Motivation: Moderate to high.

Art Therapy Group Outline
Treatment Goals:

1. Inmate/patient will improve social skills and develop positive expression skills through engaging in appropriate conversation, discussion of thoughts and feelings about artwork and listening to others.

2. Inmate/patient will develop or improve the ability to respect himself and the rights of others through listening to others' experiences in a supportive manner.

3. Inmate/patient will be able to use various art modalities as a constructive way of reducing stress rather than substance abuse or other illegal activities.

Anchor Points:

Participation: none, slight, moderate, good, active
Verbal Expression: very little, slight, moderate, good, high disclosure
Artistic Expression: very little, slight, moderate, good, excellent
Ability to Listen: very little, slight, moderate, good, excellent
Anchor points will be monitored each session.

Administered in the first and last sessions:

CES-D (depression scale)
PSWQ (anxiety scale)

Introduction To Outlines:
The use of art as therapy implies that the creative process can be a means both of reconciling emotional conflicts and of fostering self-awareness and personal growth.

Inmate/patients are comprised of a broad range of people with all kinds of abilities and disabilities. Most inmate/patients survive the pressures of prison by protecting themselves with an outer "shell."

Art therapy works in a supportive way to encourage the inmate/patients to express feelings constructively through art. If the art is of such a personal nature that it would be detrimental for the inmate/patient to reveal its meaning in group, he may choose not to participate in the discussion phase of the session. This right is stated in the Art Therapy Full Value Contract that each inmate signs prior to participating in groups.

Session I: Introduction and Evaluation

1. Purpose: to clarify goals and objectives of the art therapy group and establish an initial evaluation
2. Specific materials: 18 x 24 white paper, 12 color pastels, poster of Full Value Contract, CESD, PSWQ
3. Administration of CESD and PSWQ
4. Full Value Contract will be discussed and inmate/patient will be asked to sign the contract (see Appendix C).
5. Art therapy evaluation will be administered
6. Group discussion of artwork
7. Closure

Sessions II Through VIII

Each session will include an explanation of the therapeutic art activity, the activity itself, and discussion of group members artwork.

Materials include paper, pastels, watercolors, pencils, markers, clay, and collage materials.

Each session will include an explanation of the therapeutic art activity, the activity itself, and a discussion time for the group members artwork.

The following art therapy activities describe groups in which personal problems and potentials are explored through verbal and nonverbal expression to develop physical, emotional, and learning skills.

Feelings Exercise

Objective: Self awareness, positive and negative feelings will be identified and explored.

Materials: large box of pastels, 12 x 18 colored construction paper, 12 x 18 manila construction paper, box of tissues

Instructions—ask inmate/patients to think about:

1. Feelings as color—what color represents anger for you? (happiness, sadness, frustration, depression, joy, etc.)
2. Selecting colors that represent a positive/negative feeling. It can be one or two drawings. They will need one piece of colored construction paper and an assortment of colored pastels, one piece of manila construction paper and several tissues
3. Therapist will demonstrate...
    - tear manila paper into a shape representing the feeling you have chosen
    - use half of manila paper as a scratch pad and half for your pattern
    - place pattern on the scratch pad—rub pastel along edge of pattern.
    - remove scratch paper and place pattern on colored construction paper.

DRAWING TIME

- take a tissue and rub pastel from manila paper to the colored paper.
- repeat process until the look you want is achieved.

4. Write a description of your feelings of the artwork on a separate paper
5. Discussion of artwork
6. Closure

Art Activity—A Tree That Would Be Like You

Objective: Self awareness, the tree is a subconscious self portrait (house, tree, person projective testing).

Materials: 12 x 18 white paper, box of craypas, pencil

Instructions:

1. Draw a tree that will represent yourself
2. Answer these questions (on back of drawing):

    - What kind of tree did you draw? (Indicates self perception, strong, independent, weak, dependent, survivor, depressed, etc.)
    - How old is the tree? (This may indicate the I/P's psychosexual and/or psychosocial maturity)
    - Is your tree alive? (A response indicating the tree is dead reveals feelings of futility, depression, suicide)
    - What do you think caused it to die? death caused externally indicates that I/P blames something extrapersonal; death caused internally—I/P feels unwhole some and acceptable
    - Is your tree alone or in a group of trees? (Alone indicates I/P may be experiencing social isolation among his peers)
    - What is the weather like in the picture? (Determines environmental stress)
    - Is the wind blowing? (Determines I/P's environmental pressures)
    - Has anyone or anything ever hurt the tree? (Determines the degree to which I/P has experienced environmental attacks upon his personality)
    - What does the tree need most? (Indicates what I/P needs or wants, more trees, shelter, fertilizer, etc. Indicates he needs nourishment, support, etc. ,sunshine and water are often the reply and may not be significant)

3. Discussion of artwork
4. Closure

Lifeline

Objective: Self-awareness, identification of significant events in life as well as patterns, strengths, and needs.

Materials: 18 x 24 white paper, pencil, markers

Instructions:

1. Draw a lifeline which includes significant events in your life. Please include your earliest

memory, happiest moment, saddest moment, first drug use, first arrest, etc.
2. Discussion of artwork
3. Closure

Where Am I Going

Objective: Identification of how I/P sees past, present, and future, and their own autonomy and independence.

Materials: 18 x 24 white paper, markers

Instructions:
1. Fold paper into three sections.
2. Write one of the following titles at the top of each section.
3. Draw a representation of the titles. Please think about emotional as well as physical representation:

- Where Am I? Indication of present. (Emotional/Physical needs)
- Where Am I going? Indication of future. (Goals, hopes, etc.)
- Where Am I coming from? (Indication of past. Childhood, free world, development)

4. Discussion
5. Closure

Self Image Collage

Objective: Awareness of self as well as how others see you.

Materials: Magazines, glue, markers, construction paper. Light or overhead projector, scissors, glue.

Instructions:
1. Make a self image collage using pictures and words that will describe how you see yourself and how you think others see you. Please include both emotional and physical aspects of your self-image.
2. Select two contrasting colors of construction paper.
3. Draw a silhouette of your head in profile. (You will need someone to trace your silhouette. Paper is taped to the wall with Inmate/Patient sitting directly in front of the paper. The projector/light will provide a shadow of the profile to trace.
4. Cut silhouette out, and glue it on your other paper.
5. Select photographs and words from the magazines for your self-image collage. You may cut or tear them from the pages.
6. Glue photograph, pictures, and words on the construction paper to form a self-image collage.
7. Discussion
8. Closure

DRAWING TIME

Accumulative Drawing

Objective: Socialization and Communication, Group Cooperation, Self Awareness.

Materials: 12x18 white paper, colored markers, watch with second hand

Instructions:
1. Place your name in the bottom right hand corner of your paper.
2. Each member of the group should select a color from the marker box. (Yellow does not show well)
3. Each group member is asked to begin a drawing or scribble which will be passed to the person on their right. Each group member will begin when the facilitator says "start" and stop when the facilitator says "stop." Group members will have 20 seconds for each paper.
4. Each paper will be drawn on by every group member. (sit around a large table.)
5. When the drawings come back to the original artists, they are asked to answer the following questions:

    - Do you like the way your drawing looks? Why?
    - Do you dislike the way your drawing looks? Why?
    - Describe how the art relates to your life. You may tell a story about past, present, future, hopes, dreams, etc.

6. Discussion
7. Closure

Paint Blot Projections

Objective: Projection of feelings, socialization and group cooperation.

Materials: Colored construction paper, tempera paint, markers

Instructions:
1. Select colored paper and paints
2. Squeeze paint or use a brush to place paint on paper. (Be careful not to use in excess.)
3. Fold paper in half and gently press.
4. Open paper—more paint can be added. Repeat process.
5. Title each painting:

    - What feeling best describes the artwork?
    - Projection—What does the painting look like to you?

6. Each group member will write what they think the paint blot looks like on a paper placed beside the painting.
7. Each group member will share his description, and what group members wrote.
8. Discussion
9. Closure

APPENDIX C
Art Therapy Full Value Contract

1. All that occurs with your personal work is considered confidential.

2. If your work is of such a personal nature that you do not wish to discuss it in front of the group, your privacy will be respected. Respect yourself and other group members.

3. No judgments are to be made about any person or their work.

4. No competition with other group members. Each individual is in their own process.

5. Thoughts, feelings and emotions about specific artwork will be written on the back of that work.

6. All artwork must be titled, dated and signed.

7. Do not throw anything away. The work may take on additional meaning at a later date.

8. If working in a group, no comments are to be made about another person's work unless requested.

9. Artwork is a vital part of treatment and may be shared with the treatment team. A portfolio of all artwork will be kept by the art therapist.

Date:_____

Signature:_____

Surviving One's Sentence:
Art Therapy with Incarcerated Trauma Survivors

Elizabeth Day, MA, A.T.R.-BC

Greg Onorato, Psy. D.

It's a hot summer night and the fan just broke. Lots of the women have opted to go to the staff vs. non-staff baseball game. It's a statement for those who remain; everybody went to the baseball game! Simone stops to wonder why, in fact, she came to art therapy group. Come to think of it, why did she even decide to be in the trauma program? Spontaneously, group has begun. Almost silent last week, tonight, Simone is on a roll.

"Now why would I go stirrin' things up that I've worked so hard to forget? You'd have to be crazy to go lookin' for that pain."

She prides herself on never having talked about her incest. Then Ellen, the group's "mother," tells her story.

"Trauma? What trauma? I didn't let anything affect me—just forget it and move on. That's how I dealt with things. Remember, they had that speaker come and talk about her rape—well, then I fell completely apart. That was about three months ago.

So, I came to the trauma program kicking and screaming. I didn't want to look at this stuff either...but it came knocking on my door. I wasn't as finished with my past as I had thought. I've been doing a lot of work here and it's been really painful—but something's different. I feel alive again. I feel like something's lifted. I feel like I care—like I have energy that I never knew existed before. Maybe that's why it's worth it to look at the painful stuff.

I have my life back again. I wonder if it's like that for you, Simone. I wonder whether you have more to look at in your past."

Simone sits somber.

"Maybe," she says, "maybe."

The art therapist transitions the group at this point into creative expressions. Images of rage, hope, and integration emerge to validate the untold stories. The group honors each picture with applause. Tears and hugs, laughter and closeness become real in the ordinarily defended existence within the unit's walls.

DRAWING TIME

This vignette represents a glimpse of an art therapy group for trauma survivors. In many ways, there is nothing unusual or even remarkable about this scene. Productive art therapy groups for trauma survivors are offered in many kinds of therapeutic settings. This account of art therapy group process could have been taken from any one of them. What does, however, make this particular group unique is that it is being conducted in a female correctional institution. Group members are participants of the trauma program, a voluntary recovery program for incarcerated female offenders who present with histories of sexual, physical or severe emotional abuse.

The purpose of this chapter is to introduce art therapists to the female correctional environment as an untapped source of professional opportunities, particularly in working with trauma survivors. This chapter is not intended to provide a comprehensive understanding of psychological trauma and its treatment. For a broader exploration of these issues, the reader is directed to authors such as Briere, Chu, Herman, and van der Kolk whose writings on this topic are extensive. By sharing our experience of working with this population, we seek to demystify and destigmatize the prospect of practicing art therapy within a penal setting for women. Our goal is to entice others to follow in our footsteps beyond the artificial boundaries of traditional treatment arenas.

Current Practice, Current Need

Extremely little has been written on the topic of art therapy in jails and prisons. Editor Marian Liebmann's recent contribution, *Art Therapy With Offenders* (1994), is the only other book in print devoted to this topic and it comes out of work done solely in the United Kingdom. Aside from our chapter, *Making Art in a Jail Setting* (Day and Onorato 1989), only five articles have been written since 1967, and two of these are not in English (Andritsky, 1986; Elliot, 1987; Hook-Wheelhouwer, 1991; Levy, 1978; Welfman, 1982). Levy's (1978) work with female inmates comes the closest to our focus here. She used art therapy to help treatment-resistant inmates adjust to incarceration.

The creative therapies literature clearly documents the effectiveness of nonverbal modalities in addressing issues of sexual abuse and childhood trauma (Cohen & Cox, 1989; Cohen et. al., 1991; Glaister, 1994; Hargrave-Nykaza, 1994; Jacobson, 1994; Johnson, 1987; Levens, 1994; Mazza et. al., 1987; Murphy, 1994; Serrano, 1989; Shapiro, 1988; Spring, 1985, 1993; Ventre, 1994; Volkman, 1993). However, nothing exists in the literature which specifically speaks to the application of art therapy to incarcerated trauma survivors. Perhaps not so surprisingly, nothing whatsoever has been written about treating survivors in prison, using any modality. In fact, to the best of our knowledge at the time of this writing, the trauma program represents the sole comprehensive trauma recovery program for sentenced female offenders in the entire country.

Growth Rate of Incarcerated Women

The dearth of literature in this area stands in stark contrast to the burgeoning prison population in the United States today. Approximately 1,585,400 people were incarcerated in the U.S. in 1995. Of these, 68,500 were women (Gilliard & Beck, 1996). The number of female inmates remains substantially less than that of their male counterparts. However, the growth rate of incarcerated women has virtually caught up to that of men. From 1994 to 1995, male and female prison populations have increased by 6.8% and 6.5%, respectively (Gilliard &

Beck, 1996). One might conjecture that if current trends continue, the total number of incarcerated women could one day approach that of men. Consider that as recently as 1980, there were only 12,300 female offenders in U.S. prisons.

No systematized study has investigated the phenomena of incarcerated female trauma survivors. Therefore, one can only infer their number. Research efforts regarding the incidence of childhood abuse and adult abusive relationships in society at large are scanty and incomplete. One estimate reports that one out of every three women in the United States is sexually abused by age eighteen (Russell, 1983). Bagley and King (1992) summarize eleven studies on the prevalence of child sexual abuse. Their generalization in synthesizing the outcome of these varied reports indicates that "Serious sexual abuse in childhood (up to age 16 or 17) involving unwanted or coerced sexual contact occurs in at least 15 per cent of females in the populations surveyed, and in at least 5 per cent of males." These authors caution one to acknowledge the influence of varying research methods. Additionally they point out the fact that these studies overlooked geographically unstable and less educated persons, as well as prison and mental health populations. Therefore, they surmise the percentages listed are conservative and reflect an under-reporting of the actual incidence of child sexual abuse (Bagley & King, 1992). Neither do any of the studies reviewed take into account other, equally damaging forms of abuse.

Using the 1:3 figure (Russell, 1988) as an assumed baseline, one may extrapolate that in 1995, approximately 22,830 of the 68,500 female inmates were trauma survivors. This estimate also assumes that incarcerated women have no greater likelihood of possessing a trauma history than women who live in the free world. This assumption is one which deserves close scrutiny, and is most probably invalid.

Characteristics of Trauma Survivors

It is generally recognized that most survivors of unresolved trauma share certain characteristic maladaptive behaviors. They do not manage unpleasant feelings well. To discharge unwanted sensations, survivors often act impulsively, engaging in compulsive sexual, substance abuse or thrill-seeking behavior. They may also engage in self-mutilative or explosive behavior to deal with intolerable emotions. For survivors, interpersonal relationships often serve merely as arenas in which long standing themes of abuse and victimization can be reenacted over and over again.

The maladaptive ways in which survivors relate to themselves, and the world around them, has typically been thought of as reflecting mental illness or character pathology (e.g., borderline or histrionic personality disorder). However, from a trauma treatment paradigm, they are viewed as patterns of behaviors, which, when developed in childhood, were actually adaptive, naturally occurring, and effective responses to inescapable trauma. Indeed, these individuals may be accurately described as "survivors."

The problem is that continued use of these primitive survival mechanisms in adulthood significantly reduces a person's ability to negotiate the necessary tasks of adult life. Moreover, it comports with common sense that the self destructive behavior patterns associated with this group of women would place them in opposition to societal standards and the law.

In light of this explanation, it indeed appears likely that female trauma survivors are significantly over-represented within prison populations. Anecdotally, the second author reports that approximately 35% of the female inmates he interviewed during the routine psychological screening process acknowledge a history of some form of abuse. In his estimation, many more inmates may refuse to divulge this extremely personal information during the interview. As Chu (1991) points out, victims of trauma tend to minimize past traumatic experiences. Many regard their painful past as tightly held secrets. Additionally, initial psychological screening interviews occur when the inmate has just entered the correctional institution and before she can develop any meaningful therapeutic relationship with the examiner.

At present, all we can say with certainty is that, in our experience, psychological trauma correlates significantly with at least some types of female criminality. We also observe that the line which differentiates offender from non-offender female survivors is a very thin one, if it exists at all. Many survivors engage in behaviors that place them at potential risk of incarceration. Compare the following composite scenarios of inmate-survivors to those in the free world. The artwork of non-offenders is testament to these similarities.

Mary is doing time for putting out a contract to kill her husband who has been sexually abusing her daughter.

> Denise is hospitalized for depression. In art therapy she depicts her fantasy of killing her father by burying him alive. (figure 1)

Laura is in prison for prostitution. It's the only life she's known since she left home at sixteen. Prostitution didn't hurt a bit; she could leave her body anytime she wanted to, and no one was the wiser.

> Beth is in the acute care unit following another suicide attempt. Her sexual promiscuity and substance abuse contribute to a self concept that is filled with denigration. It is difficult for Beth to talk about the pain of her childhood sexual abuse which underlies these behaviors. (figure 2)

Katherine was convicted of attempting to murder her abusive husband. She's reliving the beatings and sexual torture he inflicted upon her in the form of flashbacks. Her greatest pain, however, is now being completely unable to protect her children from this unidentified criminal.

> Diane is diagnosed with Dissociative Identity Disorder. Her artwork recounts an occasion where "Jennifer" turned on a chain saw in the house and approached her mother who continued washing the dishes. Diane was incensed; even armed with the noise of a chain saw, she still wasn't heard. (figure 3)

Prison Environment

Prison serves at least three simultaneous objectives:

- incapacitation,
- punishment and
- rehabilitation.

Each objective reflects a particular philosophy regarding the disposition of individuals found guilty of committing some kind of felony crime. At any given time, one philosophy and corresponding objective of incarceration is emphasized over the others. Prevailing political winds and social sentiment towards criminals determine the current emphasis.

SURVIVING ONE'S SENTENCE

Figure 1: Denise—"Burying Father Alive"

Figure 2: Beth—"Collage of Denigration"

Figure 3: Diane—"Chainsaw in the Kitchen"

131

DRAWING TIME

Regardless of philosophical shifts, the fundamental mission of all prisons is to isolate convicted felons from society in a manner which promotes a safe, secure environment for prison staff, inmates, and the general public alike. Given this primary goal of incarceration, it is reasonable that security concerns take precedence over all other interests, including therapeutic ones. It also follows, that from a correctional perspective, a prisoner is regarded as an inmate, first and foremost. "Patient" or "client" status becomes a secondary identity.

The strictly regimented prison environment is not as draconian as it may initially appear. Correctional officials must maintain complete control over all aspects of prison life in order to carry out the institution's primary mission. Unbending structure within the prison environment facilitates accountability of the inmate population. It also helps ensure the physical safety of all who live and work there.

Prison Structure As A Therapeutic Tool

Management problems such as violence, drug use, and riots could easily erupt if absolute law and order did not prevail. In our opinion, art therapists, or any clinicians who seek to work inside prison walls must understand and respect the basic tenets of this unique system for at least two reasons. First, such an awareness helps to define the prison clinician's role. Secondly, it allows therapists to view the strict prison structure as a therapeutic tool.

Correctional administrators actively support activities and programs which promote the fundamental prison mission, and prohibit those that do not. Levy (1978) and Day & Onorato (1989) have already demonstrated art therapy's potential contribution to the smooth and orderly running of a prison. They point out that art therapy serves as a vehicle for safe catharsis of potentially explosive emotions. Levy also states that this modality improves conflict resolution skills among inmates.

Supporting the prison's primary goal, however, requires more than merely providing therapeutic activities which promote pro-social, non-disruptive behaviors. It also requires the art therapist to constantly think and act in a security minded manner. He or she must consistently uphold all institutional rules and regulations. For instance, depending on the security level of any particular prison, some customary art therapy materials such as clay, plasticene, plaster, knives, or even magazines may be considered contraband and consequently disallowed.

Further, scheduling of inmate-clients must conform to the institution's inmate movement procedure. One may not always meet with an individual or group of inmates in accordance with some preset schedule. Sessions may have to be postponed, canceled or cut short at the last minute because of some unrelated prison emergency or shortage of correctional personnel. The therapist must acquiesce to such circumstances. These stipulations need not be viewed as limitations to productive treatment. Instead, they can be accepted as part of the correctional environment as much as the razor wire and steel bars.

Security minded art therapists must also pay particular attention to boundary issues between themselves and their inmate-clients. Clinicians should exercise exceptionally keen judgment about revealing personal information. It is also extremely important to set and enforce consistent behavioral limits during sessions.

Furthermore, art therapists should never allow inmate-clients to split staff by pitting the clinicians against correctional personnel. In a related fashion, therapists must remain focused on the task of art therapy and not allow themselves to be manipulated into the role of prisoners' rights advocate. Most of these principles are routinely taught to therapy students. They clearly apply to all therapist-client interactions. The point is, that to work safely and effectively in a prison, therapists must follow these teachings precisely. When they do, then sound clinical practice becomes synonymous with sound correctional practice.

Congruity between therapeutic and security interests relates directly to the second reason why art therapists need to fully appreciate the correctional framework. The control, discipline and regimentation of the penal setting can be used to optimize any treatment effort. With this vision in mind, a prison can be conceptualized as a potentially powerful arena for change. Prison systems have the capacity to respond to negative behaviors much more consistently, if not effectively, than any hospital or outpatient arenas.

Consider, for example, some behavioral sequelae among female trauma survivors which regularly challenge mental health professionals in other settings. These include self mutilation, suicidality, violent rage reactions, sexual acting out and illegal drug use. In prison, all these actions represent institutional rule infractions, and consequently, are treated as disciplinary matters. They are met with sanctions which range from temporary loss of commissary privileges, to spending time in administrative detention, to loss of "good time" (days earned for good behavior, which reduce one's sentence). Such measures are powerful tools that help extinguish, or at least diminish inappropriate behavior.

Consequences for breaking prison rules can be imposed in a truly immediate and substantial manner because they are based on judicially approved inmate disciplinary procedures instead of often cumbersome mental health codes. As long as an inmate has been found legally responsible, he or she is held thoroughly accountable for his or her behavior. Additionally, the impartial, and matter of fact way in which inmate discipline is administered drastically lowers the emergence of secondary gains which are difficult to control in traditional treatment settings.

Prisons are a gold mine for clinicians who work with incarcerated female trauma survivors in yet other ways. Many of the women have had unsuccessful, often times disastrous encounters with mental health systems prior to their arrest. In our experience, however, the vast majority have never engaged in trauma-focused therapy. Survivors in prison do not glibly refer to different aspects of themselves as alters or banter about words such as abreaction or multiple personality disorder. Most seem immediately relieved of a long held heavy burden when their current pain and terror are identified as predictable, and therefore, normal human reactions from a trauma recovery paradigm. Working with these naive survivors is both fascinating and refreshing. Ironically, many of them will remain in the strict and containing prison environment long enough to experience a new found inner freedom that comes with trauma recovery.

The Inmate Code

Besides the rules and discipline imposed by prisons on their charges, there exists another set of laws which govern inmate behavior. It is called the inmate subculture or inmate code. Imposed on inmates, by inmates, these regulations are equally unyielding and much more punitive than those enforced by the authorities. This phenomenon is similar to that which sometimes takes place among school age children. There, conflicts between students are kept secret from teachers. No matter what outrage may have befallen a child at the hands of a classmate, he or she must remain silent or else risk complete loss of respect from peers. Those who "tell" are considered "tattle tales" and are socially spurned by others.

The inmate code operates with a much greater level of intensity. Within it, the doctrine of silence and secrecy stands paramount. To inform or "snitch" on a fellow inmate invites severe retribution, not only from the one "snitched out" but from the entire inmate population. A host of penalties up to and including physical assault await those who tell. There are many corollaries to the doctrine of silence which complete the inmate code. Each is somehow related to secrecy. For example, interaction with prison staff is kept at a minimum. Prolonged conversation may draw suspicion from other inmates who may fear that secrets are being divulged. Even the appearance of breaking the code could result in social or physical consequences.

Emotional displays, other than angry and rageful ones are immediately interpreted as weakness. Weakness, in turn, marks one as prey to be victimized in every conceivable way. Words such as trust and friend are anathema. Under the code, each inmate is expected to do her or his own time independently and without complaint to others.

The Female Inmate Code

The above description of the inmate code represents a secret society among male inmates. It exists in a virulent form only in maximum security facilities. In general, the lower the security level of the prison, the less stringently is the inmate code applied.

The doctrine of silence endorsed by incarcerated women works in a similar, albeit weaker fashion than its male counterpart. Generally, women do not inform on each other. When they do, however, the penalties are usually less severe. On the other hand, the acceptable parameters of emotional expression differ sharply between male and female prisoners. Whining, complaining and manipulative theatrics are not tolerated well by female inmates. However, genuinely expressed emotional pain is often responded to with enormous support and care-taking. It is not unusual for several women to keep vigil over a distraught peer.

In fact, incarcerated women openly demonstrate needs for affiliation and support. They frequently form virtual families. A "play" mother, sisters and aunts are identified within the group. Relationships are based on these designated roles. Sometimes, several "families" combine to form a large extended family. Relatedly, female inmates treat their cell or dormitory like a home. Personalized ornaments and decorations adorn living quarters to the extent permitted by institutional rules.

The inmate code is a force to be reckoned with inside any correctional setting. The point here is that the effects of this unwritten law, as it exists in female prisons, do not dramatically influence treatment. The culture in these institutions actually supports the process of change in some ways.

The Trauma Program

The art therapy groups discussed here are offered as part of the trauma program for incarcerated female trauma survivors. The fifty-two participants are housed together in a typical prison dormitory. It consists of twenty-six partial height two person cubicles, one small all purpose room which is used for group work, and toilet facilities.

The trauma program is predicated on one basic premise: trauma victims are not responsible for the pain and abuse that was inflicted on them by others. At the same time, each adult survivor is held solely responsible for her own recovery and behavior. Accordingly, members of the trauma program are required to obey institutional regulations without question. They must meet all routine inmate obligations such as holding down some sort of employment within the institution. Additionally, the program imposes rules on participants which relate directly to trauma recovery work. They include an absolute prohibition against self-destructive behavior and verbal threats against others, observing quiet time hours, and punctually attending all assigned therapeutic activities. In the trauma program, the strict regimentation of prison life reinforces clinical efforts to establish an exceptionally strong environment of containment. It is in such a milieu that inmate-clients may safely process and master powerful emotional issues. As Chu (1994, 1992) reports, working on trauma issues requires a safe environment in which the client is encouraged to maintain a certain degree of functionality in the world. The trauma program fulfills this requirement.

Women come to the trauma program suffering from many forms of trauma sequelae. They come from other prison housing units to find a place of sanctuary and empowerment. At first, many believe they are broken beyond repair, doomed to an existence of pain and terror. They are reminded that it is often darkest before the dawn. The secondary author shows them a picture he drew which illustrates that out of turmoil and confusion, beautiful things can emerge, (figure 4).

Safety is the watchword in the trauma program. Rules governing confidentiality are taught and strictly enforced. The importance of working at one's own pace is also stressed. Participants are required to reveal only that which they are comfortable disclosing at any given time.

Figure 4: Dr. Onorato—"Beauty Arising from Turmoil"

Most importantly, trauma program participants take care of one another. The naturally occurring female support system is further strengthened by encouraging members to seek out each other whenever uncomfortable feeling states are experienced. A trauma program participant who is experiencing acute crisis may choose peers to act as constant companions until she feels safe. These peers are relieved of other prison duties in order to support the peer in question.

Formal treatment takes the form of various psychoeducational and psychotherapeutic group modalities. The educational prong includes seminars in family systems, training in rational thinking, values clarification, communication skills, trauma theory instruction and a grief group. Work with individuals is limited to identifying ways to bring extremely uncomfortable or sensitive issues to group arenas for exploration. These interventions along with a rich support system and extremely structured environment comprise the trauma program. Together, these therapeutic forces help participants learn to contain previously intolerable affect and to develop adaptive skills to cope with the effects of trauma.

Group Art Therapy

Art therapy takes place in the all purpose room of the trauma program dormitory. A mural of a seascape painted by the program members is the only decoration in the otherwise barren environment. The room consists essentially of several plastic chairs, one 2' X 2' card table, and a few narrow windows reinforced, as one might assume, with iron bars. We bring this to the reader's attention to highlight what one woman termed "the group's pioneering spirit."

The inmates are so engaged in the art therapy group that they think nothing of using ironing boards or the floor as their work surface. One has to appreciate the implications of working with pastels or markers on a newly spit and polished floor for which some other inmate proudly takes credit. To ruin "her floor" is to face real fury. The group members see to it that traces of pastel are wiped away with an extra roll of toilet paper which also serves as the group's tissues.

The examples which follow are taken from the first art therapy group offered to trauma program participants. Volunteers signed up for eight weekly sessions lasting one and three quarter hours each. Collectively, the group was comprised of almost every race and color and was diverse in age. Art materials were limited to paper, pencils, craypas, chalks and markers.

Art therapy was conducted during evening hours. Therefore, the art was not used to explore trauma issues in an opening up kind of way. Instead, it was intended to help participants develop new strategies to cope with past traumatic experiences. This focus drew heavily from the strengths perspective model (Saleebey, 1996). From this orientation, individuals' assets are used to compensate for their deficits. Wellness is emphasized over pathology.

The format was a directive or theme-specific one. The art themes were adaptations of the goals of recovery as identified by leading trauma theorists (Chu, 1994; Flannery, 1991; Johnson, 1987). Most consistently, these are:

- Empowerment
- Containment
- Reaching out
- Transformation of shame
- Resolution

We were careful to advise the group members that most art therapy participants draw what they need to draw, and not necessarily what is suggested. The opportunity for self expression was maximized since it is generally limited in the prison environment. Lastly, music was incorporated into the sessions as a stimulus. Each group began by playing a song which lent itself to the evening's theme. It should be noted that the lyrics did influence the content of some participants' creative expression.

Empowerment

Empowerment may be described as one of the essential characteristics of recovery. As discussed by Flannery (1991), empowerment, or mastery, refers to experiencing control over the aftermath of trauma, as well as the ability to manage life's challenges in general. Developing a sense of autonomy and personal power helps correct the helplessness which accompanies traumatic experience.

We used the song, *A Hammer and a Nail*, by the Indigo Girls, to introduce the theme of empowerment. Many of the lyrics of this folk-rock duo promote taking responsibility for oneself. They also make the connection between personal accountability and a sense of inner strength.

The directives for this session were simply to draw one's association to the music. We did not want to "frontload" the session by labeling the song as one which addresses empowerment. Therefore, the theme was left unnamed. We anticipated that images of empowerment would spontaneously emerge in the artwork without an overt suggestion. We took *A Hammer and a Nail* to mean that one always has the power to rebuild his or her life. The image of the hammer registered differently, however, for several of the inmates. They incorporated it into their artwork as an expression of rage.

Initially we questioned whether the participants had focused too concretely on the hammer, and if, in fact, this image had interfered with their associations to the broader theme in the song. In retrospect we acknowledged that identifying and processing anger and rage plays an important part in a survivor's becoming empowered. These emotions should rightfully be directed towards one's perpetrators. Failure to own these powerful and undeniable responses often leaves the trauma survivor inappropriately directing the anger towards self or others, or masking it in denial.

• Simone said she wanted to take that hammer and pound some "understanding, compassion and loyalty" into her (invisible) ex-husband (figure 5). She wondered what makes a person mean. "Is it heredity—genes... that make generations so nasty?" Good question. Simone used this as an opportunity to express her rage about her former husband who kidnapped their children. This, she said, is the only trauma she's working on. Simone alluded to her premise (stated in the opening vignette) that what's done is done and need not be revisited. Indeed, Simone steered clear of addressing her childhood sexual abuse in any of the sessions.

Nonetheless, she was able to use this group as a vehicle to safely express rageful feelings. Her tears quickly followed. Simone cried as others offered words of support. It was an important moment for Simone who was ordinarily out of touch with her sadness. In subsequent sessions, Simone updated the group on the status of her children. The group was jubilant when she waltzed in and reported that her children had been retrieved and were now in her mother's

DRAWING TIME

care. No one dared to recognize that, only weeks before, Simone had denigrated her mother's parenting skills, as she, the mother, had allowed Simone to be abused by her own boyfriend.

• Katherine also utilized the hammer as a symbol for rage. She sat huddled on the floor and ever so briefly described her drawing (figure 6). She wants to use the hammer to smash the house of abuse, she explained. It's unclear whether Katherine was referring to her childhood home, or the one she shared with a physically abusive spouse and their children. The drawing included an obvious reference to the crucifixion, a broken heart, the earth, hell with pitchforks and devil, and a small girl encapsulated by a circle. The girl's facial features were limited to eyes. She had a torso, but no extremities. Katherine made it clear she did not want to discuss the picture further. The group respected her wishes and honored their own hunches that the drawing was about something very deep and vulnerable. Such powerful expressions may be the stepping stones to later verbal acknowledgment of a traumatic event.

Containment

Overwhelming memories and feelings often intrude upon the consciousness of survivors. A fundamental task in the recovery process is to develop the ability to modulate these terrifying recollections and affect (Herman, 1992). Even during the therapy hour, one must learn to touch the terror, then let it go. The survivor must find ways to contain immobilizing memories and affect at all other times. We chose some innocuous new age music as a backdrop for the theme of containment. We began by describing containment as a tool that helps survivors confront pain at a safe and manageable pace. We then differentiated containment from "stuffing or suppressing." Our directives helped to further clarify the characteristics of successful containment. We asked the women to create their own containment devices to hold abuse-related memories and/or feelings.

This device was required to have two features. First, it had to be adequately strong so as not to let traumatic material slip out. Second, the device had to allow one to retrieve the memories or feelings when one could more comfortably and appropriately attend to them. In concluding this session, participants were encouraged to practice using their containment devices outside of group.

The women quickly went to work. Hope depicted a manuscript (figure 7). She explained that when she told her mother about abusive incidents, her mother dismissed these stories either as being "un-talk-about-ables" or being untrue. Hope, in a self affirming way, "wrote" a book in her head. There she records all the things that have happened to her. Then Hope can validate her experience by not succumbing to her mother's denial. Hope had been "writing" in her book for years.

• Aladdin's Lamp (figure 8) came to mind for Katherine. She's been using it for ages to disappear to another land or place in time. Without knowing it, Katherine seemed to be telling the group about her dissociative coping skills. Katherine said she's had a realization—she's been using the lamp to stuff things by simply disappearing, a clear, albeit less than conscious, description of dissociation. Katherine was excited about her breakthrough. She was impressed with the difference between stuffing and containing, and intended to let the magic lamp hold things until she was ready to deal with them.

• P.B. responded to containment as a new concept. Nonetheless, her vision of a cast iron pot

SURVIVING ONE'S SENTENCE

Figure 5: Simone—"Pounding Some Sense"

Figure 6: Katherine—"Smashing the House from Hell"

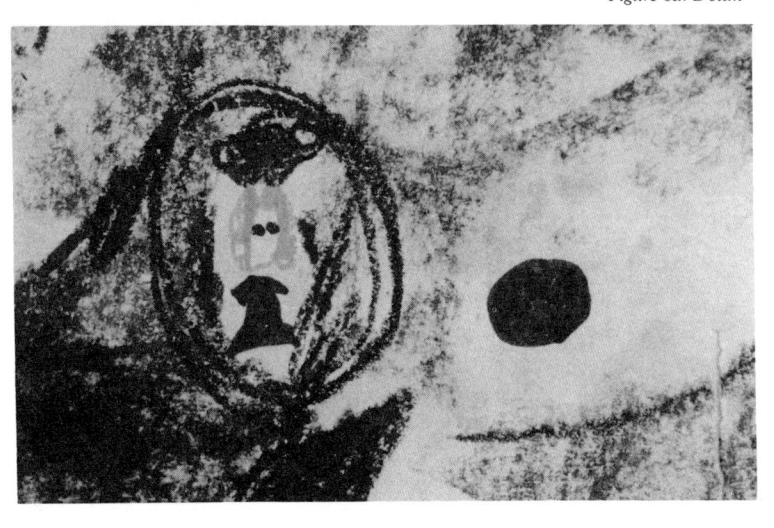

Figure 6a: Detail

DRAWING TIME

Figure 7: Hope—"The Manuscript"

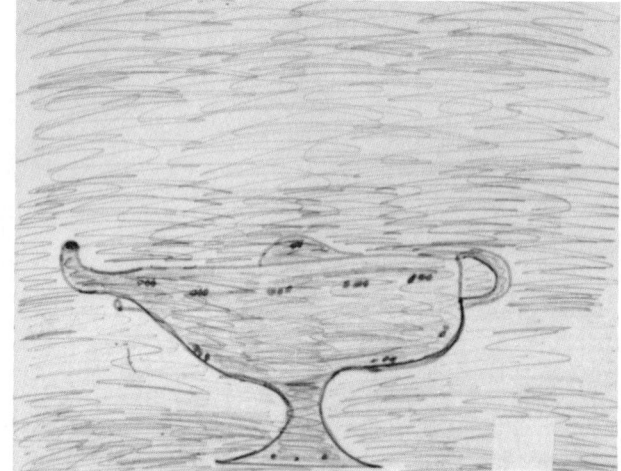

Figure 8: Katherine—"Aladdin's Lamp"

Figure 9: P.B.—"The Cast Iron Pot"

aptly met the requirements of the containment device (figure 9). The pot holds "rape and abandonment" atop some unlit logs. P.B. had not previously named these issues in her safety group which was the primary forum for open discussion about one's abuse. One group member asked why the lid was off. P.B. responded that the openness symbolized the vulnerability she felt in naming her trauma issues. P.B. went on to explain, once she's done processing the rape and abandonment, she would be able to melt them down. She clarified that she was the only one who held the match. Consider the double meaning. Perhaps P.B. was saying that only she could make the connections from the past to the present.

Reaching Out

Many survivors have the tendency to isolate. They may regard themselves as outcasts unworthy of forgiveness from a society with picket fences (Johnson, 1987). The prospect of socializing may be met with understandable fear and anxiety resulting from the burden of hiding despicable secrets. Van der Kolk (1992) reflects these concerns when he states that traumatized individuals are the loneliest people in the world. It follows, then, that another important recovery goal is to repair or establish a survivor's social network.

What words could more aptly describe a survivor's self imposed exile than Simon and Garfunkle's *"I am a Rock?"* This song speaks directly to the issues of isolation and abandonment. The inmates were asked to allocate one section of their drawing paper to symbolize isolation, and another section to symbolize reaching out.

P.B. depicted her heart and soul behind thick double layered walls (figure 10). One of the walls has come down a little. "It's taken years," she says, "to bring the wall down as much as I have."

We amplified this evidence of risk-taking. "So you've made progress," we responded. "It's really great that you were willing to lower the walls".

P.B. continued, explaining that the lightly sketched set of clothing and big green eyes were the facade. They were all she allowed of her self to be seen.

"No," others said, "we see more of you than you know, P.B. We see you hurting sometimes, being real, and being open."

P.B.'s walls were in place as she responded "I know that's what you think you see." She seemed to be informing us just how hard it was for her to use others for support. "People are mean," she said emphatically. Then she'd had enough. "Next...," she said, as a signal to the group to move on.

It should be noted that the face and figure were sketched so lightly in pencil that they were barely detectable to the camera. For the purposes of publication, we drew on top of P.B.'s lines in pen, wishing to retain the quality of her image while still making it visible to the reader. Visibility is precisely the issue for many survivors. They often verbalized a wish to be invisible with the hope of never being sexually assaulted again. It may not be accidental, therefore, that P.B. represented her clothing without a body inside. To have a body is to be at risk. Neither is it uncommon in survivor art to see the head separated from the body. This portrayal often represents a splitting or dissociation between the terrible things done to the body and the mind's awareness of it. Even in P.B.'s depiction of a face we see the features only, without the definition of a head. Those features appear to be expressing contradictory emotions. The bright green eyes are crying while the mouth forms a broad smile. Such incongruity oftentimes is another indicator of the splitting-off process.

- Zeira responded to this directive by drawing an image with vertical sections (figure 11). Her explanation of the drawing was extremely vague. She identified the arrows and then muttered some words under her breath. No one was clear about what she was trying to say, although everyone was attentive and curious. She was usually quite articulate.

Zeira's drawing fits classically into what Cohen & Cox (1989) label as a "barrier" or perhaps a "system" picture, which is typical of artwork done by individuals diagnosed with a Dissociative Disorder. The many faces had disparate expressions. One lacked a mouth, another lacked eyes. Some looked to be scowling, others appeared to be crying and worried, and still others seemed downright happy. A combination of squiggly and angular lines created the barriers which appeared to be separating the various aspects of self.

"What are those scissors about?" asks Hope.

"Nothing," Zeira replied as she stared intensely at the second author, giving him the signal that she's not ready to go further.

He affirmed her nonverbal risks, saying "You went to something really deep in that picture, didn't you Zeira?" She nodded quietly. Zeira had indeed reached out with her vulnerability, if not with her words.

Transformation of Shame

To be traumatized means that one's boundaries have been involuntarily obliterated. The result is often a sense of complete psychological nakedness. This absolute exposure translates into the experience of shame. One may react with overwhelming and intolerable vulnerability simply by acknowledging past traumatic events. Survivors must find a way to conquer shame so that they may become whole again.

We made use of Jewel's song, *Who Will Save Your Soul*, to impart both the ability and responsibility to transform one's shame. Jewel belts out the lyrics: "Who will save your soul if you won't save it on your own?"

The directive for this session was to depict shame and transform it into a less threatening image.

Katherine quickly offered her association to a group member who was confused by the instruction. "It's like, if you have a pile of shit, and then the shit gets worked into the ground so it becomes fertilizer for things to grow." Katherine could not have offered a better interpretation of the evening's art directive.

Zeira used an outline of her hands to depict shame and its transformation into a dove (figure 12). Again, Zeira was vague in her verbal explanation.

A peer asked, "Are the hands hiding the shame?"

"No," she replied, "They are the shame."

SURVIVING ONE'S SENTENCE

Figure 10: P.B.—"Bringing Down the Walls"

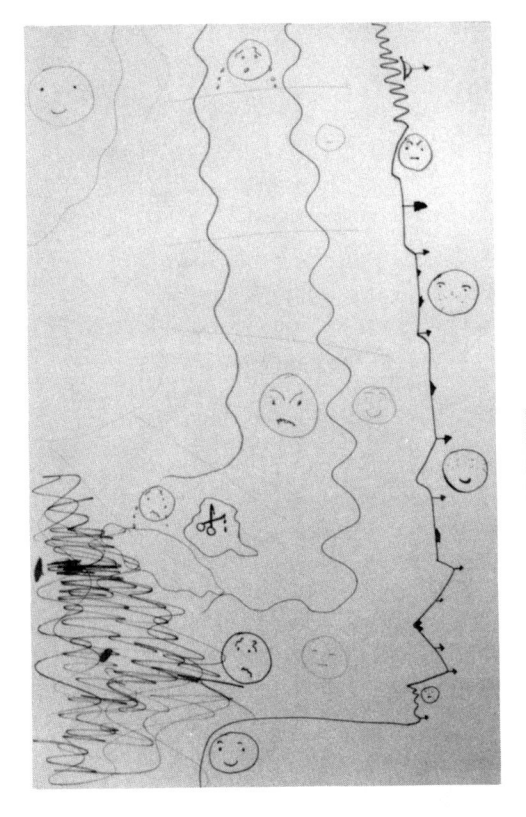

Figure 11: Zeira—"Many Faces"

Figure 11a: Detail

143

DRAWING TIME

We've touched a button. Quickly Zeira moved on to describe the dove and visually created a bird by linking her thumbs and flapping her fingers in the air. She appeared to be on safer ground again. The group wanted to go back to the first set of hands; they're curious about what seemed to be blood dripping from a pair of scissors. Zeira has replicated a previous image. The horrified expression on her face was clear: Leave this alone! She was not ready to digest the full meaning of her picture.

The art therapist asked Zeira's permission to check out one other part of the drawing. She was pretty sure she was not stepping on a land mine in inquiring about the meaning of the sun and the moon. Zeira had included these together in a few previous drawings. She lit up again; she was on safe ground.

"The sun is God," Zeira explained. "It's everywhere—even on a cloudy day, the sun is there. And the moon—that's God, too. When the sun goes down, the moon comes out, and so God is always there to keep me safe, day and night."

The faces below the dove were smiling, clearly under the protection of a higher power. It appeared that Zeira's spirituality was vital in her recovery and did have the ability to transform her shame into the bird of peace.

- Kim confused shame with guilt. She depicted herself under the needle of a giant sewing machine. For each thing she had done wrong, another stitch would be made (figure 13).

"No, that's guilt," the group corrected her. "That's when you did something wrong and you're remorseful. Shame is when somebody else violated you, and you're embarrassed."

Kim, a prolific artist, had several other transformation images to try on the group: a rose blooming beside a snowman, a tree with strong incredible roots (figure 14), a woman on a deserted island crossing a river to join society. Now it was Kim's turn for applause. She looked surprised and then beamed. Kim had just transformed shame into pride before the group's very eyes.

Resolution

It is difficult if not impossible to define the word resolution as it applies to traumatic experience. Questions such as "Why me?, Was it my fault?, Did I deserve the abuse?, Will I ever see the light at the end of the tunnel?" often plague survivors.

Some ask, "Do I have to forgive the people who hurt me?" or "Wonder if I still love the people who hurt me?"

Each traumatized person must come to terms with these questions. Making sense out of senseless acts is the task that faces all trauma survivors in order for them to reclaim meaningful and productive lives.

For this theme it was important that we select music without lyrics, and without a clearly defined mood. We did not want to influence the women's responses in any way. We settled on a compact disc by the Modern Mandolin Quartet titled *Pan-American Journeys*. This eclectic music was indeed suggestive of a journey and lent itself to a metaphor of the road from victim to survivor.

SURVIVING ONE'S SENTENCE

Figure 12: Zeira—"Transformation of Shame"

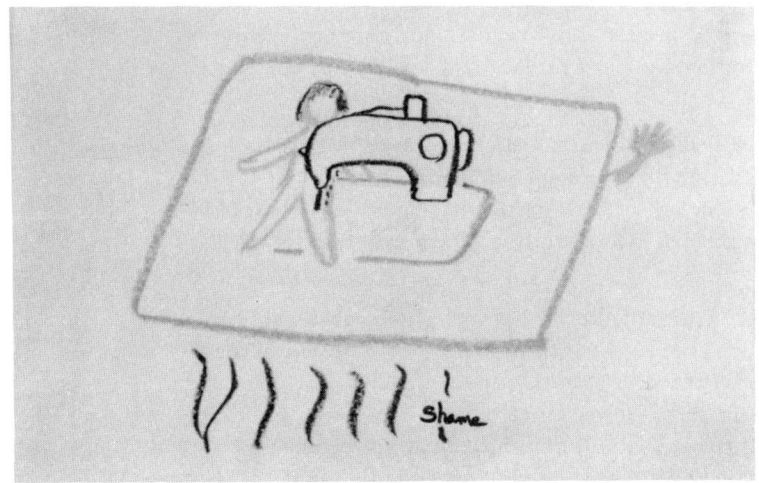

Figure 13: Kim—"The Sewing Machine"

Figure 14: Kim—"A Tree Survives"

145

DRAWING TIME

We directed participants to represent their journey to healing and recovery or a segment of it. We also asked them to symbolize important events which have occurred or may occur along the way.

Bobbie drew her path (figure 15) with many pitfalls. Interestingly, she didn't appear to actually be on the path until the last three quarters of the drawing. How true that is for many survivors who may spend years in treatment without getting anywhere.

In the middle section, Bobbie depicted a cross. This, she explained, represented the burden of her trauma which she had to carry. By the time Bobbie was near the latter part of the journey, she pointed out that the cross had become solid, but lighter. Her trauma was still a burden, but one that she could manage. The dark clouds turned to sunshine, the pitfalls were fewer and smaller, and a frightened expression turned into a smile. This may seem simplistic, as though Bobbie dutifully complied with the drawing task and inferred that a happy ending was expected.

However, compare Bobbie's body image in figure 15 to that depicted in her first art therapy session (figure 16). There Bobbie communicated her sense of internal imprisonment, feeling unable to get outside of herself, nor to let others in. Her existence had solely consisted of a head and torso.

In subsequent sessions Bobbie came to draw herself (albeit as a stick figure) having arms, and finally with all four limbs. If we allow the two pictures to speak about Bobbie's journey from victim to survivor, it appears that she has come out of her internal incarceration. Bobbie now has legs upon which to stand, and very long arms, indeed, with which to gain control over her world.

- Joan became sheepish about showing her picture (figure 17). Others, she complained, presented "happy" pictures. The group enticed her to show them her drawing. Instantly they were saddened as they saw the drawing and listened to Joan talk about her children who were caught in the civil war in Ghana and Liberia. She believed three of them had been picked up by a refugee boat (depicted in the top right corner). She had no idea what has befallen her other children.

Joan was clearly powerless over this situation. She was devastated by the separation and by the ambiguity of these circumstances. Joan's hope was that her journey would take her back to Africa where she would be able to reconcile with her children. She cried for a moment, and quickly regained her composure. The group gave Joan two rounds of applause. She was a mother figure to many of the women and was greatly revered.

- Jen's journey from victim to survivor took her from one side of a river to the other (figure 18). She built a bridge herself out of huge boulders. Jen identified the victim segment of her journey with "sadness, fear, horror, abuse, loneliness, loss, no God, prostitution, drugs and jail." The contrasting green side represented aspects of her life which she has reclaimed: "God, family, peace, dignity and forgive(ness)." Jen appeared to make visible progress in both building her bridge and crossing it during the art therapy sessions. Initially she was skittish and sometimes left the group quietly without explanation. In the last few sessions it was evident that Jen was stronger and more impassioned about her struggle toward recovery.

SURVIVING ONE'S SENTENCE

Figure 15: Bobbie—"The Road to Recovery"

Figure 16: Bobbie—"Self Portrait"

Figure 17: Joan—"The Road to Reconciliation"

- Sharlene offered four "snapshots" along the way to her recovery. Her first drawing showed her getting into trouble as a teenager by loitering on street corners. The second (figure 19) depicted Sharlene's arrest for the sale of illegal drugs.

She and her "associates" lived in the housing projects. One "associate" told Sharlene to pick up the ringing pay phone and make the deal. Little did Sharlene know that her gang brothers had just sold her down the river, leaving her to take the rap alone. The voice at the other end of the line was an FBI informant. Hidden cameras were photographing her unsuspecting face.

Although not verbalized as such, it appeared this event marks the crossroads on Sharlene's journey from victim to survivor status. Her crime and punishment are what have given her pause to think about her life, her values, and most importantly, her children. She actually acknowledged her time in prison as beneficial and critical in getting her life back on track.

- Luisa's flight of stairs (figure 20) recorded what she identified as her personality change from being "big" (hardened and tough) to being "small" (vulnerable and sensitive). "Other inmates have even commented on this," she said. "People who knew me at another institution, and who see me now, are surprised at how much softer and friendlier I am."

Luisa seemed happy with the feedback. She attributed the change to her stepping down the trauma stairway. As she went down (and inward) she became smaller, "like a little girl," she said. Luisa had intentionally decreased the scale of her self image to convey the vulnerability she experienced in investigating her childhood trauma. This, she said, allowed her to shed her armor of toughness even from behind the walls of prison. Luisa expected that once she "gets to the bottom" of the stairs, there would be sunlight and flowers.

- Zeira's journey (figure 21) is shown chronologically. She guided the group quickly through painful references to her childhood abuse. The scissors showed up for a third time, smaller and less ominous in appearance. Zeira looked much more comfortable than the last time she drew the scissors. However, once again she declined the group's invitation to talk about them.

Zeira's path continued, leading her to a convent where she was taken in by the nuns. Zeira acknowledged the strength that faith, yoga and meditation provided her throughout her life. Despite being victimized again in her adulthood (shown on the lower left side with orange and red), Zeira's spirituality remained strong. Further on the path, and centered in the middle of the drawing, was Zeira's son whom she considered to be a miracle. The prison was represented in the top right corner with the various influences that have helped her use her incarceration as a healing environment.

"Don't get me wrong," Zeira said, "I don't want to be here. But the prison has definitely been a life saver for me." The group discussed this paradox of being healed instead of hardened within the prison walls. The women expressed outright gratitude for the opportunity to accomplish so much more while incarcerated than merely surviving their sentences.

Summary
This chapter devoted a great deal of time to demystify and reframe the world behind bars. When the rigors of the penal system are understood, they can be appreciated as representing a potentially powerful therapeutic environment. In our experience, it is clear that psychotherapy, including art therapy, can be effectively practiced within prison walls. This is especially true within female prisons.

SURVIVING ONE'S SENTENCE

Figure 18: Jen—"Building a Bridge"

Figure 19: Sharlene—"The Crossroads"

Figure 20: Hope—"The Stairway Down"

149

DRAWING TIME

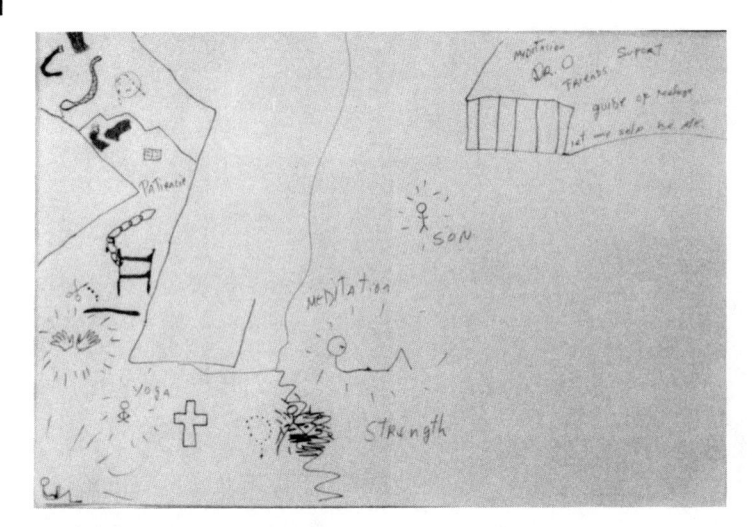

Figure 21: Zeira—"The Healing Walls"

We have reported that imprisoned female trauma survivors can be treated during their incarceration. Specifically, we illustrated how art therapy can be productively applied to this seemingly enormous population. Unfortunately, there exist no comparative reports or studies which can validate (or invalidate) our experience. The actual number of incarcerated trauma survivors remains unknown. Systematic exploration of the treatment of this population is sorely lacking. Such efforts would be welcomed. Perhaps inquiry into the reasons for the dearth of relevant art therapy literature should also be made.

It is impossible to predict how the objectives of incarceration may change in the coming years. There are powerful political forces that push prison systems to eliminate all but the bare essentials for convicted felons. From this perspective, criminality represents immutable behavior. As such, any form of psychotherapy may be considered an expendable frill, if not outright irrelevant.

Simultaneously, other movements urge prisons to offer increasing opportunities for self improvement to inmates. This viewpoint suggests that inmates are entitled to such services because the prison population is composed mostly of the poor, minority groups and the underprivileged. In any event, treatment and research efforts in this area assist a needy population. They may also result in data which could help society decide if any form of rehabilitation is a cost effective objective of incarceration. Art therapy and art therapists could contribute greatly to this pursuit.

References
Andritsky, W. (1986). *Maltherapie im strafvollzug.* (Painting therapy in prisons.) Gruppendynamik, 17(3), 273-286.
Bagley, C. & King, K. (1992). *Child sexual abuse: The search for healing.* New York: Routledge
Becker, K. [Producer], van der Kolk, B. & Wolfe, J. (Speaker), (1992), PTSD: Beyond survival [Videotape]. W. Newton, MA: PTSD Video

Chu, J.A. (1994). The rational treatment of multiple personality disorder. *Psychotherapy, 31*(1), 94-100.
Chu, J.A. (1992). The therapeutic roller coaster Dilemmas in the treatment of childhood abuse survivors. *Journal of Psychotherapy Practice and Research, 1*(4), 351-370.
Chu, J.A. (1991). The repetition compulsion revisited: Reliving dissociated trauma. *Psychotherapy, 28*(2), 327-332.
Cohen, B.M. & Cox, C.T. (1989). Breaking the code: Identification of multiplicity through art productions. *Dissociation: Progress in the Dissociative Disorders, 2*(3), 132-137.
Cohen, B., Cox, C.T., Mills, A., & Sobol, B. (1991). Art by abuse survivors: A life cycle. In *Image & Metaphor: The Practice and Profession of Art Therapy*, Proceedings of the 22nd Annual Conference of the American Art Therapy Association, Nov. 13-17, 1991.
Day, E.S. & Onorato, G.T. (1989). Making art in a jail setting. In H. Wadeson, J. Durkin, & D. Perach (Eds.), *Advances In Art Therapy* (pp. 126-147). New York: John Wiley & Sons
Elliot, J. (1987). The treatment of serious juvenile delinquents in Massachusetts. *Educational Psychology in Practice, 3*(2), 49-52.
Flannery, R.B. & Harvey, M.R. (1991). Psychological trauma and learned helplessness: Seligonan's paradigm reconsidered. *Psychotherapy, 28*(2), 374-378.
Gilliard, D.K. & Beck, A.J. (1995). Prison and jail inmates, 1995. *Bureau of Justice Statistics Bulletin*, Aug. 1996, p. 4-10.
Glaister, J.A. (1994). Clara's story: Post-traumatic response and therapeutic art. *Perspectives in Psychiatric Care, 30*(1), 17-22.
Hargrave-Nykaza, K. (1994). An application of art therapy to the trauma of rape. *Art therapy: Journal of the American Art Therapy Association, 11*(1), 53-57.
Herman, J. L. (1992). *Trauma and recovery*. New York: Basic Books
Hook-Wheelhouwer, J. (1991). Protective-custody: A lifestyle in prison. *Pratt Institute Creative Arts Therapy Review, 12*, 36-40.
Jacobson, M. (1994). Abreacting and assimilating traumatic, dissociated memories of MPD patients through art therapy. *Art Therapy: Journal of the American Art Therapy Association, 11*(1), 48-52.
Johnson, D.R. (1987). The role of the creative arts therapies in the diagnosis and treatment of psychological trauma. *The Arts in Psychotherapy, 14*(1), 7-13.
Levens, M. (1994). The use of guided fantasy in art therapy, female survivors of sexual abuse. *Arts in Psychotherapy, 21*(2), 127-133.
Levy, B. (1978). Art therapy in a women's correctional facility. *Art Psychotherapy, 5*(3), 157-166.
Liebmann, M. (1994). *Art therapy with offenders*. London: Jessica Kingsley Pub.
Mazza, N.; Magaz, C.; Scaturro, J. (1987). Poetry therapy with abused children. *Arts in Psychotherapy, 14*(1), 85-92.
Murphy, P.S. (1994). The contribution of art therapy to the dissociative disorders. *Art Therapy: Journal of the American Art Therapy Association, 11*(1), 43-47.
Russell, D. E. H. (1983). The incidence and prevalence of intrafamilial and extrafamilial sexual assault of female children. *Child Abuse and Neglect, 7*, 133-146.
Saleebey, D. (1996). The strengths perspective in social work practice: Extensions and cautions. *Social Work, 41*(3), 296-305.
Serrano, J.S. (1989). The arts in therapy with survivors of incest. In H. Wadeson, J. Durkin, & D. Perach (Eds.), *Advances In Art Therapy* (pp. 126-147). New York: John Wiley & Sons
Shapiro, J. (1988). Moments with a multiple personality disorder patient. *Pratt Institute Creative Arts Therapy Review, 9*, 61-72.
Spring, D. (1985). Symbolic language of sexually abused, chemically dependent women. *American Journal of Art Therapy, 24*(1), 13-21.
Spring, D. (1993). *Shattered images: Phenomenological language of sexual trauma*. Chicago: Magnolia Street Publishers
Ventre, M.E. (1994). Healing the wounds of childhood abuse: A guided imagery and music case study.

DRAWING TIME

Music Therapy Perspectives, 12(2), 98-103.

Volkman, S. (1993). Music therapy and the treatment of trauma-induced dissociative disorders. *Arts in Psychotherapy, 20*(3), 243-251.

Wulfman, R. (1982). Art-therapie en milieu penitentiaire. (Art therapy in penitentiary surroundings.) *Psychologie Medicale, 14*(9), 1425-1428.

This chapter includes the opinion of Dr. Greg Onorato, and does not necessarily represent the opinion of the Federal Bureau of Prisons or the U.S. Department of Justice.

Easing the Transition
From Prison to the Community

Dorrie Mosel-Gussak, MA, A.T.R.

People diagnosed with schizophrenia or other mental illnesses generally have poor social skills, inappropriate affect, and grandiose delusions. They may lack insight, behave in antisocial or sociopathic ways (APA, 1994) and thus may eventually end up in conflict with the police via "5150." This is the penal code number for a required 72 hour police hold in a psychiatric unit or facility for psychiatric evaluation, the judicial system, and finally, the prisons.

When these mentally ill patients are ready to leave the institutional setting of prison or psychiatric hospital, they have difficulty adjusting to the outside world. They often find themselves in halfway houses, residential treatment centers or psychiatric facilities, lacking skills in communicating and making appropriate choices.

Art therapy is an effective tool in working with these forensic patients in a locked psychiatric health facility. Art therapists ease their difficult transition back into the community by training them in needed social skills.

For three years I have worked with the mentally ill in an eighty bed facility in northern California. Our patients, adult forensic and non-forensic "residents" of all cultures, some having lived in state hospitals, have difficulty succeeding in the community. Many referrals to my facility have come from acute care facilities after "5150" incidents, and the residents have been stabilized.

The Skills to Make Significant Choices
Our facility adopted the "psychiatric rehabilitation" philosophy following the Boston University model which stressed the provision of skills and supports to enable the residents to chose where to live, learn, work, and socialize, (Cohen & Forbess, 1992). All our residents were assessed for their capacity to make significant choices for the direction of their lives. Only 5 percent made important or significant life choices, illustrating how unprepared they were for returning to the community.

Residents with both forensic and psychiatric experiences coped in different ways depending on their mental availability (IQ, internal preoccupation, delusional systems, etc.) and past proficiency in manipulating their forensic environment. Their conduct depended on what survival behaviors and tactics they used in the prison/jail/forensic prison, and how effectively they satisfied their needs without negative consequences. These learned behaviors were a means to survive a hostile setting, where residents were either prey or predator.

The Victim Versus the High Functioning Psychopath

The residents with severe psychiatric symptoms affected by developmental delays and/or mental retardation were most often prey to their peers (i.e. sexually abused) in the prison from which they came. The victim role continued in their communal living experiences.

The facility's level system and community rules protected them from most predatory peers. However, the more antisocial residents with higher verbal skills and less disorganization or mental confusion could inevitably circumvent any organized system. They used their developed prison savvy and manipulated the system with relative ease because the facility's philosophy promoted providing choices and positive reinforcement rather than punishment. Truly high functioning "sociopathic" residents were rare but when a few came through the facility, they quickly established themselves as leaders of their community (unit) with the full support of their peers.

The facility adopted a multi-disciplinary approach with an extensive rehabilitation program, including a variety of creative arts therapies, and verbal and recreation groups, providing the residents with skills and support for their eventual discharge. Each resident had a rehabilitation therapist aiding in the choice of groups appropriate to their particular problems.

The physical plant was divided into four units of twenty people each. The front half of the facility had two distinct and separate units which shared a Day Room. The Family Room was between two locked doors which incorporated two open smoking patios. All units had access to a large backyard with a basketball court and patio with lawn chairs and tables. The Rehabilitation Center was situated at the far end of the yard.

The Level System

The facility's rehabilitation program used the level system from one to six, each level having a specific number of tasks residents had to fulfill to move up the levels and earn more privileges.

The residents entered the facility on level one where they were limited to groups within the main building of the facility, and were not allowed family passes or outings.

Level two residents could go to groups at the activity center, and on van rides.

Residents on level three could go to any groups, activities, and outings to different cities and community events. They could take two half-hour passes either within facility grounds or into the community.

Level four allowed for longer passes into the community or facility grounds as well as overnight visits to their families.

All levels were reviewed weekly in treatment team and raised or lowered, depending on the resident's ability to maintain appropriate behavior and follow staff directions. AWOL attempts and assaultive behavior automatically dropped the resident's level to one. Thus, residents had to follow unit and community rules, respond to limit-setting and demonstrate non-violent behavior in order to attend creative arts therapy, symptom management and discharge planning groups which were located at the Rehabilitation Center. They also could earn canteen credit on several on-site jobs requiring a specific level of behavior.

The philosophy of the facility, psychiatric rehabilitation, provided staff with a dual dilemma. Not only did clinical and rehabilitation staff have to offer residents choices as to the direction and disposition of their lives, but at the same time, they had to act as auxiliary egos, establishing structure and setting limits necessary for corrective responses to an often out-of-control population.

The dilemma was also keenly felt by many of the residents who had either never been given the opportunity to make choices in their lives, due to early onset of their illness and long periods of institutionalization or had lost the freedom of choice during incarceration because of their poor initial choices (violence, drug addiction, alcoholism).

The Art Therapy Program

At the art therapy groups once a week, the group had specific rules regarding safety and respect of peers and their artwork. On some days, the therapist would select art projects and on other days, residents could choose their projects if they wished. However, even when it was their choice day, the residents would often ask the therapist for a project idea.

Art therapy group sessions would focus on skill building, as per the psychiatric rehabilitation model (socialization skills, values clarification, goal setting) as well as increasing an understanding of emotions and their impact on behavior, and increasing non-verbal self expression in a non-violent manner. The following case study of Peter, a diagnosed paranoid schizophrenic resident, describes aspects of the art therapy program.

Peter

Although neither large nor imposing, Peter, a thirty year old resident, had a long history of assaults both in the community and the facility. His DSM-III-R (APA, 1989) axis I diagnosis was Schizophrenia-chronic, paranoid-type.

Peter responded to internal stimuli by pacing or rocking back and forth while standing. He often played music in his room, reportedly to cover the auditory hallucinations he experienced. He did not respond to reality testing and voiced grandiose delusions, claiming to be a millionaire and to have trained a wild bear to do tricks. He aspired to be a professional dog trainer and often discussed his Labrador retrievers, whom he called "prize-winning." At times, Peter seemed pleasant, responded to humor, and was quiet in groups.

The younger of two boys whose parents divorced when he was nine years old, Peter was expelled from school after he struck an eleventh grade teacher. No psychiatric symptoms were noted at that time and his social history described no significant personal relationships or work history.

Peter was arrested the first time at age 19, for assault with a deadly weapon and intention to commit rape. On other occasions, he was arrested for battery and parole violation. While serving time at a state prison, Peter fought inmates of a different race on several occasions and assaulted a correctional officer.

He later expressed racist delusions and claimed to be superior due to his German heritage, as evidenced by his artwork. Peter also turned his anger inward and inflicted fairly deep wounds on his body until he was treated successfully with a behavior modification approach.

Separation/Individuation

One of the ongoing issues Peter dealt with was his ceaseless separation/individuation conflict with his mother who could neither set limits nor care for him. He seemed to be unable to individuate, which, according to Blos, (1979, p. 142) "...becomes in adolescence the shedding of family dependencies, the loosening of infantile object ties in order to become a member of the society at large."

Peter constantly sabotaged his discharge planners by refusing to go anywhere but home to mother. Admitting she could not control him, she allowed their dysfunctional enmeshment and tolerated Peter's abusive behavior towards her. His relationships with women residents at the facility were not successful either. Peter would try to manipulate and jealously guard his "girlfriends" and was verbally and physically abusive to them.

On several occasions, Peter was able to form relationships with the clinical staff or female mental health workers. Their eventual departures brought up feelings of abandonment, causing him to regress and resort to violence. However, although he was difficult to motivate, he did respond to firm limit setting and the communication of expected behavior.

Peter attended art therapy groups regularly, for three years, often waiting at the art therapy room for the session to begin. Because his verbal communication was minimal at best, through art therapy he could express himself and his issues non-verbally. It was one of the few groups he attended even when he decompensated.

Through Peter's seeming devotion to art therapy, he was able to accept the relationship he and I developed over time. Pointedly, I was a woman authority figure who did not accept his negative attitude toward women. Perhaps through our interacting, he began to resolve his poor relationship with his mother on a subconscious level.

Collage

A favored art therapy project was collage, generally successful in the process of execution and in pleasing products. "The collage medium is particularly useful while initiating group art therapy for it tends to lessen the anxiety level related to artistic performance," (Landgarten, 1981, p.66). The process of making collages seemed to raise the residents' self esteem, required little internal organization, and produced a calming effect on agitated or hyperactive residents.

For those residents who feared they could not draw, and those who were paranoid, collage seemed to be the least threatening art activity. It gave weaker artists the choice of photographs to express their feelings. They avoided facing embarrassment describing the unrecognizable images they might have drawn or painted.

Reminiscent of childhood activities, collage helped reduce defenses, so that they could talk more freely about the significance of their artwork. Residents with forensic histories were able to use pictures of guns, police, jails, drugs, as well as words to express their experiences. Often, art was the only tool that enabled them to do so in a socially acceptable manner.

To eliminate the use of scissors and time spent looking through magazines, pre-cut pictures, textures and words out were kept in labeled folders of words, animals, people, objects, landscape, and places. To structure the session further, if needed, I would give a topic or residents would choose one of their own. The following episode demonstrates how the process of art helped Peter resolve some of his conflicts non-verbally.

Peter's Response: Preoccupied With 'Power'

Peter enjoyed making collages and over time, his efforts became more complex and increasingly self-expressive. Figure 1 shows a collage of cars. Often associated with power, both in terms of the engine size and capabilities, cars demonstrate independence and financial status. When driving a car, one has control of the direction and speed.

Peter's preoccupation with power (as he described it) reflected his current difficulties with a female peer. Peter was possessive and controlling in his relationship with a woman who used many men to get her needs met.

Despite the metaphoric assertion of power, Peter neither had the freedom (being in a locked facility) nor the power to go anywhere due to his continued insistence of being discharged to his mother's home. He thus pursued a stagnating relationship and a continued dependent living situation. Despite the bluff of using powerful cars to lure women, Peter's fundamental inability to relate to women in a socially acceptable way virtually left him "parked at the corner."

Figure 1: Peter—collage

The instructions for his next collage (figure 2) were to tear the pictures from the magazines and form interesting patterns with the torn edges. Peter complied with the instructions, but was unable to get past his rigidity and need to control the page and images. The women are neatly lined up. When Peter could not find women to fit into the spaces, he chose to leave blanks.

Interestingly, he preferred to tear out images of young women, those he

Figure 2: Peter— collage

DRAWING TIME

Figure 3: Peter—collage

Figure 4: Peter—collage

had the most conflict with in life. No elderly women or children were represented. Peter discussed dating and outlined his personal preference for women who would "listen." Again he expressed verbally and nonverbally his need for power and control in his artwork, illustrating his problems about relationships with women (his mother and current "girlfriend").

Peter's Expressive Ability Increases

Peter's later collages, figures 3 and 4, showed his increased involvement and ability to express himself. Peter's new social worker and treatment team had made progress in mediating his relationship with his mother, and Peter survived the discharge of his "girlfriend" (though he did some property damage to the unit).

In viewing the bulk of Peter's artwork over the course of treatment, it was evident that Peter seldom used people in his artwork, graphically illustrating his tendency to avoid social interaction. He seemed to identify himself with animals he had aspirations to control, evident in his grandiose delusions of being a wild bear and dog trainer.

In figure 3, the collage topic was to create a collage about your future goals. Peter juxtaposed Linus and Sally of the Peanuts Gang with a Dalmatian. Linus declares, "Animals and children should be saved and not abused."

Though Peter's collage remained somewhat linear and rigid, it helped him describe to the group his dream of training dogs for show and obedience trials (control, power). He reflected on how dogs gave unconditional love to their owners.

The Use of Animals in Collage

In my experience, people with antisocial traits frequently use animals in collage. This may illustrate the artist's inability to follow societal norms, thus the rejection versus total acceptance given by animals. Did Peter identify with the animals which he claimed were abused, or

EASING THE TRANSITION

was Peter identifying himself as the abuser in wanting to control them by "training" them? Though in denial about his illness, past abuses and inability to make and keep relationships, his discussions and artwork indicated that he wanted to be "saved."

In figure 4, completed several months later, with the theme of "Save the Animals," he seemed to favor this concept. This time Peter asked me to find additional specific animals to fill the page completely, while he continued his composition. He could not fill the page enough, in contrast to his usual style which demonstrated a poverty of feeling and content. Previously, perhaps metaphorically, he was as empty as his compositions, illustrating his inability to form and keep healthy relationships with his peers or his mother. In this project, however, Peter was willing to ask for and accept my help. This increased social interaction and cooperation seems illustrated in the abundance of animals and fuller compositional style.

The Feelings Chart

Another successful but sometimes disliked project was the Feelings Chart. As a warm-up exercise, reluctant residents often illustrated their feelings and then discussed them with the group. Frequently they were unable to label their feelings despite obvious demonstrations of anger, depression, etc. This project enabled them to briefly 'check-in' for the day or illustrate previous unresolved feelings, increasing their ability to discuss relevant issues.

Instructions were fairly complex for the disorganized patient, but verbal cues such as "what color are you going to use for anger" kept them up with the rest of the group. The residents were asked to respond to a word describing an emotion, (for example, anger) by choosing a color, (for example, red), and covering the page with as much of that color as they were feeling the emotion. If they did not feel that emotion, they could place a dot in the space. All emotions were labeled for ease in the discussion period. (As a secondary gain, residents also learned to spell.)

Peter had difficulty acknowledging and expressing his emotions. Figure 5 was his typical response to the project. None of the emotions are labeled except "happy," which is depicted within an empty circle. Unlike the other emotions, it is concrete, contained, controlled, and hollow, possibly how Peter experienced "happy."

Figure 6 shows a yellow swastika, another version of "happy." Although many cultures associate yellow with happy, few would agree that the swastika represented a

Figure 5: Peter—oil pastels on paper

Figure 6: Peter—oil pastels on paper

159

DRAWING TIME

pleasant emotion. Perhaps because artwork was not censored in my groups, Peter felt free to draw this provocative image, opening up racial and social issues for discussion.

Peter's continual use of the symbol, despite objections from peers, illustrated his provocative antisocial behavior, and demonstrated his need to be powerful and in control. As one of the original residents, with many of his peers already discharged into the community, he provoked powerful reactions with the constant use of this symbol. It deflected attention away from Peter himself, who still remained at the facility.

Figure 7: Peter—colored pencil on paper

Figure 7 was completed after the Feelings Chart exercise and his yellow swastika. Peter depicted himself as a devil in a mountain of flames. After a trying week of relationship difficulties and an inability to control his anger, he was able to express his feelings quite easily through the artwork.

Residents with past forensic experience generally did not discuss their actual incarceration. However art tasks helped them reveal and discuss aspects of such incarceration (e.g., sexual abuse, helplessness, anger). In this picture, the solitary encapsulated figure, fire covering the page, specifically the genital area, and devil/evil theme, seem to portray his impotent rage and thus perhaps his inability to form relationships with women, sexually or otherwise.

Create A World—Team Building

Another technique used to build group identity, increase social skills and verbal and non-verbal communication, was the Create a World group project. Residents were to create a world in which they could all live together. They had to negotiate what type of world (real, or fiction/fantasy) they would create. Taking several group sessions, this project emphasized team building. Residents could choose to work in two or three

Figure 8: Peter—oil pastels on paper

160

dimensions, using all materials except clay, considered too regressive for many residents.

In doing this project, the residents, especially those with forensic experiences, learned to become aware of their own boundaries, their basic needs, accepting compromise during group negotiations and improving their experience in making choices.

First, choices—the residents could chose where they wanted to live, which paralleled the psychiatric rehabilitation philosophy of the facility. As mentioned earlier, many of the residents had never made important choices in their lives.

Second, social interaction—the residents had to interact appropriately. No manipulation or forceful coercion was allowed. All residents, regardless of level of functioning, participated equally.

Third, transition to the community—the therapist provided reality testing and focused on preparedness for community living throughout the course of construction and during the discussion period. Very often, for example, the residents forgot to provide themselves with food, and this was addressed both as part of the art project and in planning for the future.

Fourth, self esteem—given the investment of time and creative effort, the residents were proud of their work, and discussed it long after it had been completed.

Peter's response to the Create a World project was predictable. When he did participate, he drew animals but did not participate in many of the group negotiations. Several times the issue of swastikas cropped up and Peter finally heard that the group did not want swastikas in their world.

Teaching Art Techniques

With an art as therapy approach, working from life, or from photographs has also proved successful with the residents. New techniques have been introduced to the group as they choose what they paint and draw. The "techniques" groups have a relaxed atmosphere, helping residents increase their ability and confidence using art materials. Since most residents have chosen paint or mixed media, the projects are usually completed in two or three sessions.

Still life paintings are difficult for some less organized residents, but with more individual attention, they are able to complete their work. Focusing outside themselves and onto an object, even the most hyperactive residents are able to increase their attention span and their self esteem. As an added bonus, they are allowed to sell their artwork in the annual art show. Since the artwork is not to express issues or to be processed in group (any issues revealed in the artwork are discussed privately) the residents are supported and empowered through the display and sale of their work.

Figure 8 was done by Peter in a techniques group. Though the residents were shown how to blend and mix colors, Peter chose not to, again indicating his rigidity and inability to adapt to change. Peter insisted on drawing from one of his collages, and added an environment.

Figures float on the page, the trees, bushes, and fawn's face, scribbled and fragmented. The sun adds little warmth, and the overall feeling is that of emptiness and loneliness. It was nonetheless a good effort, considering Peter's aversion to messy materials. His paintings were usually very good copies of whatever subject matter he chose, and he permitted technical

DRAWING TIME

interventions as he worked on them. Most of Peter's work sold immediately in the shows, often to his mother.

Topics That Elicit Discussion

Art projects topics geared to reality testing draw out the residents' personal preferences for future community living, and a small amount of insight as to what obstacles (internal and external) they face. Topics are chosen according to how the group members deal with their daily life on their units. For example, when there is violence on the units, the topic might be, "Draw a safe community where you would like to live." The group would then illustrate and discuss what it would take to make each of them feel safe.

The concreteness of the project is beneficial to the most psychotic of patients. It also gives residents the chance to compare where they have lived in the past and exchange ideas about future discharge plans. Even for the forensic residents, this project seems to instill hope, and a greater understanding of community living.

Figure 9, Peter's response to "Where I would like to live," was predictable. He drew his mother's house where he said he would like to continue living. Despite comments from peers about his inappropriate choice, Peter remained adamant. His image contained the most elements he ever drew in one picture.

The large trees make the house feel isolated. No path to the house make it as unapproachable as Peter. "Drawings of houses and trees are also likely to be associated with relevant aspects of the person," (Groth-Marnat, 1990, p 386). The odd perspective and color choice gave the house a closed look, with the windows like lidded eyes. The overall impression of gloom and Peter's offhand description seem to match the feeling of the house. Peter knew he would not discharge home to his mother.

Figure 9: Peter—oil pastels on paper

Peter's Progress

Throughout his four year stay at the facility, Peter had eliminated his self injurious behavior, possibly because it no longer served as a defense mechanism, nor attracted the amount of attention he desired. Though his treatment team had tried to help him understand his dysfunctional relationship with his mother and thus his treatment of women, Peter showed little if any insight.

Sabotaging efforts to discharge him into the community, Peter seemed to know just what level of violence would keep him at the locked psychiatric hospital and not returned to a state facility. He maintained that level, claiming that he had no control over his anger. Peter had increased his social skills in the art therapy sessions, though his fixed delusions of grandeur with regard to his superior Nazi views continued. His treatment team had begun to set up board and care visits for Peter, as he was seen to be ready for that transition.

How Art Therapy Worked for Peter
Art therapy was valuable for Peter on many levels. First, it allowed him to form a healthy relationship with a non-punitive authority figure who encouraged him to express his feelings. Unlike verbal groups, in which Peter rarely participated, art therapy groups provided Peter with an external focus where he could symbolically express his fragmented feelings. He could then talk about his artwork in his concrete manner, allowing his underlying issues to emerge in further discussion.

When Peter developed enough trust, he began to draw swastikas, and was outspoken about why he drew them. The reaction by his peers was loud and clear. Luckily, no one responded violently to his racist comments which he may have made to incite his fellow residents. It demonstrated his lack of insight into social interaction. If he had been in a forensic setting, or even in the community, people who were the brunt of his racist comments might have reacted otherwise.

Finally he was able to "hear" some of the comments his peers and I made and understand how his images affected the community. His peers asked that he not display his swastikas publicly and finally, he agreed.

Peter was increasingly verbal in art therapy groups and eventually learned to joke with certain peers. He participated in interactive projects appropriately, and even his behavior on the unit was less assaultive.

Reinforcing Basic Rehabilitative Concepts Through Art Therapy
Aside from specific art projects geared to specific issues, all art therapy sessions reinforce basic rehabilitative concepts key to residents' successful transition back into the community. These are:

- improving social skills
- understanding what skills are needed to be successful in the community
- making choices and managing symptoms
- increasing self esteem, hope and confidence to work through any difficulties encountered.

All these goals are achieved through art therapy, as well as through the total rehabilitation program which reinforces these concepts. The art projects especially provide paranoid residents with a forum where they express their needs and comfort level with the group.

Social interaction, a sense of community, and communication, some of the residents' most difficult problems, are addressed through the process of art, nonverbally, then verbally for satisfactory resolution.

References

American Psychiatric Association (1989). *Diagnostic and statistical manual of mental disorders.* Fourth ed. Washington, D.C.

American Psychiatric Association (1994). *Diagnostic and statistical manual of mental disorders.* Third Ed, Revised. Washington D.C.

Blos, P. (1979). *The adolescent passage: developmental issues.* N.Y.: International Universities Press, Inc.

Cohen, M. & Forbess, R. (1992). *Reference handbook: developing readiness for rehabilitation.* Center for Psychiatric Rehabilitation: Boston University.

Groth-Marnat, G. (1990). *Handbook of psychological assessment.* New York: John Wiley & Sons.

Landgarten, H. (1981). *Clinical art therapy: a comprehensive guide.* New York: Brunner/Mazel, Publishers.

Part 3

SPECIAL FORENSIC POPULATIONS

The Lucky Ones:
Probationary Students in a Special Education School

Claudia Ronaldson, Ed.D., A.T.R.-BC

This private school was specifically designed to meet the academic challenges of seriously emotionally disturbed (SED) boys in residential treatment. The boys' ages range from 7 to 18 years, some are learning disabled, and many have average to above average intelligence. The majority of these students were placed in our facility by the courts and local departments of social service.

The school's population has undergone a considerable change during the last two years with the introduction of pre-adolescent and adolescent boys who exhibit more typically conduct-disordered behaviors. These children exhibit such characteristics as aggression, destructiveness, fighting, tantrums and defiance of authority (Tibbetts, Pike, & Welch, 1986). Many also are on probation. Part of this change is the result of the community's need to use private special education resources to place students who do not fit easily into traditional special education categories or other county educational resources. The result is an uneasy mix of students whose behaviors are not always adequately addressed by the school's internal systems of behavior management. Including more conduct-disordered probationary students into a program initially designed to address the serious emotional and academic needs of children has created an imbalance in the school's environment and in the attention of staff to the student population as a whole.

Probationary students often become confrontational leaders in the school environment, creating a power struggle by intimidating other students and defying the staff. Although probationary students currently make up less than 14% of the total student population, they take a much larger percentage of the staff's time and attention dealing with their behavior. They seldom verbalize their feelings and are more resistant to prompts or counseling interventions that address underlying emotional issues.

Characteristics of Seriously Emotionally Disturbed Children
The expanding number of probationary students has changed the dynamics of the school far beyond what their increase in numbers indicate. Children who fall under the special education category of seriously emotionally disturbed (SED), although often aggressive, also are very

vulnerable and sensitive to the varying personalities and misbehaviors of others.

To meet eligibility for the special education category of SED, a child must have exhibited at least one of the following characteristics to a marked degree over a long period of time, adversely affecting educational performance:

- an inability to learn which cannot be explained by intellectual, sensory or other health factors
- an inability to build or maintain satisfactory interpersonal relationships with peers and teachers
- inappropriate types of behavior or feelings under normal circumstances
- a general pervasive mood of unhappiness or depression, and
- a tendency to develop physical symptoms or fears associated with personal or school problems (United States Department of Education, 1977).

Characteristics of Children with Conduct-Disordered Behaviors

Generally speaking, children with conduct-disordered behaviors would have been described as juvenile delinquents in the past. In the nineteenth century, the term "delinquency" was used to legitimize the incarceration of any child who, in the judgment of a court or of a reform school's administration, might benefit from a highly structured school environment of discipline and instruction (Schlossman, 1995).

The American Psychiatric Association's (1994) definition of Conduct Disorder describes a repetitive and persistent behavior in which the basic rights of others or major age-appropriate norms or rules are violated (p. 85). Although conduct disorder is not a special education category, many children with these behaviors nevertheless qualify under the categories of learning disabilities or serious emotional disturbance (i.e., Major Depression or Dysthymia).

Consistent with national data, learning disability was the most common form of disability among incarcerated children in California. In addition, although delinquent behavior is typically considered to reflect social maladjustment rather than emotional disturbance, a large number of delinquents are diagnosed as having serious emotional disturbances. In the delinquent population, national estimates of emotional disturbance by school administrators range from 16.2% to 50% (Warboys, Burrell, Peters, and Ramiu, 1994, p. 35).

Most children in residential treatment have been court-ordered through Department of Social Service and Probation Department referrals to be qualified to attend our school as the least restrictive educational setting (P.L. 94-142, Education for All Handicapped Children Act of 1975). Children from the local community enter the school through district referrals (some of these children also are on probation) supported by the Special Education Local Planning Agency (SELPA). In both cases, the students have an individualized education plan (IEP) that addresses their educational and behavioral needs. Depending upon the placement agency, each student also receives individual therapy at least once a week from either the residential treatment facility or from community mental health services.

Characteristics of Probationary Students

Students on probation who enter our school are under much closer observation than other students. Probation officers for these children are notified immediately of serious misconduct (i.e. destroying property, assaultive behavior, going AWOL, etc.) in the school or residential programs. Probationary students from the community also are closely monitored by their parents and the school, in turn, has closer contact with these parents in monitoring their children's behavior. There are few "second chances" given to children on probation. They may be placed in juvenile hall and relocated to another placement immediately after unfavorable reports to their probation officers.

As stated earlier, children with more conduct-disordered behaviors are quite different from children who are described as seriously emotionally disturbed, although many of their behaviors are similar. Probationary students frequently fall into several categories. Although some students on probation are learning disabled, most of their school problems result from truancy and a defiance of authority. They tend to lack direction and have a general sense of either not "fitting in" or being attracted to the "fringe group" of the school's population. Entitlement issues often mask a poor self-concept that is reinforced by the consequences of their misbehaviors. A form of depression results when such children view themselves as "bad," an image that is maintained when an individual shows little remorse for acting-out behaviors that appear to be more controlled in nature (i.e., breaking and entering).

Art, an Integral Part of the School's Curriculum

The art program has been an integral part of the total school curriculum since the formation of the school ten years ago. As a nontraditional art therapy intervention, the program was developed by this writer, an art therapist with an art education background, as a curriculum in which art would be used therapeutically with children in a school setting. Kramer's (1971) definition of "art as therapy" was used as a foundation for the program within the context of complementing and supporting psychotherapy but not replacing it.

Art materials supply students with the opportunity to find pleasure and satisfaction in the artwork they create. Such experiences become meaningful and valuable to the total personality, according to Kramer, through the process itself and through the insight and skill of the art therapist. The use of self-expression in art by students in our school is a combination between art therapy and art education. The role of the facilitator of this process becomes a dual one as art therapist/art teacher.

The art program, as it has developed over the years, exists as an integral part of the personalities of this writer and of the students who are the heart of it. In this way, the school acts as a secondary environment that protects the value and integrity of the program that is created by its participants and the art process itself.

The Process of Sublimation

Another important aspect of the art program involves the process of sublimation. Sublimation (Kramer, 1979) occurs in experiences when fundamental changes in the balance of inner forces within a child are observed. To allow for such changes, a child must be ready "to contemplate what is painful and conflicted and to take pleasure in finding a way of mastering such feelings through his art" (p. 104). Although sometimes dramatic, the process of sublimation often occurs in subtle ways over a period of time by the introduction of art materials in the art studio and in the classroom.

John, for example, would draw on small pieces of paper whenever he had the chance during

DRAWING TIME

the school day. An accomplished artist, he would usually hide his drawings and be unwilling to show his artwork to others when it was noticed and admired. During classroom art sessions, John would begin a drawing assignment and then either tear his paper into pieces or fold the paper several times and put it into his desk.

One classroom art activity was titled, "My Favorite Place." Most of the students drew restaurants, theme parks, or places where they had lived. John began painting a beautiful landscape with watercolors that depicted shaded palm trees, textured mountains and dotted fields of flowers. Before he was finished, John crossed out the images with black and blue paint and sat at his desk with the results of his work for all to see. In the process of asking the students to say something about the artwork which they created, John replied, "I don't have a favorite place." The art therapist/art teacher replied, "It looks like something happened to your favorite place that changed it." John sat silent and wide-eyed, allowing his painting to be collected and stored with the other students' artwork.

In the following weeks, John drew other images that he enjoyed such as motorcycles and action figures that he gave to students and staff. Although not as intimate, John's later drawings reflected his creativity and individual interests that could be shared with others. He became the class "artist," receiving praise for his artwork and helping other students with their drawings whenever requested.

Recently, John gave a drawing to me that is now hanging in my office. A colored pencil drawing of a turtle with a mass of "hair" pointing in different directions, the turtle's long neck is thrust out in front of him. There is a doubtful, vulnerable expression on the turtle's face but he is, nevertheless, poised to move forward (figure 1).

The beauty of the turtle drawing goes beyond the image itself. John took an incredible risk in destroying the image of "My Favorite Place." It was an authentic moment for him that he was not expecting and, because it was genuine, it could be accepted by himself and others. Such moments are rare but are repeated through the art experience. The turtle drawing represents an equally vulnerable image for John that he did not destroy but gave as a gift to someone for safekeeping. The sequence of these images illustrates an amazing growth in John's emotional ability to accept himself.

Figure 1: John—10 years old, colored pencils

The Growth of the Art Program

The art program began in a small room in a building separate from the main school building and the classrooms. Students were pulled out of their classrooms individually or in small groups, once a week, for thirty minutes. As the school population grew, so did the size of the art groups with four to five students being seen during one class period. The time for the art program also was extended to forty-five minutes. Three years ago, another art room, twice as large as the original, was provided which created an art studio atmosphere.

In the art studio, students are allowed to work independently on different art projects. A variety of art media is always available, and students come to the art room with their individual ideas. The goal of the program is to provide an open environment for students to explore their creativity and to experience satisfaction in their self-expression. Many students come with limited skills that are developed over time. Their progress is slow but sure as the art media directs the students' exploration as much as the art therapist/art teacher's interventions.

In recent years, the art program also has expanded into the classroom. Using an art education model, students are taught how to use the elements of art (line, shape, color, texture, value and form) abstractly, thereby expanding their degree of self-expression. With increased awareness, students are able to draw, paint and work three-dimensionally with clay without being tied to representational images or limited abilities.

An important part of this process involves a student's being able to talk to the class about his artwork at the end of the period. A by-product of this part of the art period is the ability of other students to listen and to make positive comments about the artwork of their peers. Thus, the art allows students to experiment with self-disclosure and its impact on others, risking vulnerability in the process. Authenticity occurs as a result, giving students an opportunity to experience different ways of being.

Seriously emotionally disturbed students and probationary students are combined in the classrooms and in many of the art studio groups. Compared to the SED population, the probationary students rarely seek help, believing they already know how to successfully complete their projects, and they are rarely aware of their mistakes in the process.

In the art studio, they typically select wood as a material for building useful objects (i.e., cabinets and bookcases). It becomes the art therapist/art teacher's responsibility to be firm and consistent in directing the probationary students to take time to evaluate their work and to be more aware of the sequential nature of the building process (Step A must be completed before Step B, etc.). Time and patience is required, creating frustration in most students.

Probationary students often are resistant to imposed structure that doesn't have logical rules and concrete explanations. For example, students understand that rules in the art room are made to maintain safety and that, if these rules are not followed, a student may be suspended from the art program.

The same students, however, don't believe that it is fair to receive a consequence for swearing in class. A rule prohibiting swearing appears arbitrary and unimportant to them.

Different Kinds of Difficulties

Following multiple directions to complete tasks also is problematic for probationary students

DRAWING TIME

and the SED students, but for different reasons. While SED students have more difficulty with the internalized processing of information, the probationary students usually have difficulty with more externalized stimuli (i.e., being impatient and irritated by the request to follow directions). Issues of fairness often arise that sometimes split students and staff in their resolution.

Imbalance in the mixture of SED and probationary students occurs naturally in the classroom. As the art therapist/art teacher working with groups of twelve students per classroom, students are dealt with individually, based upon their responses to the directions for the group. In the art studio, however, groups are formed through the collaboration of the art therapist/art teacher and the classroom teachers. Students are worked with individually from the beginning, depending upon their choice of available art media.

Art activities are individually based upon either classroom curriculum or art media that is selected by the student or the art therapist/art teacher. In this way, the activities are not always clearly defined and are flexible, according to students' abilities and emotional needs.

Many probationary students are resistant to being taught skills in using loose and expressive media such as clay and paint which tend to be fluid and not easily controlled. Such students are most interested in a physical construction of art that is structured and can be controlled by the use of tools. A sense of mastery becomes a very important aspect of the art process with a feeling of "a job well done."

The rules and structures provided by the art therapist/art teacher also increase the opportunities for positive experiences within the art process. In this way, the environment and the necessary tools for construction support the underlying creative process.

The interest in building things becomes a positive intervention that balances the destructiveness of their behavior. The tendency to have to "bang" things together, and create something from nothing becomes a cathartic experience, and a way to channel their aggressive and insecure tendencies.

Judith Rubin (1984, p. 93) writes: "Another common goal in art therapy is to help patients to express or release strong feelings, like aggressive impulses. While catharsis alone is never enough, genuinely experiencing the expression of any affect and finding that it can be controlled and need not be destructive makes for a very useful learning experience."

In essence, the students learn to channel their aggression into the physically demanding construction of three-dimensional wooden objects. Only hand tools are permitted in the art studio, making the creation of the forms direct and immediate. With the exception of power tools, there are no other limitations on the art tools used by the students under the direct supervision of the art therapist/art teacher. If safety issues arise, students are suspended from the art program for a defined period of time. This rule is strictly enforced and supported by the school.

When probationary students do use more expressive art media, they choose more rigid materials such as felt-tip markers to create designs with egocentric qualities (i.e., making a design from a schematic self-symbol or from their own name). Artwork is created that enhances the student's self-concept in a literal sense, while exhibiting the student's current level of functioning.

A Classroom Puzzle

During one art assignment, a classroom puzzle was created that included individual abstract pieces that represented each student and staff member. The direction was to draw something on a puzzle piece that was important about the person and would identify the person as unique within the group. Some suggestions were favorite activities, teams, foods, places, colors, etc. A person's name also was suggested as something important about an individual that was instantly identifiable. Multiple images were encouraged.

Mike, one of our probationary students, quickly printed his first name in black letters and framed it with black dots. He then added the words "class art" twice and "cal skate" once, underlined in black dots. Mike outlined his puzzle piece in wide black and blue lines and was finished with his design in approximately five minutes. When asked if there was anything else he could add that would be important about him, he replied, "No." A few minutes later, he used a fine-pointed black pen to scribble over his name and remaining white areas of the design stating, "This is important about me, too" (figure 2).

At first, scribbling over his design appeared to be an act of defiance by Mike to the art therapist/art teacher's suggestion of adding more images to his artwork. On a much deeper level, however, Mike was giving an emotional response to his current level of functioning. By scribbling over his design, Mike was visually trying to decrease its importance. The scribbling was random enough, however, that it served to enhance the design, allowing it to remain an equally important part of the classroom puzzle.

A week later, the class was asked to design a sign identifying the puzzle which was already on display in the school's hallway. During a group discussion concerning a title for the puzzle with the classroom teacher, Mike and another student worked together in thinking of the perfect title - Puzzle of Unity. The other students agreed, and the sign was created to reflect the group's creative process, both verbally and nonverbally.

Other examples frequently occur where probationary students work on assigned artwork in

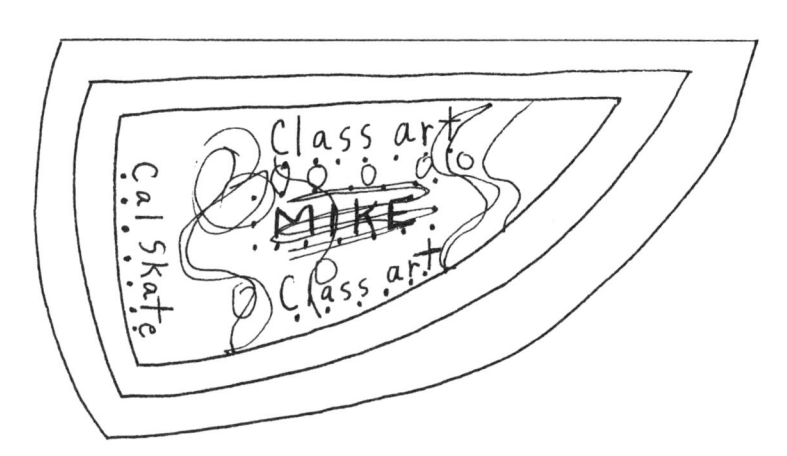

Figure 2: Mike—12 years old, (drawn by the author in the manner of the artist)

the beginning but will either stop working when frustrated or throw their work away after completion. It is often difficult for these students to allow others, especially staff, to see and acknowledge their artwork as being good. In some cases, a student may exhibit bravado during the art process but form no attachment to the finished product afterward.

The Student and His Artwork Have Value

In all cases, the art therapist/art teacher's intervention is critical. The consistent message is that the student's artwork has value and the student has value. This point cannot be stressed enough.

During a face-painting activity on Halloween, two adolescent probationary students volunteered to help staff paint the faces of younger students. Although it appeared that their most obvious motivation was to not be in class for the morning, the older students put themselves in the position of positively interacting with other students and staff. They also allowed themselves to be in the service of younger students by helping them create temporary alternative identities without manipulating the process or the results. It was a new experience for all concerned that had a positive effect on the entire school environment.

The "lucky ones" are those students who receive the services they need and continue to benefit. In the art program, these same students allow their innate creative processes to develop into satisfying experiences. Although not always lasting, few students miss this opportunity. The goal is that such experiences will be repeated over time with greater frequency and a foundation will be developed that combines internal and external trust within the child. Authenticity is the result. When this occurs, the future holds promise for all of us.

References

American Psychiatric Association (1994). *Diagnostic and statistical manual of mental disorders* (4th ed.). Washington, DC.

Kramer, E. (second edition 1993). *Art as therapy with children.* (Second ed.) Chicago: Magnolia Street Publishers

Kramer, E. (1979). *Childhood and art therapy: Notes on theory and application.* New York: Schocken Books

Rubin, J. A. (1984). *The art of art therapy.* New York: Brunner/Mazel, Inc.

Schlossman, S. (1995). Delinquent children: The juvenile reform school. In Morris, N., & Rothman, D. J. (Eds.). *Oxford history of the prison: The practice of punishment in western society.* (pp. 363-389). New York: Oxford University Press

Tibbetts, T. J. (Chair), Pike, T. R., & Welch, N. (1986). *Identification and assessment of the seriously emotionally disturbed child: A manual for educational and mental health professionals.* Sacramento, CA: California State Department of Education

United States Department of Education (1977). *Federal Register, vol.42,* (163). Washington, DC: Author

Warboys, L., Burrell, S., Peters, C., & Ramiu, M. (1994). *California juvenile court special education manual.* San Francisco, CA: Youth Law Center

A Barbed Wire Garden:
Art Therapy in a Maximum Security Prison for Adolescents

Linda Milligan, MPS, A.T.R.-BC

There is no doubt that working with the adolescent males incarcerated at the Bensalem Youth Development Center, a maximum security prison, is difficult. To work effectively with a youthful, aggressive, and chronic population like this, a therapist must understand and develop balance among three issues:

- the adolescent's struggle to become an adult,
- society's need for law abiding citizens, and
- the therapist's need for a safe, professional space in which to work.

I view the adolescent from different perspectives—as an individual and as a member of a family, neighborhood and prison. I also work with the developing relationship between client and therapist, as well as with transference and countertransference material that forms throughout treatment. My goals and interventions are often behavioral and cognitive, yet based on object relation and developmental theories.

As an independent contractor, hired under a grant by a mental health center in Philadelphia, I have two goals: to facilitate growth and change in each youth I see and to help staff design interventions they can use in the day to day activities with the inmates.

Each day I enter a private world, defined by fencing and razor wire. At first glance, one wonders about the life inside this institution. I think of this Youth Developmental Center metaphorically—as a barbed wire garden entered with care. I find ways to help the flowers live, grow and maybe bloom. This metaphor developed from a piece of art I made at work (figure 1).

Following is a discussion of the youth and the art they create during therapy as understood from Erikson's (1985) developmental theory and issues of countertransference. Developmental levels are usually presented, but rarely observed, level by level. When working with each youth, many levels are seen and worked with during each session. However, for clarity, I will follow one level at a time.

The Inmates
I try to view each inmate from the prospective of the self, family, and community, trying to build on the strengths that allowed this person to survive in a very hostile environment. We

DRAWING TIME

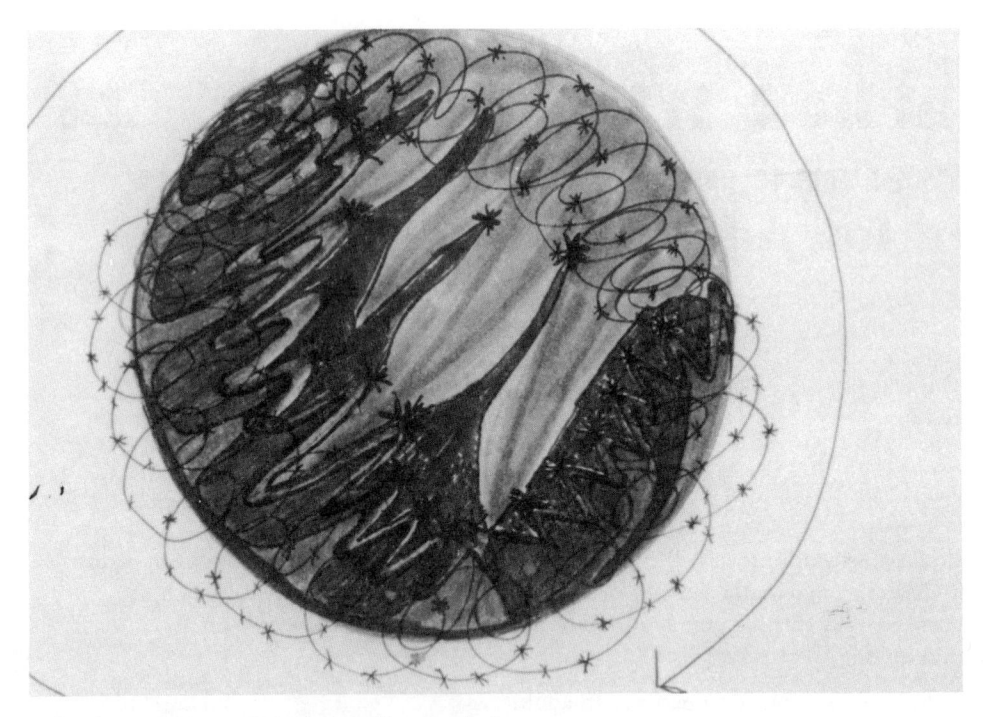

Figure 1: L. Milligan—"My Barbed Wire Garden"

start with what the youth knows about his world and begin to discover how he may create a new world. As our working alliance forms, I can easily see the teenage struggle for competence, one area to gauge healthy change and improvement.

Recently, a profile of the individuals sentenced to the center was made (Popowski). At present, the 118 males housed at the YDC are between the ages of 14 and 21, with an average age of 18. The average length of commitment is one year. Some leave after 9 or 10 months and a few are sentenced until the age of 21, their juvenile life. The ethnic mix is 60% African American, 20% Hispanic, 15% White and 5% other.

The youth are repeat offenders and can best be described as predatory. For the most part, their crimes are against people; armed robbery, drive-by shooting, assault, rape, murder and drug dealing. They have been in less structured and more therapeutic placements before arriving at this secure facility. They have either failed to adjust elsewhere or have committed another offense against the state.

It is important to keep in mind that the individuals here represent a very small percentage of youth. In a recent article in the New York Times, *Stop Crime Where It Starts* (July 31, 1996, op-ed) John DiIulio places predatory youth at one half of 1 percent of the teenagers arrested for violent crimes yearly.

To understand the gaps in development and its impact on treatment and the possibility to reoffend, it is necessary to look briefly at the inmate's lives before they arrive at YDC Bensalem. The boys mainly come from Philadelphia and the Pittsburgh area and strongly identify with their local inner-city neighborhood groups and gangs.

The average youth has dropped out of school by fifth or sixth grade and reads on a third grade level. The average I.Q. is 85 but there is a full range from 75 to the upper end. Attendance is mandatory at the internal school until an inmate obtains his GED, graduates or leaves the prison. Motivation for graduating or obtaining a GED is usually to impress the judge and obtain an early release. I offer books to them, work on reading skills, and have them draw as I read stories to them. Few know the standard fables and fairy tales of childhood that taught many of us human values.

In a culture where children have children, fatherhood is a badge of adulthood. An inmate may have one or more children and each child will have a different mother who is frequently older than the incarcerated youth. Mother and child are seldom referred to by proper names but are de-personalized and objectified by being called "my baby and my baby's mother". Since their fathers were often absent, leaving no role model for male parenting, I encourage these young fathers to explore fatherhood and parenting skills. Sometimes this can lead to a change in attitudes and a better understanding of their own childhood.

The fragmented families lead chaotic lives with a high rate of incarceration among other members. Many are the product of teenage parents themselves. The social dynamics of the family makes developing an effective aftercare plan, which includes a sense of connectedness and responsibility, difficult. In spite of this chaos, the inmates I work with are verbally protective of their families and tend to discount family life as part of their problems. Many have romanticized their role in the family and believe that the money they give in aid excuses their deeds and elevates their status.

Diagnostic Drawing Series

The primary diagnosis given by the state psychiatrists and psychologists is Conduct Disorder followed by Attention Deficit Hyperactive Disorder.

When I first begin to work with a youth, I administer the Diagnostic Drawing Series (DDS) (Cohen, 1994). The DDS requires three images drawn on 18" x 24" 70 lb. white paper with soft, flat sided, chalk pastels (box of 12 Alphacolor) on a flat surface. The three drawing tasks given are:

- make a picture using these materials
- draw a tree, and
- make a picture of how you're feeling using lines, shapes and colors.

The client has 15 minutes for each image and the paper may be oriented in either direction.

As a result of this diagnostic tool, I become aware of depression and post traumatic stress symptomatology. Art made in sessions will often reveal issues of unresolved grief, sexual identity confusion, poor boundaries, and a poor sense of self. Issues of mistrust, low self esteem, and poor social skills are often expressed within the art.

Typically, and not surprisingly, the youths I see are impulsive, immature, self-centered, aggressive, manipulative, dependent, stimulus seeking, and lacking in empathy. The defenses I most frequently encounter are denial, repression, suppression, projections, fantasy, displacement, reaction formation, minimization, and acting out.

Inmate Art

Inmate art is art of the teenager, otherwise known as "gang art" (Lowenfeld, 1987), which strives for naturalistic representation. I see a wide range of developmental levels, artistic abilities, and interests. For the most part, the boys fall into two groups. One group enjoys art, drawing, and seeking ways to develop that skill. I encourage this group to draw frequently and when possible, give them a drawing pad for a private journal. I encourage them to draw when feeling frustrated, bored, stressed, sad, or unable to talk to staff.

The second group tends to be uncomfortable with their artistic ability and are often very critical of their art. With this group, I try to connect with non-drawing activities, such as collage (Linesch, 1988) and beads.

Both groups are striving to develop a level of competency. I try to be mindful of the different developmental levels that may need repair before moving forward with the tasks of adolescence and the developmental level of identity *vs.* role confusion (Erikson, 1985)—the fifth level.

Developmental Levels

Erikson's first four levels are: *trust vs. mistrust; autonomy vs. shame and doubt; initiative vs. guilt; and industry vs. inferiority.* One goal of art therapy is to help adolescents achieve an appropriate degree of accomplishment in each level.

Briefly, with the successful completion of the first level, the individual has come to expect consistency from self and others—his needs can be met and his environment will be safe.

To help repair this basic level of trust I involve each youth in a discussion based on issues central to therapy—confidentiality, respect, safety, and consequences. Working towards that goal, I work individually with each youth in a closed room without support of security near by. I try to be consistent with weekly schedules. We maintain simple rules based on respect for each other, the art materials, and the therapeutic space. I keep clear boundaries, am careful of the clothing I wear, and avoid touching the youth as it can too easily be perceived as a threat or sexual invitation.

I work hard to build an alliance before working on active change. I actively listen, mirror their feelings, confront negative behavior, and respect their anger and their need for defenses. I am constantly aware that they are rarely seeking therapy by choice and therefore see no reason to change. Rather, they believe others are the reason for their discomfort.

Safety is an important issue in prison for staff and inmates, as well as building trust. Therefore care is taken with the art supplies offered. Obviously, things that can be used as weapons, such as razors and knives can not be used. Glass, rigid plastic, and metal are not allowed. Scissors are short, with rounded tips. Thread for beading can not be so strong that it can be used to strangle. I limit the number of items out on the table at any one time, reducing theft of materials. The art room has poor ventilation, therefore materials must be free of toxic fumes.

Many objects that are made must be locked up rather then kept in their rooms. As an artist I find these limitations frustrating. To work through the frustration, I use the same materials I offer the inmates for my own art. I have found with experimentation that it is possible to create meaningful art with the materials available. This knowledge allows me to be empathic and give guidance when needed.

Although the limitations are accepted by the youth as a fact of life, this doesn't stop them from asking for materials that may be off limits. I now check with unit staff before accepting their assurance that something is okay.

When manipulative behavior arises, it becomes an issue in treatment. I resented the need to double check them on their given word. I felt deceitful if I did not believe what was said in session. The need to confront deception, at first, fueled my feelings of fear. But by accepting my fear, I have avoided many behaviors that would be counter-therapeutic.

Exploring my feelings, I realized the desire to nurture can be related to fear. Unrealistically, I thought that if I were nice to the inmate, he would be nice in return and not harm me. This proved unrealistic. As a group, they have little capacity for empathy and their actions are opportunistic, impulsive, and self-centered.

Feeling remote or aloof is the flip side of the desire to nurture when fear is the driving force. If I am far enough away—above the situation—I cannot possibly agitate the inmate enough to cause physical acting out. The inmates too will use this same defense to deal with fear and pain. Self awareness of feelings is necessary to stay connected to each inmate.

Fear is Everywhere

In the beginning, I could not imagine that the youth at the center ever felt fear; however, I have come to see and hear their fear—it is everywhere for them. It manifests itself in hypervigilance and paranoia—believing it is better to strike first. They are afraid of the unknown and afraid to try something new. This manifests itself in oppositional and rigid behavior. To defend against fear they use reaction formation and denial, acting fearless, and showing anger to maintain control.

By touching my own fear, I have begun to touch their fear. They often create collages that include terrified children screaming or holding onto something, or people running away. How frightening it must feel to be out of control—in a world spinning out of control as well.

Anger

Anger is the most carefully monitored feeling throughout the agency. In a 1992 review of eight recent studies, Lewis and Bucher noted that activities encouraging clients to vent their anger led to increased feelings of anger, helplessness and a sense of being victimized (Tafrate, 1995). Once angered, they are slow to cool down (figure 2).

On the other hand, art-making gives safe expression to anger. It is contained on paper. Collage-making helps define the anger and events leading to the outburst and solutions can be explored. Sculpty clay, stiff when cold, helps release anger and gives form to the feelings. Anger management skills can then be developed. In this way the youth begins to learn to trust himself and his ability to control his level of anger.

DRAWING TIME

Figure 2: Unknown inmate—"Untitled"

Rarely do I need to take action due to out-of-control anger. However, when I notice early stage anger or agitation, I address the feelings beneath the anger. If the anger continues, I involve the youth in the decision to continue or discontinue the session. Sometimes we walk back to the unit, other times we move into a calming activity, such as slow focused breathing. Other times the inmate chooses a less stressful activity, such as playing with one of the simple toys I keep on hand or playing the squiggle game with me—a simple game in which one person draws a scribble and the other person turns it into a picture.

Developing skills to successfully choose between opposites happens during the second developmental level—*autonomy vs. shame and doubt*. Erikson states that it is important for the growing child to have freedom of choice. At the same time the child must believe that his environment will protect him from the danger of poor choices. Art therapy, an excellent metaphor for living, offers choices with positive and negative results and as the youth becomes comfortable with art's limitations, he begins to accept society's limitations.

Fear of Failure Often Gets in the Way of Creativity

To help develop autonomy, I offer a wide range of supplies from which to choose, such as pencils, paint, paper, wood, clay, beads, and fabric. I encourage experimentation; however, fear of failure often gets in the way of creativity. Many of the boys have clear ideas as to what makes "good art," defined and limited by past experiences. I start with what they know, which is more often than not, drawing with pencils. I slowly offer a wide range of pencils, very hard to extremely soft lead, color and gray tones, regular and water soluble pencils, different erasers, tissue, blending sticks, as well as books on pencil technique. This gives the youth the opportunity to have a wide range of experiences while feeling comfortably in control.

For youth who are less skilled and less attentive, I offer crafts. The youth with whom I work place value on material possessions and are more likely to become invested in an activity with an end product. Creative crafts, such as beading, appeal to them because beading lends a sense of order, mistakes are easily corrected, and designs are endless. Recently, a youth was so pleased with his beaded necklace he favorably compared it with the gold necklace he wore on the street.

As *trust and autonomy* build, requests are made for different materials, guidance is sought to learn a new technique and projects may take more than one session to complete.

Initiative, Erikson's third developmental level, brings the desire and ability to choose, plan, and carry out a task. If the task is well chosen and successfully completed, the individual has a sense of well-being for a job well done. I ask each inmate to help get and clean up materials. This is a basic act of respect and is presented in a matter-of-fact manner. I acknowledge help and jobs done well. Logical consequences are given for the few problems that arise.

At this level, the youth is able to take responsibility for his art making. I understand and respect their ideas or lack of ideas. I give freedom of choice with the understanding that tasks will be monitored as to their appropriateness for a prison setting. Once, I innocently replied "yes" when asked by one youth if he could make *anything* from the newspaper and flour paste. He proceeded to make a gun. I allowed this with the understanding that it would never leave the art room and when the project was finished, we would explore the role of guns in his life and society, and the possible impact a gun, even fake, on the institution. This exploration led to a poetic expression of excitement and fear in his violent world.

Graffiti is another art form that needs to be monitored as it can cause tension between rivals. However, I find it a good way to get to know the youth, their family, and neighborhood. Many enjoy teaching me their skills. As the alliance develops, graffiti usually disappears. Reappearance often signals anxiety, depression, or pending release. Again, it is a springboard for communication.

Art fits well into Erikson's fourth developmental level—*industry vs. inferiority*. At this stage, the individual begins to place drives and impulses on hold in order to acquire the skills needed to be a productive adult. As the youth progresses in treatment, a desire develops to create a better image or object. Questions of technique arise, along with the patience to listen and follow directions. Finished art is often presented to others with a sense of pride and a desire for recognition.

The making of greeting cards is a good place to observe developmental levels. At the first level, the desire to make a card will come from a suggestion by staff or peer. The youth will give little thought to the holiday or person receiving the card, preferring the activity to the sentiment.

As the youth matures, he slows down and thinks about the person and reason for sending the card. A wide range of materials are used to create meaningful images that relate to the message. Rub-on letters and rubber letter stamps are valued for their professional looking finish.

Later, students enjoy learning calligraphy to enhance the card's appearance and others use their own graffiti. Individual styles are as unique as each youth. One youth clearly entering the fifth stage, *identity vs. role confusion*, designed his own company logo for the back of the card. The desire to maintain an age appropriate level of competency is clearly seen with this activity.

The fifth stage is the task of adolescence. It is a time of rapid physical, emotional, and sexual change—peer groups become self mirrors, past developmental levels are revisited and the need to separate further from the family all come together to form a new whole. Failure to succeed at this level leads to role confusion, over-identification with others, doubt as to one's sexual identity, and prematurely advancing into and failing at the next level, intimacy *vs.* isolation.

Exploring Inside And Outside

Small wooden boxes with covers are an excellent media to explore the idea of "inside" and "outside" with paint, paper, fabric, ribbons, and found objects. I have been intrigued by the many styles created—from plain black boxes to very fancy frilly ones. One youth decorated his box with ribbon, lace, beads, and paint, reminding me of a young girl's boudoir. A bell was attached to the under side of the cover as an "alarm" to warn of intruders. Another youth covered the outside of his box with pine cones, old leaves, and weathered silk flowers (figure 3). The act of gluing these objects onto the box was very comforting for him, helping to fill the empty hungry space inside. A third youth glued stiff, knife-like leaves on the inside of the box—clearly making an uninviting space.

Mask-making is another art form used to express the self. Crayola makes a light weight modeling compound that is clean, easy to work, and dries overnight. The youth paint and add yarn and other objects to these masks. One mask created had a tribal look, some have blank or alien appearances, and others strive to look older and very masculine.

The Importance of Books

Understanding words, spoken and written, is very important in our society and is needed to complete the fourth developmental level—*industry vs. inferiority*. Since the youths' education has been interrupted, I try to integrate books into the treatment and the art process—reaching many developmental levels. For the strong reader, I lend fiction, nonfiction, poetry, and art books. A favorite, *Makes Me Wanna Holler* by Nathan McCall, is the autobiography of an African-American male from street-hood to journalist. It's a story about their life style and his success makes him a good role model.

Reading skills are at about a third grade level and many are self conscious of that fact. I have found reading out loud nurturing. It opens new areas for future exploration. I encourage them to do art work while they listen to the stories. Other books I recommend are: *The Knight in the Rusty Armor* by Robert Fisher—a playful, metaphorical story of the hero's journey of self discovery and change; and *Harlem Horses* by Bernard V. Finney Jr.—a short, easy-to-understand volume of poems about prison life. The fifth developmental level is the journey of *identity*. By offering and reading stories I present heroes, roles, and actions for the youth to think about while traveling the path of self discovery.

Cognitive Distortions

My emphasis up until now has been the youth's development, their striving for competence,

A BARBED WIRE GARDEN

Figure 3: Unknown inmate—wooden box

and the effective use of art to understand developmental levels, create the possibility for growth, and evaluate change.

Another area that needs to be kept in mind when working with this population is the youth's distorted thinking and comfort level with their own life style. This thinking leads to ego-syntonic behavior and is difficult to change. The inmate's thinking tends to be vague, inconsistent, circular, and global in nature. Art is an effective intervention here because it is concrete, permanent, and hard to deny. As progress is made, one can look at problems expressed in the art work and explore new solutions.

Yochelson's 1993 edition of *The Criminal Personality, Vol. I: A Profile for Change*, has been extremely helpful to me in identifying some of the patterns of distorted thinking. The youth justify negative behaviors by:

- externalizing their problems
- projecting their thinking and feelings onto others, and
- identifying themselves as victims.

The youth lack the ability to empathize with others, are self-centered, impulsive, and easily frustrated. They interpret unmet needs as a form of put-down and/or disrespect. They see themselves as unique, above others. This thinking excuses their crime, allowing them to take pride in their M.O. (mode of operation). They are sentimental, believe themselves good people who make mistakes, and excuse themselves of crimes that "help" the family.

The youth fantasize about family, relationships, and goals—believing they are protective and denying interpersonal problems. In reality, they see girl friends and children as property. They lack feelings and are unable to understand the feelings of others.

They tend to be perfectionists and fear failure (Yochelson, 1993). Magical thinking permits them to believe a wish to be reality. When the wished-for goal is not reached, they believe others have blocked or cheated them, denying them what is rightfully theirs. Anger and acting out compensate for the pain and frustration of failure. Some of this thinking is learned through example but I also believe some is self-protective, allowing them to compensate for early deficiencies in the developmental levels.

Countertransference

To nurture and be nurtured in a therapeutic setting is very important. Clearly, as an art therapist, I enjoy offering art materials to nurture self expression. Without the awareness of countertransference issues, I could misuse materials and my role. Instead, I try to guide the youth's need to be dependent towards being independent instead.

Their childlike neediness is often a mask for their fears and uncertainty in new situations. I would like to nurture the small frightened child within them but I would then diminish the emerging adult.

They often ask for solutions and then become oppositional to those solutions, setting up a push/pull scenario which can lead to anger in both therapist and inmate.

A primary task in art therapy for many is learning to take risks and make choices. Inmates have very few choices in jail and art therapy is a wonderful place to give a healthy sense of power and control.

Robbins (1988) maintains that the therapist's emotional connection to the client and his environment is a basic tool of treatment. Trusting that connection can lead to creative solutions that may otherwise be overlooked. To neglect feelings that develop when working with aggressive individuals, staff, and the institution can block the therapeutic process. The frustration of repeated blocks and failures can lead to ineffective treatment and burnout.

Schaverien (1992) states that a therapist must develop effective ways to distance oneself from strong feelings without becoming cut off from those feelings. Exploring inner feelings reduces the chance that one's feelings will contaminate the therapeutic environment.

To help monitor, identify, and contain feelings related to daily stress, I draw mandalas (figure 4). The Sanscrit word for *circle*, a mandala represents the self, wholeness, and healing in Hinduism and Buddhism (Fincher, 1991). With my constant use of mandalas, I have become keenly aware of my fears, the desire to nurture or flee, as well as the feeling of being stuck, overwhelmed, and helpless. Images of birds, feathers and kites identify the desire to flee.

My feelings are of frustration with the institution rather than the inmates. Splits within the art reflect my response to the mixed message from society to warehouse and/or provide treatment. On hot days, the lack of an air conditioner or a window in my office can produce thoughts and images of tropical islands. Unpleasant working conditions help me connect with the powerlessness the inmates express in their art. My art helps me to identify and connect with their fear, anger, depression, and sometimes optimism due to conditions and treatment at the center.

Mandala art is a container, keeping strong, negative feelings safely within. I also see the mandala as a metaphor for prison—safe but limiting and restrictive. A number of youth have

A BARBED WIRE GARDEN

Figure 4: L. Milligan—"Countertransference to Neediness"

said they feel safe in the prison—no longer needing to look over their shoulders. Most feel frustration due to the restrictions.

Art-making does not need to take a great deal of time. Simple magic markers on paper often release and identify feelings and issues. The inmates and I use the activity of art making to safely discharge feelings that otherwise build in a prison. It can be pleasing, expressive, and nurturing. It helps me refuel for another day. It has helped me to process the subtle interaction between inmate and therapist. I am fortunate that my art is seen by my employer as a therapeutic tool—helping me to better understand and treat each inmate.

Working with these thorned flowers in a barbed wire garden is a journey of self discovery. Being playful and maintaining one's sense of humor helps the flowers take their places in the sun and grow. It is a rewarding task for the gardener.

References

Abdullah, O. (1993). *I wanna be the kinda father my mother was.* Syracuse, NY: Laubach Literacy International, New Readers Press

Brandell, J. R. (Ed) (1992). *Countertransference in psychotherapy with children and adolescents.* Northvale, NJ: Jason Aronson Inc.

Cohen, B. (1994). *Diagnostic drawing series* (revised rating guide 1994). Alexandria, VA: publ. by author

Dilulio, J. J., Jr. (1996, July 31). Stop crime where it starts. *New York Times.* op-ed.

Erikson, E. H. (1950). (1985 ed.) *Childhood and society.* New York: W.W. Norton

Fincher, S. (1991). *Creating mandalas for insight, healing and self expression.* Boston: Shambhala

Finney, B.V. Jr. (1991). *Harlem horses*. Albany, NY: Zone 5 Press

Fisher, R. (1987). *The knight in the rusty armor*. California: Melvin Powers Wilshire Book Company

Lewis, W.A. & Bucher, A.M. (1992). Anger, catharsis, the reformulated frustration-aggression hypothesis, and health consequenses. *Psychotherapy, 29* (3), 385-392.

Linesch, D. G. (1988). *Adolescent art therapy*. NY: Burner/Mazel, Inc.

Lowenfeld, V. & Brittain, W. L. (1987). *Creative and mental growth*. (eighth edition) NY: MacMillan Publishing Company.

McCall, N. (1994). (1995 ed.) *Makes me wanna holler: A young black man in America*. NY: Vintage Books

Popowski, W. (1996, July) Personal communication.

Robbins, A. (Ed.). (1988). *Between therapists: the processing of transference/countertransference material*. NY: Human Sciences Press

Schaverian, J. (1992). *The revealing image; Analytical art psychotherapy in theory and practice*. NY: Routledge.

Tafrate, R.C. (1995). Evaluation of treatment stratefies for adult anger disorders. In H. Kassinove (Ed.) *Anger disorders: Definitions, diagnosis and treatment*. (p. 124) Washington, D.C.: Taylor & Frances

Yochelson, S. and Samenow, S. E. (1976). (1993 ed.). *The criminal personality, vol. I: a profile for change*. NJ: Jason Aronson Inc.

Helping Criminally Insane Men Who are Hearing-Impaired Through Art Therapy

Renu Sundaram, Ph.D., A.T.R.-BC

The term, "criminally insane" defines a wide range of prisoners from actively psychotic people to those under the influence of drugs or alcohol at the time of their crime, and those unable to function in traditional prison settings. I worked for two years at a state hospital where 1000 male offenders, judged "criminally insane," are housed. Their crimes range from misdemeanors to repeated felonies and most are on medication.

Several of the prisoners' problems are caused or exacerbated by their hearing loss. As an art therapist with a hearing-impairment, I have been particularly interested in working with them.

Doing art therapy with criminally-insane males requires breaking away from the traditional applications of art therapy. Naumburg's psychoanalytic theory, Kramer's child-oriented emphasis, Kwiatkowska's family-oriented philosophy, and other more traditional theories appear unsuccessful with this hard-core population.

The Setting

The men are housed in twenty-eight wards grouped into "programs," each dealing with different problems including sexual offenses, physical impairments and medical illnesses. Generally, there are three or four wards within each program.

Because the hospital emphasizes community and biopsychosocial rehabilitation, the inhabitants are allowed more freedom and leisure activities than found in a prison or jail setting, despite the criminal history of its inmates.

The ward on which I worked was part of a program that served mentally-disordered offenders (MDOs); patients who were found incompetent to stand trial; and patients who were found guilty by reason of insanity. There were approximately 40 patients. The ward staff included rehabilitation therapists, psychiatric technicians, nurses, a unit supervisor, a psychologist, and a psychiatrist. The patients were required to be in at least 12 hours of rehabilitation groups per week.

Although I am an art therapist, my role was primarily that of a rehabilitation therapist. I was responsible for conducting other groups besides art therapy as well as interpreting for patients who are hearing-impaired during all groups, therapeutic community meetings and interdisciplinary team meetings. I conducted socialization skills groups, helping patients to develop appropriate interpersonal skills; and mock trial preparation groups with the patients who are hearing-impaired, teaching court procedures and how to present themselves in court.

I, myself, have a profound hearing-impairment and am able to hear only some environmnental sounds with the use of a hearing aid. However, spoken language and reading lips are my primary modes of communication.

Being hearing-impaired in a setting where I was constantly surrounded by criminals who were insane heightened the challenge to my safety. Had anyone approached me from behind with aggressive intent, I could have been an unsuspecting victim. However, my safety was never jeopardized due to my hearing loss. I was all the more vigilant and took care not to place myself in harm's way.

I also believe that being candid with patients about my deafness helped me to reach them in a way that I might not have otherwise. While growing up, my deafness had isolated me from the mainstream; I felt like a misfit, trying to adapt to a world geared toward the "norm." On a subconscious level, I might have empathized with the patients more than most staff, since the inmates, too, were misfits due to their crimes and felt society's subsequent rejection. Having experienced isolation, I identified with them and they could relate to me on a level that they could not with anyone else on the ward. Our link was our deafness.

I had recently learned Signed Exact English (SEE), which was different from American Sign Language (ASL), the signing system all the patients use. So I learned their language. Aside from myself, only one other staff member knew sufficient sign language to communicate with these patients. I also spoke a little Spanish.

By teaching hearing patients and staff ASL, I facilitated communication between the patients and the rest of the ward, thus reducing the hearing-impaired patients' feelings of frustration, loneliness, and isolation. Previously, most patients and staff resorted to writing their messages.

Being a woman was another challenge in this setting. I was frequently the target of sexual innuendoes or hallucinations and delusions of a sexual nature. The patients frequently needed reminding of proper staff/patient boundaries. According to Aulich (1994), setting a firm distinction between patient and staff is vital in order to develop appropriate treatment. In addition, due to the mental instability of most of the offenders, vigilance for unpredictable behavior was constant. Despite the presence of security officers, staff and other patients were assaulted by patients.

The patients often had difficulty in understanding ward, hospital, and court procedures. Most of them did not even understand why they were in the hospital and had thought that they would simply be dismissed and sent home. Much of my time was spent simply teaching them the seriousness and consequences of their crimes.

Many of these patients had been in prison for years. Like their hearing co-inmates, some preferred to remain on the ward than to be released to a community in which they did not know how to function. Also, most came from poverty with little education; consequently, they had not acquired productive social or cognitive skills needed for successful integration into society (Aulich, 1994; Isaac & Armat, 1990). Habits which helped them survive in hostile surroundings were ingrained; changing to more constructive behavior seemed overwhelming.

Groups and Media

Due to safety hazards and the patients' unpredictability, most of the groups were held in a central dayroom, next to the nursing office where other staff were able to monitor the group and come to my aid if my safety or the patients' safety was jeopardized. Rarely were there opportunities to develop group cohesion due to constant surveillance and distractions.

Art supplies were limited due to security issues. The ward was not equipped with the space or the facilities to house a wide array of art media. Patients were capable of turning the most rudimentary materials into lethal weapons. For example, toilet paper and toothpaste could be easily mixed together. The result: a dangerous rope made out of thick, rock-hard braids, which could be used as a tool for escape or assault. Pencils could become tools for stabbing; clay could be secretly hoarded to create makeshift weapons; scraps of metal could be sharpened into knives; vapors from permanent markers could be inhaled, sending patients with a substance abuse history on "highs."

Most of the sessions were restricted to using colored tissue paper and construction paper, making magazine collages, and drawing with markers and pencils. Colored pencils and scissors were counted before and after being given to the group. Patients were often searched at the end of each group to make sure they had no hidden cache of supplies.

Many patients had to be encouraged to attend groups. If they participated in their assigned regimen as required, their chances of having their sentences reduced improved. For those who had life sentences or were ineligible for parole, there was little motivation. However, many patients seemed to enjoy coming for art therapy groups.

Group themes usually focused on:

- teaching them responsibility,
- discussing respective crimes,
- developing interpersonal and self-expressive skills,
- exercising behavior modification techniques, and
- discussing effective communication strategies.

Some of the patients had difficulty remaining reality-oriented. For them, group sessions focused on reality issues such as:

- orienting patients to person and place,
- why they were in the hospital, and
- what they hoped to get from rehabilitation.

"Here-and-now" tasks were important not only in helping patients who had difficulty staying reality-oriented, but also those who, like patients with a hearing-impairment, relied more on concrete and visual modes.

The most important element of the art therapy group was providing patients with the creativity and the flexibility to express themselves through art media (Karban, 1994). The opportunity to communicate nonverbally through art media was especially powerful for the patients with a hearing-impairment. Artwork as a channel for communication helped both the hearing

DRAWING TIME

and hearing-impaired, giving them a degree of control and freedom.

Case Study—Weldon
Weldon (pseudonym) was a 37-year old male with a hearing-impairment, originally committed to another state hospital for assaulting his brother with a knife while under the influence of drugs; thus, he was considered guilty by reason of insanity. While there, he sexually assaulted a staff member. Due to the seriousness of his crime, Weldon was transferred to a maximum security ward in this state facility, after his sentence was extended for another two years. Weldon was diagnosed with schizophrenia, and had a history of suicidal attempts, assaults, sexual aggressiveness, and polysubstance dependence.

Weldon was able to speak, but communicated primarily through sign language. Although the staff worked intensively with him, Weldon expressed little desire to change. The habits that brought him to the state hospital appeared so deeply ingrained that he preferred to maintain them rather than to strive for more productive habits (Isaac & Armat, 1990). In addition, Weldon's mental status fluctuated, making him prone to episodes of psychotic and assaultive behavior. Weldon was assigned to join the art therapy groups.

Goals
Weldon's hearing impairment required the use of concrete concepts and highly visual modes of communication. He did not fully comprehend the seriousness of his crime nor the consequences. He didn't understand that he had to account for his actions in court. His inappropriate sexual and aggressive behavior with patients and female staff consistently led to extensions of his original sentence. Developing Weldon's interpersonal and communication skills were crucial to his rehabilitation; he needed to learn how to survive in challenging circumstances.

Although these goals were appropriate for the general population, they were very specific in Weldon's case. They were tailored to his hearing impairment by attempting to decrease his naiveté, isolation, and pent-up frustration and aggressiveness, and to improve his channels of communication.

Sessions
Weldon had been on the ward for two years when he joined the art therapy groups, in which he was the only person with a hearing-impairment. He had no previous exposure to art therapy, but appeared interested in participating. He attended for six months. Although the group met weekly, Weldon attended sporadically, frequently missing groups for a variety of reasons. He often forgot about the group, or the side effects from his medications interfered with his ability, or willingness, to attend. Sometimes he was prohibited from attending group due to assaultive behavior.

In the first session, the group members introduced themselves by constructing individual collages. Weldon's collage had two messages, illustrating both a desire to leave the hospital and things that he liked doing at the hospital (figure 1). Weldon simultaneously spoke and signed that the bed reflected his desire to sleep; '7' was his lucky number; and that he liked taking showers and eating breakfast, but did not like taking his medication. Weldon added that he wished he could travel, go back to his family, eat Mexican food, and go horseback riding. He willingly showed his collage to the rest of the group.

During Weldon's next session, the group members focused on their families and what they enjoyed the most about them. Weldon drew an Indian figure on a horse, which he verbally said was himself riding on his family's farm (figure 2). He did not volunteer any extra information about his family, although he did say he was sorry for assaulting his brother.

During the next session, Weldon was emotionally labile and inappropriate. Group members were asked to choose an animal they would want to be and explain their choice. Weldon drew a rabbit, laughing loudly for no apparent reason. He then drew two more rabbits with a nest of eggs. The picture appears fragmented and disorganized; the flowers and trees appear impoverished; and one of the rabbits' bodies is cut off by the paper (figure 3).

Weldon's psychotic episodes impeded his ability to function on the same level as the rest of the group. His two drawings of the rabbits contrasted with his artwork from earlier sessions. In the previous sessions, Weldon adhered and appropriately responded to the theme of the

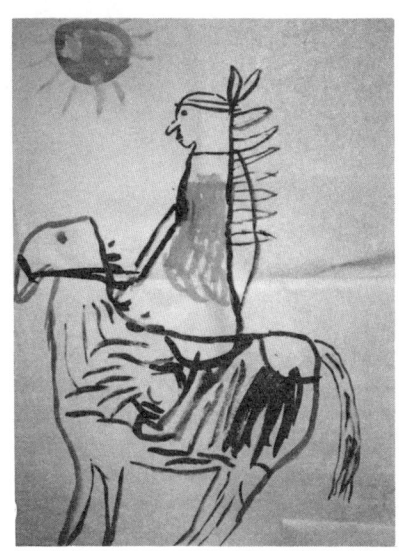

Figure 1: Weldon—collage　　　　　　　　　　　　　　　*Figure 2: Weldon—drawing*

session. However, in this session, Weldon was unable to make associations between the rabbits and himself. His frequent spontaneous laughter and behavior didn't fit with his drawings or the group. Yet the presence of the two rabbits with the nest in the middle suggested that Weldon wanted to find some sense of belonging.

Due to his assault on another patient, Weldon was not allowed to attend the group for several sessions. After returning, he remained under surveillance by a psychiatric technician and a security officer. In the session that Weldon returned to, the group was asked to think of constructive ways to help them handle stressful situations. Weldon drew himself as a "yoga man" being taped by a video camera (figure 4). He frequently laughed during this session, but, otherwise, presented no behavior difficulties.

DRAWING TIME

Figure 3: Weldon—drawing

Figure 4: Weldon—drawing

In the drawing of a "yoga man," Weldon still seemed to have remnants of his past psychotic symptoms. The bulging eye of the "cameraman" appeared to depict the staff members watching him. Weldon may have felt paranoid when watched by the psychiatric technician and the security officer. In addition, he drew himself again with no hands or feet. Possibly, this drawing communicated Weldon's feelings of being secluded and restrained. The hearts suggest feelings of grandiosity and narcissism.

In the following session, Weldon continued to present psychotic symptoms. He kept laughing for no apparent reason, "blanked out," had difficulty staying focused, and signed and spoke about hearing voices telling him "bad things," but was not able to state what the "bad things" were. Weldon had just had his medication increased. In his drawing, Weldon drew the injection that he had received to stabilize his psychosis. He signed and said, "I feel as if my brain is about to explode from the shot." He then drew a sundae, a fish, and a face, (figure 5), which he called "Pig."

During the next two sessions Weldon continued to draw random images and still had difficulty staying focused. The group had the opportunity to express themselves with any theme they chose. Weldon selected several images: a bird, a necklace, an asthma inhaler, an ambulance, and a waterfall. His next drawing consisted of a camel, a women, and a flower (figure 6).

Concrete versus Unstructured Tasks

In the next session, Weldon's attention span had improved, possibly because of increased medication. I felt that because of Weldon's shifting states of reality, it was important to take advantage of his improved mental status to "ground" him to more concrete concepts. This might help to re-orient him and allow him to participate constructively in the group. He was asked to choose a picture from a coloring book. Here, his behavior changed remarkably. Given a specific task with clear lines, he diligently worked on the picture with a variety of colors. He also took his time in working on the picture, which was different from his usual quickness in previous sessions.

Weldon was not able to finish the picture during the session and asked if he could finish it on his own. This was the first time he had expressed any interest in completing his work. Other than "grounding" Weldon, the coloring book may have also given him the encouragement and

Figure 5: Weldon—drawing

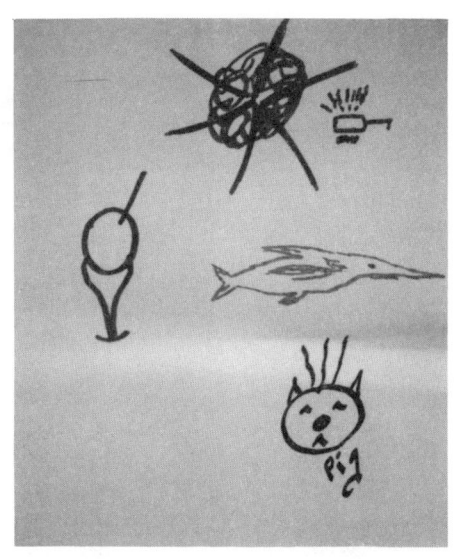

Figure 6: Weldon—drawing

support that he needed. Through the structured drawing, Weldon may have felt more able and self-confident in producing an acceptable product.

Patients tend to prefer that the picture "look right," and choose stereotypical matter such as crafts or step-by-step drawings to attain that goal, rather than explore unfamiliar techniques and communicate ideas (Riches, 1994). Unstructured drawing tasks appeared too disturbing for Weldon. Providing concrete and structured tasks helped him achieve a more reality-oriented performance. He selected a picture from a coloring book that appropriately addressed the theme of the session, "friendships." He diligently attended to the task and finished it after the group had adjourned. The colors he selected were appropriate, and he remained within the drawing's boundaries. This was the first drawing in which Weldon had taken a serious interest and seemed happy that he had successfully finished it. The drawing appeared to instill the self-confidence that Weldon needed to succeed at a task. He appeared more stable in this session than in the previous sessions.

In the next two sessions, Weldon's receding psychotic symptoms allowed him to participate more fully in the group. The winter holiday season was approaching, and the group focused again on their families and their homes. Some of the members, eligible for parole, were excited about the possibility of release.

Weldon drew what he called his home with a fire lit in the fireplace, smoke emerging from the chimney, and a cat on top of a tree (on the left). Hammer (1980) states that a house is significant because it represents the patient's view of his home environment. However, in the background, clouds obscured the sun and, according to Weldon, it was raining. Weldon quickly drew the jagged and rough lines. The trees appeared unable to withstand the onslaught of the rain (figure 7), appearing shaky as evidenced by faint, incomplete lines and no trunks to stabilize them. It is possible that the absence of the trunks reflected feelings of instability and loss of security and control that Weldon might have been experiencing. The

DRAWING TIME

Figure 7: Weldon—drawing

Figure 8: Weldon—drawing

cat in the upper left quadrant of the drawing is high up on the page, on top of a tree. According to Hammer (1980), the placement of the cat could reflect Weldon's shifting state between reality and fantasy. Futhermore, the cat embodies the concept of femininity and identification with females, and is one of the three most commonly drawn animals by prisoners and patients with psychotic symptoms (Hammer, 1980). It is possible that the cat reflected Weldon's psychosis and inappropriate boundaries with female staff.

When asked how he felt about spending the holidays at the hospital, Weldon angrily said, "It's not fair that some of the patients get to go on parole, and I don't." Although Weldon expressed his feelings appropriately, he still did not acknowledge the seriousness of his crime or the danger that he still posed to others.

In the first session after the holidays, Weldon drew a boat taking him far out to sea (figure 8). Although he had a brighter affect and appeared more stable, he still would not discuss the here-and-now of his treatment, choosing to escape his present reality in a boat that "will take me far away where there are no problems."

The boat was already in the distance, moving away from the rocks and crashing waves. As in figure 7, Weldon also drew a red sun. This time the sun was not obscured by clouds or rain as in the previous drawing. Although Weldon constructively expressed feelings of anger and sadness in his drawing, his artwork suggested that he still preferred not to deal with his issues.

A Group Project: Waterfall Mural

The next two months of art therapy was spent making a large 3.5' x 6' mural, consisting of four wood panels, to be hung in the ward. The entire group actively brainstormed for ideas for the mural, drawing an outline, and finally, painting the picture. They chose "Waterfall" as their theme; as one of the patients said, "Water is a passage; it takes us anywhere." The mural took two months to complete with tremendous group effort. Weldon played an active role in painting; it was one of those few projects in which he consistently attended, interacted well with the other patients, and appeared to thoroughly enjoy himself.

In a setting where feelings of isolation and despair are predominant, Weldon became part of a group that supported and encouraged each other. The mural enabled Weldon to feel comfortable working with other group members (Karban, 1994). Also, the mural was structured and concrete enough to give him the self-confidence to understand and complete the activity. Further, by giving Weldon the opportunity to actively participate, feel comfortable in talking about himself, and practice turn-taking and listening skills through this task, he was able to work on developing constructive communication strategies (Landgarten, 1981). He had increased his social repertoire by learning how to work with a team of patients.

Shortly, thereafter, Weldon was transferred to another ward due to the hospital's restructuring of its programs.

Through the art therapy groups, Weldon had the opportunity to express his feelings in a constructive manner. As shown through his artwork, Weldon often appeared unable to control his cognitive processes; thus, he was unable to accurately depict his thoughts (Landgarten, 1981). However, despite his displays of psychotic symptoms such as hearing voices and not focusing, art therapy gave him the opportunity to safely express himself, as well as to orient to reality. Even more important, with his hearing impairment and inability to verbally express himself sufficiently, Weldon used his artwork as a channel of communication.

The "Waterfall" group mural probably was the highlight of Weldon's efforts. His medications had significantly improved his level of functioning and he no longer was under surveillance. Weldon actively invested himself in this major project, frequently working on it outside the art therapy sessions. The most important aspect of this project was that Weldon learned to work with the other group members as a team. The completed mural demonstrated Weldon's capacity to contribute to the group, and helped to instill needed self-confidence.

Summary

Art therapy in a setting for the criminally-insane is a challenge. Not only will the art therapist encounter resistance from the patients, but also from an environment poorly equipped to conduct art therapy programs (Day & Onorato, 1989). Safety will always remain a higher priority than providing a rich array of media with which to work. Trying to instill new and more productive habits in individuals who are either mentally incapable or strongly resistant to change requires persistence and stamina.

My deafness served as a challenge in this setting, yet it was also my forte. I understood the experience of standing out in a crowd, and I could empathize with what the hearing impaired patients experienced. I fully understood the limitations imposed by their disability and I served as their link to the "hearing community."

Art therapy proved to be a valuable tool for patients like Weldon who have difficulty communicating with other patients and staff. Weldon used his artwork to express his feelings, to develop more appropriate behavior, and to discuss his crime. A balance was sought between understanding the dimension of Weldon's disability and dealing with his resistance to provide a most beneficial rehabilitation in a resistive setting.

Art therapy can be successful only when the therapist accommodates to both the needs of the patient and the demands of the setting. In Weldon's case, concrete "here-and-now" tasks seemed to work best for him while metaphorical tasks were not as successful. Through images produced in the artwork, he developed a sense of safety and trust with me in a setting that lacked these qualities. As Liebmann (1994) says, the concrete and visual productions arising from drawing sometimes enables the patient and therapist to discuss the significance of the product in a non-threatening manner.

I quickly learned on the job to be creative and flexible, constantly ready to shift gears, and adapt to the many rules of the hospital. Although most of my art therapy training had been psychoanalytic, I quickly learned how ineffective that approach was in this particular setting. In order to address the patients' level of functioning and the nature of their crimes, I had to use more behavioral and gestalt approaches. Here-and-now and behavior management became the focus.

Ultimately, I found the most effective way to work with inmates was to accept them as individuals, as human beings, no matter how heinous their crimes. By recognizing patients have contributions of worth, clinicians can help both staff and patients break down some long-standing barriers of resistance and hostility and move toward healing and growth.

References

Aulich, L. (1994). Fear and loathing: Art therapy, sex offenders, and gender. In M. Liebmann (Ed.), *Art therapy with offenders*. 165-196, London: Jessica Kingsley Publishers

Day, E. S., & Onorato, G. T. (1989). Making art in a jail setting. In H. Wadeson, J. Durkin, & D. Perach (Eds.), *Advances in art therapy*. 126-147, New York: John Wiley & Sons

Hammer, E. F. (1980). *The clinical application of projective drawings*. Springfield, IL: Charles C. Thomas

Isaac, R. J., & Armat, V. C. (1990). *Madness in the streets*. New York: Macmillan, Inc.

Karban, B. (1994). Working as an art therapist in a regional secure unit. In M. Liebmann (Ed.), *Art therapy with offenders*. 135-164, London: Jessica Kingsley Publishers

Landgarten, H. (1981). *Clinical art therapy*. New York: Brunner/Mazel Publishers

Liebmann, M. (1994). Art therapy and changing probation values. In M. Liebmann (Ed.) *Art therapy with offenders*. 251-289, London: Jessica Kingsley Publishers

Riches, C. (1994). The hidden therapy of a prison art education programme. In M. Liebmann (Ed.), *Art therapy with offenders*. 77-101, London: Jessica Kingsley Publishers

Growing Old, The Hard Time Way
Art Therapy as an Intervention in Gerontology and Criminology

Marcia Taylor, Ph.D., A.T.R.

The older prison inmate population, those 55 and over, has until recently remained fairly constant at 3 to 5% of the prison population, or between 20,000 and 30,000 people. This number, however, is rising; Sol Chaneles of Rutgers University forecasts that inmates over 55 might double every 3 to 4 years. By the year 2000, their population is estimated to reach 100,000 nation wide. This increase in the older prison population can be attributed in part to tougher sentencing laws, longer sentences, changes in demographic populations at risk, increased unemployment rates, changes in prison capacities and decreasing use of parole (Castle, 1992).

Many older inmates are repeat offenders. Others, however, are first time offenders who have committed a crime at a later age, generally sex offenses, larceny or homicide. Some career criminals are apprehended because they are slower or less sharp than when they were younger—some have grown old in prison due to the length of their sentence. Inmates incarcerated for the first time after fifty-five or sixty rarely led productive or successful lives prior to their arrest (Zamble & Porporino, 1988).

Historically, women have received shorter sentences in part because they were not the primary perpetrators but accomplices to crimes, for example, driving the getaway car during a robbery. However, as women commit more serious crimes and receive longer sentences, state prisons will be required to cope with aging female offenders as well as males.

Older Prisoners Pose Formidable Problems

• In general, most prisons are designed for a younger population. As this population ages, their medical problems and health costs will increase. Some corrections experts estimate an average cost of $75,000 to $100,000 a year to house and care for an elderly inmate—as much as three times the cost for a younger inmate.

• For older inmates, the prison environment can be extremely threatening. Most older inmates are mixed in with the general prison population unless they are non-ambulatory or critically ill and on a medical unit. They can be prey to younger inmates who steal their belongings and harass them, both psychologically and physically.

DRAWING TIME

- For the few inmates who will gain freedom in old age, there are additional problems to face. Many have lost or are estranged from family and friends, have no home or job skills, and little or no savings and medical insurance. While elderly prisoners do not pose as obvious a security threat within the prison or to the community if released at a geriatric age, society shows little compassion toward them, and longer mandatory sentences and excessive stipulations follow.

- With prison overcrowding, the needs of the elderly inmates are often overlooked as more critical issues arise.

- The topics elderly inmates list as their main concern during incarceration include freedom, family, power, loss and doing or serving hard time.

The development of innovative and cost effective programs is part of good prison management. Any disruption in prison management, whether in additional health costs or handling troubled inmates, translates into a tighter budget and lost opportunities for better use of those dollars. Most correctional staff acknowledge that older inmates need ramps for inmates in wheelchairs, special housing arrangements as protection from younger, more violent and aggressive inmates, individualized medical diets and special recreational, vocational and therapeutic programs. However, with other overriding concerns, such as overcrowding and AIDS, the development of programs for older inmates has far less priority.

Goals and Benefits of Art Therapy with Older Inmates

No research is available concerning art therapy with the older prison population, however, we know that engaging older inmates in art activities and art therapy presents them with a creative means for self-expression to communicate their concerns in visual art form. Working with an art therapist provides them an opportunity to deal appropriately with their issues through discussion of their art work in a psychotherapeutic setting. Further, inmates receive positive feedback from staff and other inmates for their creative pursuits. In addition, the final art product is a tangible object in an environment which has little space for personal belongings.

Art therapy can address the following needs and concerns:

Doing Time: There is a need to have constructive ways of using time to improve problem solving skills, improve quality of life and change destructive attitudes. Many inmates, especially those in maximum security, may be "locked down" in their cells for 18 hours a day. This time is referred to as *dead time* and it is a real and overwhelming concern of the inmate on a day to day basis. In group discussions, younger inmates agree that being released or transferred to a minimum security institution is their main concern. For older inmates, there are other more important issues of time. When they finally accept the fact that being released is improbable, they turn to how best they can serve long periods of dead time. Structured art programs allow them to constructively use and even take advantage of this *dead time*. They can make short term goals to deal with present time and making art in their cells is viewed as better than doing nothing at all. Inmates are resourceful in using supplies available to them. For example, handkerchiefs and cotton pillow cases available for purchase from the prison commissary are transformed into canvases, which, when decorated with acrylic paints, or pens and markers make gifts for family, friends or other inmates in exchange for food or favors.

Expression in visual art allows the older inmate to constructively use time and overcome the pervasive sense of "present time" without a future. This is supported by a statement of an older inmate, serving 3 consecutive life sentences, and not eligible for parole until the year 2070: "I didn't draw for 45 years. Now I get up at 5 am. and start drawing. There isn't enough time to do all the art that I want to do. I need a 36 hour day!"

Support: There is a need for more in-depth, preventive type of attention in helping inmates adjust to growing old with dignity in prison. Inmates in general have a relationship with their keepers, the correctional staff and administration, that is usually rooted in distrust and anger. Seeking an emotionally supportive and accepting relationship may appear to show weakness on the part of the inmate or elicit retaliation or violence from other inmates. Custody implies a situation in which inmates are locked down, counted and controlled while a supportive environment would seem to suggest care for the inmates' welfare and attempts to introduce freedom through dignity.

Art therapists can provide a supportive environment for inmates to explore creative means of expression that encourage risk taking and experimentation and challenge critical thinking. Art involves feeling, judging, manipulating materials and communicating ideas, (Greenberg, 1987). Creating art offers inmates a sense of control, a feeling of being in charge.

Prison generally concerns survival rather than enhanced living. Participation in art therapy helps bring into conscious awareness talents and values the inmates never realized they possessed. This awareness results in better self-image and increased self-discipline which are conducive to better adjustment to their incarceration.

Safety: There is a need to be insulated from the intrusion of younger, more aggressive inmates. Forming an older group of inmates, such as the Senior Men's Group described later in this chapter, helps them function as a cohesive and supportive unit.

Developing a group to which they can belong, helps those whose family ties have deteriorated due to aging and lack of contact.

Emotional rehabilitation: Older inmates often suffer from depression and feelings of hopelessness and anxiety. Their pre-prison experiences often left them with low self-esteem and a feeling of powerlessness. The liberating feelings and increase in self-esteem that art can sometimes provide can be the basis for attitudinal changes. For those who will grow old or die in prison, rehabilitation can be redefined in terms of attitudinal changes. For the few who will leave, it translates into a better chance for a successful life on the outside.

Privacy: There is a need to have personal space in an overcrowded and impersonal environment. The art experience allows them to withdraw into themselves—perhaps into fantasies, perhaps into self-reflection—qualities often lacking in inmates.

Coping Skills: There is a need to learn strategies for coping with prison life. Zamble and Porporino (1988) have demonstrated that prisoners are notoriously poor decision makers, and prison does not help this deficit. One aspect of coping skills is the ability to visualize and verbalize problems clearly and correctly, to meet the problem directly and solve it. The impact on problem-solving of prior lifestyles, and lack of culturization adds to their inability to think through and verbalize a problem. Structured art therapy provides an opportunity for the catharsis of negative emotions, otherwise spent on prison infractions. This in turn, leads to better decision-making which leads to better adjustment to the environment.

New Jersey State Prison

I volunteered for more than 4 years with the Senior Men's Group at the New Jersey State Prison, a maximum security prison. Built on one large city block of approximately 12 acres, it houses more than 2,000 men, inmates described as the most difficult and dangerous adult offenders in the state—most serving sentences of at least 20 years.

In 1978, the new penal code requiring mandatory sentences for crimes involving firearms or other weapons was enacted, removing discretionary power from judges and courts in sentencing decisions. This means more criminals receive longer sentences, further increasing overcrowding with no new plans for prison expansion. Those serving less time present other disciplinary problems such as escape risks or long criminal histories. This rather volatile and crowded living situation was exacerbated by the new penal code.

As a volunteer, one must pass security and receive clearance to attend designated classes or events on specified days. Entering the prison through metal detectors, civilians are escorted by a guard or staff member to their final destination. No civilians are allowed to pass through the halls during inmate movements. When one door is unlocked electronically by a guard behind protective glass, the door at the other end is locked, sealing the hallway.

The atmosphere dramatically changes from maximum security to school environment upon entering the two story school building within the prison where the Senior Men's Group meets. Classrooms, offices, meeting rooms and a library of general reading and law books fill the building. Classrooms are decorated with student-inmate work including test papers, written work and poetry, art work and inspirational posters—similar to an urban middle or high school.

The inner wall of each room is glass but besides this and the guards' presence in the hallway, the impression is one of a supportive school environment. A variety of classes are held during the day and evening. Here, in a second floor all purpose classroom, the Senior Men's Art Therapy Group meets.

The group, made up of older inmates, was formed at the New Jersey State Prison to be studied by Dr. Eamon Walsh for his doctoral research into the needs of the aging inmates. The title, Senior Men's Group, de-emphasized the word "inmate", to give the group focus and dignity. Over several years the group was directed by volunteers and topics ranged from current events to music to inmate concerns, all depending on the interests of the group members and leader.

Just Killing Time

I first met the Senior Men by their invitation following two events I coordinated at Trenton State College. In 1989 I organized a conference entitled *Art in Prison: It's More Than Just Killing Time*, featuring speakers from corrections and art backgrounds.

Of particular interest was the information shared by Dr. Walsh. Having worked in corrections for over 35 years he stated that inmates, especially those growing old in prison, who had a creative involvement in art, whether alone and self-directed in their cells, in art classes and/or in art therapy, were better adjusted to their overall prison situation. In other words, he implied that art had an ameliorative effect on the harshness of prison life.

Another noteworthy speaker, Howard Beyer, Superintendent of the New Jersey State Prison concurred that creative arts programs provide a humane and viable approach to prison management.

Examples of prison art were shown as slides at the conference, sparking the interest of the conference participants. As a result, in 1991, I curated a statewide exhibition of inmate art work from all the correctional facilities within the New Jersey Department of Corrections. The exhibition, *Hard Time Art*, which also included a book of poetry published for the exhibit by inmates, was reviewed in several newspaper articles. Interviews of the many people instrumental in organizing the exhibit and of several inmate artists were included in these articles.

It was at this point, having read my comments, that the Senior Men's Group invited me to join Dr. Walsh to visit their group and talk about the possibility of starting an art therapy group with them. Some of the men had been in art classes in other correctional facilities or had positive experiences working with the art teacher at the New Jersey State Prison during the day school session. Others still remembered their childhood art experiences and were skeptical about their talents. Several feared their art work would be analyzed and interpreted and used against them. As one succinctly said, "This is going to be the nut class!" A few associated drawing the House-Tree-Person and other projective tests as intrusive and threatening or conversely, something in which they could manipulate the results.

Art therapy was described as a form of self-expression in visual art, the discussion of which is meaningful as it relates to the concerns of the individuals or group who created it. The focus of art therapy is addressing the process of expression, not the final art product, as might be expected in an art studio class. Quite interestingly, when the group actually got under way, the reverse occurred, with the final art product being equally, if not more important, than the process. They were able to take ordinary art material and transform it into something extraordinary and uniquely personal... and this, in an impersonal, harsh environment.

The initial reaction to art therapy varied with different members of the group. Some reacted with skepticism and distrust—others with eagerness at the idea of trying something new; but most, with a sense of curiosity. If for no reason other than the fact that all the Senior Men would receive their own art supplies, the group began.

The majority of the group was serving sentences for murder or multiple murders, with sex offenses and miscellaneous convictions being in the minority. Most were serving a sentence of 25 years to life with many having already spent 5 to 18 years behind bars. The repeat offenders, serving their third or more sentence, had spent more than half of their life in prison. The oldest was in his seventies, the youngest in his late forties. Most ranged in age from 55 to 65. This is a representative sample since one half of the total inmate population in New Jersey correctional facilities is serving 10 or more years and the 60 plus age group totals 51% of all older inmates.

The number of men allowed in the group was 20, based on classroom capacity. Actually, a core group of 10 to 12 men participated on a regular basis, the rest coming infrequently. It was my understanding that the group had a waiting list although this was never confirmed.

DRAWING TIME

Limitations in Art Supplies And Related Materials

Materials used in prison must conform to security regulations. Some supplies present risks: turpentine for oil painting can be volatile, clays and some chalks can jam locks and dark ink from permanent markers can alter prison uniforms to resemble the color of those worn by guards. Working in three dimensions as in mask-making can be a security risk in maximum security if the materials and finished products are used as dummies in escape attempts.

Greenberg (1987) points out an additional problem when the elderly are involved with art making. Physiological changes due to aging affect all three routes through which toxic materials enter the body: skin contact, inhalation and ingestion. When working with a potentially violent population, the risk of toxicity increases to themselves or if used against others. Also, there may be an interaction between medications, food and toxic substances.

For these reasons, art materials were limited to washable markers, various drawing and colored pencils, crayons, oil pastels, watercolors and appropriate papers, as well as acrylic paints and canvas boards.

For collage, assorted colored paper and magazine clippings were used with white glue, which is also available in the prison commissary. Even these basic supplies presented some problems. Pencil sharpeners are not allowed because of the sharp metal blade. Either permission was needed to use an office pencil sharpener or the inmate artists devised ways of filing the soft lead into usable points. Because scissors are not allowed, collages became tedious and time consuming. At first the men were encouraged to select pictures from magazines, postcards, museum catalogs, etc. The pictures were trimmed outside the prison, then returned the following session. To save time, hundreds of pictures were clipped and brought to the sessions at regular intervals.

Both Greenberg (1987) and Hoffman (1992) agree that copying limits creativity. But in the case of the Senior Men, using pictures stimulated visual expression and provided images readily available to their senior citizen counterparts through field trips and museum visits. Spending long years incarcerated in places where even the recreational yard is concrete, many inmates can live the rest of their lives without even seeing a real tree! While copying from pictures may be a limit to creativity, in prison it can be a window to exciting possibilities.

Group Format

After retiring from the Department of Corrections, Dr. Walsh continued his active role with the Senior Men's Group and accepted a faculty position in the Department of Law and Justice at Trenton State College. As colleagues in the same academic setting, we applied for and were granted two substantial grants in 1991 and 1992 from the college research committee to finance the group's initial needs.

The sessions were held once or twice a week for an hour and a half in the evening, keeping in line with the inmates' daytime work responsibilities and other time conflicts like A.A. meetings and religious instruction. The evening time slot was consistent with the regular schedule of the evening school, at no additional cost for more guards.

The group began with workshops demonstrating art techniques with the available supplies to encourage experimentation, develop confidence and foster creativity in inmates needing basic instruction in the use of art materials. This was done with all the supplies as they were introduced to show the range of possibilities within the medium. Instructional art videos describing techniques and ones documenting the lives of famous artists and art movements were also incorporated into the sessions. Pocket folders were given to the men to organize books and handouts. In this way they each had a copy of materials for personal reference in their cells.

Local artists were invited as guest speakers to show slides of their artwork, demonstrate their techniques and talk about the importance of art in their lives. These sessions were particularly animated and energizing since the men posed numerous challenging and insightful questions to these guests "from the outside." A few also enjoyed sharing their art work to receive critiques from an aesthetic and technical point of view.

In the beginning I suggested certain drawing topics, although it wasn't long before the men suggested topics on their own. All participation was voluntary with the understanding that any and all attempts at artmaking would be treated with respect. Greenberg (1987) suggests that adult learning styles are influenced by prior experiences and age and that after 30, adults learn by doing. They need encouragement to compare their work with what they did at the start. Learning for older people is not compulsory, so they can select what they want to learn and how they learn it. This worked for the Senior Men's Group. The members were free to decide their level of participation and the extent to which they shared information with each other.

Some of the topics they most enjoyed also illustrated insightful information without revealing the nature of their crimes. Asking them to draw your family of origin and the house you grew up in offered understanding about their family relationships, the roles or importance of family members and the way the inmate used his own family role to cope in prison. At the same time they were encouraged to reminisce about earlier times, an activity typical in the older population, but often avoided by inmates with an intense focus on the present.

Drawing themselves as a vehicle of transportation brought out memories of happier times, at least in comparison to their current situation. Fancy and fast cars, taxicabs, trains, military vehicles and naval vessels to name a few, required reflection about past events and showed how they maneuver their way through prison life.

They were able to share through storytelling, as Hoffman (1992) suggests, emotions and involvement in historical milestones that they experienced collectively. "Imagine a large expanse of open water with no land in sight, then draw the first boat that comes to mind..." challenged them to problem-solve and think in terms of future events. Who is on the boat? Where is it going and how will it get there?

A group round-robin activity had interesting results. Each group member selected one color crayon, made a mark (a dot or an x) on one side of a drawing paper to indicate the person/color who began the drawing and then started a drawing of their choice on the other side. After a few minutes, each person passed the drawing to the person on their right, continuing until each drawing arrived back to the original artist. They were amused by the novelty of the activity but quite serious when the drawings were displayed for discussion. They saw the similarities in the work as a universal group expression, with remarks like, "We're not alone" and "We're all in this together" as common responses.

DRAWING TIME

In the beginning, the group followed a specific structure, with opening hellos and discussion, a decision on a theme for the evening, followed by time to draw or paint and concluding with discussion of the art work. Group members were encouraged to use their art supplies to continue drawing and painting in their cells and bring the art work to the group sessions for discussion and sharing with the group. This evolved into a preferred way of working. The men even asked for themes to do as cell work, their version of homework. While creating art in their cells was outside a therapeutic framework, it fulfilled an important goal, that is, to help inmates "draw" away hard time and serve as an immediate release of emotions. They were responsible for their own art supplies. It was easier having their art supplies available at all times and safer than leaving the supplies in a locked cabinet that could be easily vandalized.

Creative writing workshops were also presented by guest speakers. The group members were encouraged to maintain a journal in poetry and prose. They were given writing tablets (one without spiral wire binding—another potential dangerous object) to focus on creative writing, as opposed to a diary approach. This was to allay any fears that their written work would be taken in the wrong context and viewed as possible infractions.

The artwork was displayed at the college, in local libraries and at community events. At the end of each significant event, completion of a series of projects, and good attendance at the end of a year, each inmate received a certificate of participation. While this is unusual for a therapy group, it is a common practice in the prison to recognize inmate accomplishments. These forms of recognition, kept by inmates in journals or folders, can be important material presented to parole boards or during their case appeals.

Case Example

Primo, a nickname derived from his full name, was 64 years old when I first met him and serving three consecutive life sentences for the murder of his second wife and their three young children. He had already spent 14 years in prison and knew he would most likely die in prison.

He openly spoke of the murders although the crimes were never the main focus or intended topic of any group discussion or drawing theme. The amount and nature of disclosure was up to an individual. (Many of the group members had high profile cases—the trials and details of their crimes being headline news. In addition to local media coverage, a few were the basis of books and TV movies and documentaries.)

Primo told his story with such frankness that even the other group members were surprised. "I'll never get out. I have to face my sins. It's a hard thing, killing your family," said Primo. Apparently he had problems with alcohol and difficulty getting and keeping jobs. As he explained, coming home drunk one day he had an argument with his wife. As the argument escalated, he took a gun from his gun collection and shot his wife and the children. Realizing what had happened he attempted to kill himself, the gun jammed and he passed out in what he described as an alcoholic blackout.

At first he seemed to just enjoy the companionship and social atmosphere of the group but said he would, "give art a try." By the time of his death in 1995, presumably of a stroke, he was one of the most prolific artists of the group.

GROWING OLD, THE HARD TIME WAY

His early attempts were sketchy pencil lines scribbled on the page and filled with printed or written phrases about his life. The sketches included designs, crosses, guns and references to bottles of alcohol. He used familiar images while also practicing his skill at drawing. Primo had not engaged in any art activity during his adult life, however his interest in art as a child and teenager was being awakened after a long period of inactivity.

His early sketches parallel what Hoffman (1992) describes as dormant skills. He contends that what is learned in art is rarely forgotten and that adults, being reintroduced to drawing, may travel through some of the developmental stages identified for children. Primo used his early art experiences to his best advantage, drawing for hours each day to fill the idle time. He seemed pleased with the sheer number of drawings and his satisfaction of being able to get ideas down on paper.

His next group of drawings involved the use of color with more planned arrangements of the earlier images and usually limited to four objects or four areas of the paper. Figure 1 shows a family shield drawn inside a mandala shape that was prepared for the group. The shield is divided in four sections which he compared to the four family members he killed. He never identified or spoke of his family by name but continued the repetition of "four" in conjunction with his exploration of color. Each section is separate yet becomes part of a large configuration. Drawn in pencil then outlined in black or dark color and colored in with crayons, the drawings resembled coloring books.

He continued with an almost playful use of color, overlapping different shades of crayons and experimenting with skin tones. I suggested trying oil pastels but he felt unable to control or blend them stating they were too messy. Though the men kept their art work, Primo was not as attached to or possessive of his early drawings as we will see with his later work. However, right from the beginning it was clear that "family" in the real or abstract sense was very important to him.

He expressed an interest in drawing people and portraits. He started using pencils exclusively and abandoned color, then requested charcoal and a variety of soft lead pencils to emphasize shadow and depth. Though many of his subjects were copied from magazines and newspaper photographs, his best subject was himself.

Self Portrait

Triple Lifer (figure 2) illustrates one of several self-portraits he completed in his cell by copying his reflection in a mirror. It resembles himself remarkably. In both upper corners he included a winged foot which he used in earlier drawings and referred to as "winged victory." The expression on his self-portrait is both stoic and painful. At his request, I duplicated copies of several different portraits which he gave to other members of the

Figure 1: Primo—"Family Shield"

DRAWING TIME

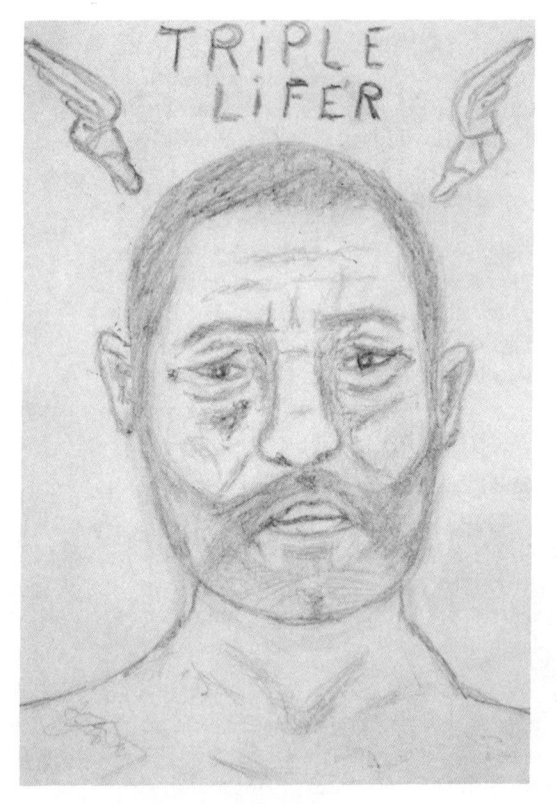

Figure 2: Primo—"Triple Lifer"

group. To his surprise, the other Senior Men were quite impressed by his developing drawing skill and honest expression, giving him positive feedback and encouragement. He was a well-liked member of the group and was missed on the several occasions he spent time in the medical prison unit of the local hospital. He was arthritic and had medical complications stemming from diabetes.

As I would only keep art work he felt comfortable sharing, his next distinct group of drawings was unavailable. It was a significant time for Primo. He spoke about the limited contact he had with two grown children from his first marriage which ended in divorce. His son had died but it wasn't until months later that he was notified. The loss without closure was difficult for him.

At this point his drawings took a dramatic turn. Using pictures as guides he selected separate elements from each—a person, clothes, an environment, and condensed them into one drawing. He requested markers and developed these new images into colorful party scenes and family-like gatherings. He asked if they could be laminated to protect the waterbased markers. Before returning them, I suggested displaying them at the college with artwork samples from the other men. While on display, two were published in the local city newspaper along with an article about the Senior Men's Group.

Primo was happy to have positive recognition. He sent a copy of the article and the artwork to his daughter, who lived in another state, thereby re-establishing a relationship which continued for about two years. She never visited, possibly because of the distance. He created composite pictures mixing magazine ads with famous paintings and adding creative ideas of his own. After each was laminated, he sent it to his daughter. Devising the composite pictures took him beyond an art technique and into the creative act itself. He was self-directed—fulfilling an emotional need for family contact through his art work.

An Integrating Process

In October 1994, Primo brought figure 3 (see color plate 8) to the group. It was one of his few later images without people or animals. He described it as a double mountain, a landscape, a nice place to be. The double mound or mountain image was the basis of my earlier research (Taylor, 1972) into the way art reflects the changes that hospitalized psychiatric patients undergo during their hospital stay. The double mound is a visually balanced picture and when it occurs in patients' art work, it indicates a significant change, an integrating process or turning point for the patient. The image is one of the oldest symbols in Egyptian art symbolizing transformation and rebirth. Curious about it, I asked him whether or not something out of the ordinary was happening with him, the group or in the prison. He said he just wanted to try something different, however, he had just received word that his daughter died of a heart attack at the age of 47. Thus began his final transition in art.

His drawing retained the bright quality of markers enhanced by skin tone markers and a fine line black pen he used for outlining. During the last five months of his life, he completed between 15 and 20 drawings, incorporating religious themes, sailing ships and images of death with scythe in hand and redemption. But most importantly, the majority of drawings referred to his daughter and the real or imagined events from her life. After his daughter's death, he still wanted his drawings laminated, keeping them for himself... though he suggested that I make color copies for myself.

Figure 4, *Little Girl and Reflection*, was not an exact image of his daughter but made him realize he could cope with her loss, his last real outside contact, through his drawings. The fish, frog and lotus flowers, all symbols of rebirth or rejuvenation, continued the theme of transformation and change as seen in the double mountain drawing (color plate 8).

Undoing Past Events

In figure 5 (see color plate 9), he pictured his daughter on her death bed, a nurse praying at her side and the reflection in a mirror of a doctor entering the room. He noted the picture had many possible interpretations and offered a few. The doctor appears hesitant and is only a reflection. It could be himself cautiously entering and possibly having the power, as the "doctor," to make everything better, even undo past events. The nurse and daughter are crying for the loss of lives and relationships. The quilt he designed as the bedcover includes objects he thought might have some meaning. The crab, star and other symbols in the room such

Figure 4: Primo—"Little Girl & Reflection"

as the horseshoe, cross, horse and dog all hold symbolic reference to change, transformation and passage. He seemed to transcend life in prison through his art.

His last drawing (see color plate 10) was a colorful interpretation of Grant Wood's *American Gothic*. He died during the week between our sessions without ever sharing his comments about it with me or the group. We never knew if he realized the couple he portrayed was a father and daughter rather than husband and wife. I never knew what happened to his artwork but I have the color copies of the last significant group of drawings.

Following his death, the Senior Men talked at great length about Primo's use of art as therapy. It wasn't the first time a member of the group died but in Primo's case, it was the first time they brought closure to a death by discussing art work. What most impressed them was the intensity with which he approached art. With encouragement and his own self-direction, Primo used art to fulfill his emotional needs. While others worked on their case appeals, he drew for hours in his cell.

Discussion

With the 65 and older age group the fastest growing segment of our population, it is realistic to expect the aging prison population to increase at a similar rate. Programs will be needed to deal with this special aging group. The "lock them up and throw away the key" attitude will not work for elderly inmates in already overcrowded prisons. Art therapists can use the primarily sedentary quality of creating art in helping inmates learn skills to cope with life in prison. Goals should include helping the men deal with the pervasive sense of doing *hard time* and as an immediate release of emotion.

An aging group in maximum security, possibly the harshest form of institutionalization, has been the focus here. Similar groups in medium or minimum security settings may require other goals, for example, assisting inmates as they prepare to cope with life after release. The primary goals would remain constant: to help them use time more constructively and improve their quality of life by raising self-esteem and lowering stress.

Older inmates need special health care, new prisons or new facilities in existing prisons and innovative educational and social programming. By rethinking traditional approaches, art therapy can contribute to therapeutic programs for older inmates. Strengthening group interaction and cohesiveness in a creative environment encourages recognition of similarities which helps them confront conflict more easily—especially important for inmates who will spend lengthy periods of time together.

References

Burnett, C. (1989). Introduction. In S. Chaneles and C. Burnett (Eds.) *Older offender: Current trends*. New York: Haworth.

Castle, J.C. (1992). *The history of Trenton State Prison: A study of the development of the correctional system in New Jersey 1797-1991*. Unpublished Masters thesis, Jersey City State College.

DePalma, A. (1991). About New Jersey, Jan. 27, *The New York Times*, 19

Fry, L.J. (1988). The concerns of older inmates in a minimum prison setting. In B. McCarthy & R. Langworthy (Eds.), *Older offenders*. New York: Praeger.

Greenberg, P. (1987). *Visual arts and older people*. Illinois: Charles C. Thomas, Pub.

Hoffman, D.H. (1992). *Arts for older people*. New Jersey: Prentice Hall.

Sander, S.L. and Johnson, D.R., (1987). *Waiting at the gate: Creativity and hope in the nursing home*. New York: Haworth.

Taylor, M.F. (1972). *Implications of ego integration in the mound drawing evaluated according to Freudian theory*. Unpublished masters thesis, Hahnemann Medical College.

Toch, H. (1977). *Living in prison: the ecology of survival*. New York: Free Press.

Walsh, C.E. (1990). *Needs of older inmates in varying security settings*. Unpublished doctoral dissertation, Rutgers, The State University of New Jersey.

Zamble, E. and Porporino, F. (1988). *Coping behavior and adaptation in prison inmates*. New York: Springer, Verlag.

Part 4

HEALING OURSELVES THROUGH ART

Red Rope and Blue Veins:
The Importance of Self-Monitoring in a Prison Setting

Beth Merriam, A.T.R.

During the first few months working at a Canadian federal prison for women, several times I found myself at the staff entrance when I had intended to be in another area of the prison. I laughed and joked with the correctional staff about needing reassurance that I could leave at any time.

In therapy sessions with inmates, as I listened to stories of terror, rage and despair, I became conscious of similar feelings within me. Fragments of their experiences left me overwhelmed, confused and fearful. My opportunity for expressing these emotions was minimal.

Therapists can, like their clients, experience emotional affects that sometimes result in emotional withdrawal from their therapeutic alliances. Fortunately, art therapists can use their creative abilities for continuous self-exploration and self-care. However, we should also seek ongoing support and supervision when working with traumatized clients in correctional institutions so that we can continue working with people who desperately need to learn how to express themselves.

By doing creative writing, I resisted withdrawing and stayed connected emotionally with these women.

Following is my fictional account of an inmate's internal experience which I wrote, out of my own despair. I was beginning to feel overwhelmed working with this young woman. In writing her story as fiction, I shifted from listening and observing from the outside to listening and feeling from the inside.

Red Rope and Blue Veins

I saw a girl inmate go into segregation. It was either that or kill herself. There's no telling what a girl will do in anger. Four steps into the cell to the back wall and she banged her fist against it just to hit something. For eight months she had played house, wanting connection with a partner. She imagined making tea just as any couple might, and sharing kisses and strokes to give pleasure. Her house. Five by eight feet. Cement and steel. Toilet. Sink. Shelf. Curtains to cover the bars. Feigned domestic tranquillity.

No sound was made though her knuckles ached. That would come later when a noise in her head would leave tremors throughout the walls of her body. Her body was a house built in

DRAWING TIME

Beth Merriam: "Red Ropes, Blue Veins", watercolor on paper

layers and each layer sealed up feelings. Lying on the bed she covered herself with the sandpaper blanket and licked a finger to glide over the scar on her neck. Biting off a finger nail she held this between her front teeth and scratched her tongue in a rhythmic motion. She did this for a long time and thought about swallowing it. If the nail got caught in her throat she might have another feeling to think about. She spit it out and scanned the concrete floor, trying to find that piece of herself.

She hated small rooms. Mother had always locked her in the small back room before going out with friends. "Just for a little while," was usually all night and sometimes the next day.

RED ROPE AND BLUE VEINS

Once, after two days and nights, she returned with tears of guilt and a half eaten bag of chips. Sprinkling some on her hand she offered these to her daughter, but the girl did not like this mother and bit the offering hand, scattering the chips. When mother left again that night, the door stayed open and she soothed herself by picking the chips from her hair and eating them like the sacrament. The salt on each piece was sucked until the crispness became a soft mush that could be pushed to the back of her throat and swallowed. The taste of freedom was salty.

Her favorite story was Snow White. She liked the idea of eating something and falling asleep. Once she took a handful of pills and drank red wine as a ritual. She woke in the hospital with a tube down her throat and heard the doctor welcome her back. She lived, but not happily ever after. The doctor gave her a diagnosis instead of a kiss.

Tiny body, big eyes, quivering mouth. When words failed she would tease the back of her throat with a finger. Her vomit was very articulate. She imagined a gun shooting poisonous vomit. "I hate you. I hate you. I hate you." She loved to hate, and thought that she might just hate everyone in the world, including herself. Her-fat-self. Her-fat-self was bigger than ten segregation cells. Her-fat-self could grow until seams split and bars bent, until windows cracked and buttons popped. Zippers and doors would not close. She started pacing her cell. Getting to know her limits.

Every weekend had been a party. Waiting under the pile of coats thrown on the floor by Mother's friends, she watched them drink and listened to the noise level slowly increase until the time was right to creep out from her shelter. She would drink until her tummy felt hot, and imagined a tickling finger making a line from her nose to her belly button. The hot liquid always brought a squeal from somewhere deep inside.

Finally, mother didn't come home at all and she went to live with Mrs. Myers who always had a cigarette and blew the smoke out of her nose like a dragon. Mrs. Myers finished each sentence by mingling the last word with smoke. As if the last word were the most important. The one you had to catch. Sometimes she would lie on the floor where Mrs. Myers couldn't see her under the cloud of smoke. The words would drift away and she would be like the ashes that remained.

It was forbidden to ask about her mother. Her real mother who left and no longer had a face. Sometimes she went to church to look at the picture of Mary whose gaze never strayed from baby Jesus. Once she sat in a different seat and thought that Mary's gaze had searched for her. When she told Mrs. Myers this, the dragon broke her bottle of wine in one swoop against the side of the table and ordered her to clean up the mess. She saved one piece of glass to keep under her pillow. She liked blood. It made her like Jesus and now Mary might look at her too.

At the home she was told to change or else she might never be forgiven of her sins. Finger wagging lectures made her think about grabbing that finger and biting it off. The finger that scratched, checked for dust, tasted, turned off lights, rang door bells, tapped on shoulders, pushed open curtains, pulled up things, tested water temperatures, pointed and beckoned. She learned to wait out the finger.

Good girls don't cry. You only cry if you've done something wrong and if you've done nothing wrong then you're good and have no need to cry. Good girls eat everything on their

DRAWING TIME

plate. You only leave something on your plate if you've been bad, so eat everything on your plate. Good girls don't ask. If you ask questions you must not have listened right and that's bad, so don't ask. Good girls don't see things they're not supposed to. If you see too many things you might become curious and that would be bad so don't look. Good girls don't listen to the big people talking. If you listen to the big people talking you'll hear what isn't fit for girls to hear and that's bad. Good girls don't go where they're not supposed to. If they do they'll get a knock on the head.

Good girls don't cry. You only cry if you've done something wrong.

Her hair was always a mess and so they cut it off. That was when she had her first period. There were warning signs. Cramps. Each month she would check her panties for red. Blood was the best thing she had and she watched every month to see. Every month was penitence. When she bled she cut.

She had the same dream about a drowning baby every time she went to segregation. In the dream she would push her way on foot through the water in a desperate attempt to save the baby, but was always too late and watched it slowly sink and disappear into the black water. She would wake in a sweat, waving her arms and screaming silently, angry that she could not swim to save the baby.

The man who delivered groceries to the home told stories about ships. Some were made of wood he told her, but others were made of steel and could still float.

How could something so big float she wondered, and thought that she might step onto the water and float away too. Wet shoes made the women at the home angry and the man laugh. The man laughed because she had tried to get away and the women screamed because footprints made her visible.

Red rope and blue veins. The words repeated in her mind over and over like a lullaby, but it kept her awake instead of putting her to sleep. Red rope and blue veins. She tried putting a tune to it and started humming an old country song that she used to know. One of those never-ending sad songs about lost hope and tangled memories, and if she ever got out of here she would write her own song. She talked herself out of it, as she always did, remembering the past that everyone would want to know. How she ended up in here. Red rope and blue veins always made her cry.

It had been a difficult delivery. Fifteen was too young to be having a baby the doctor said, and looked angry that he should be put through this. She kept the screams inside her head, not wanting to trouble him anymore than she already had. The nurse soothed her with a wet cloth. She thought that everything inside of her was being pulled out. A girl. With a cord around her neck and a blue face.

She had not been a good mother. She quit drinking for awhile but soon found herself needing the alcohol to calm herself when the baby cried and wouldn't stop, no matter how much she fed her and walked her and sang to her. She started sitting out on the front step, sipping her drink and leaving the baby to cry. It worked for awhile, but soon the apartment door and front door couldn't hold the crying and so she sat across the street. Not for too long. Then she heard cries coming from the window and ran to the bar down the street where the noise and music kept the baby good and quiet.

They said the baby must have been alone for three days. Must have just slowly given up, the neighbors said. Had been a pretty little thing too. Cried sometimes, but real pretty. The mother? Well she was quiet too. Never spoke to anyone. Never had men in like that other one up in 301 either. Shame. Damn shame what happened to that baby. Yes, she thought. It was a damn shame. Her whole life was a damn shame when she thought about it. She didn't like thinking about it.

Mandala Healing:
My Recovery from a Hostage Crisis

Joan Pakula, M.Ed, A.T.R.

For six and a half years I worked on an acute psychiatric unit in a prison. Most of the male inmates were in their twenties and thirties, the youngest, eighteen. They arrived on the unit delusional, agitated, and possibly suicidal. Some were filthy and smelled of feces and urine. A few were returning patients with a smile for familiar faces. Staff cleaned and fed, medicated, responded to demands and insults, and encouraged and cajoled.

The program promoted stabilization by providing medication, groups, some fresh air, TV., and individual evaluations. I provided art therapy.

The patient's response to art therapy was good. In small groups they relaxed and created the images that told their stories. Patients with limited social skills were able to participate, giving them opportunities to make choices and take control over the images they created.

In prison, staff never knew what might be around the next corner. It could be quiet for a few days, and then we would hear one alarm after another. The alarm generally sounded as an alert for assaults, but could also be for a hanging, a fire, or an escape. With an alarm, everything on the unit came to a halt, and staff ran to assist the unit in need. At any time, potential for grave danger was present. For patients, this kind of instability and inherent danger was something they had known much of their lives. Since adolescence, they grew up in state hospitals and prisons. Unpredictable and unthinkable events were not unusual.

My Experience

On what was to be my last day in this facility, a much dreaded event occurred. During a creative arts group, two staff members, four patients, and I were taken hostage by another patient. We were seated around a table when the patient quietly stood up and announced he was taking us hostage.

The patient—young, agile, and well over two hundred pounds—was a "lifer" with nothing to lose. He had even killed one of his cellmates. Holding two sharpened pencils and in complete control, he threatened to kill one of us.

I was incredulous. My first reaction was "Is he serious?" The answer was obviously "yes" and a shocking, sickening feeling came over me.

He was to my left; I kept looking at him, trying not to take my eyes off of him. Yet I was also aware of the door to my right. Although I was pretty sure I could make it to the door if I ran, I did not dare move from my chair because of the possible consequences.

Rocking from side to side, ready to spring, he demanded to see the warden and the media. As time went by, his demands increased. His statements became more bizarre and less organized. Claiming to be "superman" he said he was "in control of this whole thing."

A silent alarm had been given, but we could see only a few staff members outside the door, so we did not know what was evolving.

Different people came to the door and attempted to reason with our captor, but he warned them not to enter the room. He was not satisfied with anyone until two associate wardens appeared.

When a staff member hostage offered him one of her cigarettes, a change took place. The power of the smoke! After smoking two cigarettes, he became less agitated. He rocked less. Negotiators made repeated ineffective requests to let the hostages go. Although the phone rang, no one dared move. As time went by, I began to feel exhausted. I didn't know how long I could stay in this hypervigilant state.

Eventually, staff negotiators made progress. The patient let one of us leave the room. I now was a larger part of the target because he was physically closer to me; only an arm's length away. More time passed and I was the next to be released. The remaining hostages stayed for another thirty minutes before they too were released without physical harm. Out in the hall, I was surprised to see staff in "battle gear" waiting. Most staff had never experienced a hostage-taking before this. They also appeared frightened and shaken. I was relieved that I was no longer under the control of a desperate and potentially homicidal man.

For weeks, I was physically exhausted. That hour had been an ugly roller coaster and my neurological circuitry was in disarray. Immediate "post trauma" sessions brought more exhaustion. I started working with a skilled and caring therapist, and received much support from my family, friends, and co-workers. However, despite all the positive attention I was receiving, I did not feel whole. I spent most of my time at home on a couch, needing to be in a safe, comfortable place. I felt satisfied just to sleep, or stare out the window, watching spring flowers grow and bloom.

After about three weeks of resting, I got the sudden urge to draw. Not surprisingly, it turned out to be a mandala, as I had been working with this archetypal symbol for a long time.

Mandalas

Mandala, the Sanskrit word for *circle*, is the symbol of the self, wholeness, and healing (Jung, 1959). Mandalas are created by Buddhist monks and, at times, are unintentionally created by children and adults. The inmate/patients also drew mandalas.

I had received training in the Mari Mandala Assessment, developed by Joan Kellogg (1981). At the prison, I used this method with the patients, paying attention to color choice, archetypal symbols and their placement within an empty circle. During groups, there was always paper available with the circle penciled on, giving the patient an unspoken invitation to create a mandala. Some patients responded to this well and the process appeared to be a satisfying, pleasurable, and healing experience. It's possible that looking at a circle, instead of blank paper, decreased their anxiety about drawing. Using this process I was able to get greater patient participation and see images I might not have otherwise seen.

Drawing at home became a ritualistic process. I would sit on the floor with a drawing board, using oil pastels on 12" x 14" paper. I took time to relax and "turn off" my thinking. I intuitively chose a color that was made known to me before I even sat down to draw. Although I previously used a pattern to make a circle, at home I drew it free hand. Now, drawing my own circle seemed to be a natural part of the process. I took on the challenge of making a good circle, but accepted my less than perfect shapes.

I drew over sixty mandalas in the first year following the hostage event. Looking back at them, I saw sixty mirrors reflecting and clarifying my world in a unique way. Often the content of the mandala surprised me.

In the first months, the mandalas obviously reflected the regressive, raw side of the hostage event. One of my first mandalas, figure 2, still scares me with the sharklike teeth and bloody mouth. With each mandala completed, I felt better. Each gave me something I needed at the time, or released something that needed to be released.

I believe that we have answers inside of ourselves, a body wisdom which can be tapped into in many different ways. Mandalas are one of the ways to reach our body wisdom. Mandalas give freedom, within a perfect containment—the circle.

Because of my beliefs, the mandalas became a significant part of my healing. The hostage-taking had left me anxious, exhausted, and depressed—feeling that my life would never be the same. I was startled by the slightest hint of danger. I found innocent sounds and people threatening. At its worst, the trauma left me feeling extremely vulnerable. To my relief, creating the mandalas dealt with the darkness and brought me strength and hope.

The content of the mandalas was unpredictable. Some grew out of my dreams. The most difficult to write about now are those which show my own regression, fragmentation, and terror. They look like the work of acutely psychotic patients. There was little room for denial here. I am surprised that I even made the move to draw the first one.

In figure 1, the circle was drawn free hand in a weak line of gray pastel crayon. Tentatively, lines of pink and yellow followed, and then the burst of red/orange. The mandala looked like it was sitting in an angry boiling fire, unable to contain the inferno. From the upper left, a red/orange, missile-like object pierced the circle. At that time I had somatic and dream experiences of a sharp object coming at me from the left. The inmate had been to my left. In the first months, I experienced much physical discomfort.

Figure 2, which speaks, or screams, for itself, was drawn about six weeks after the incident. The colors are blue and black. Snaggled "teeth" ring the red "mouth." The raging monster made an appearance.

I then drew some "earth mandalas." They appeared spontaneously, bringing the healing of nature. When each drawing was finished, I felt as though I had been hiking in the hills. In actuality, I had not left my bungalow, but I felt the nurturing of the earth, and a release from stress.

DRAWING TIME

Figure 1

Figure 2

MANDALA HEALING

Figure 3

Figure 4

DRAWING TIME

Morning or Mourning

I called figure 3 *The Morning/Mourning Demon Brings Relief, Thank You*. The morning I created this image, I felt anxious and restless. A landscape of red hills appeared in my mandala. With arms raised, a blue demon appeared. For some reason she was not threatening and, of all things, a snake bit or kissed her chest!

As I drew, the mandala became light and whimsical. My mood had changed and I looked forward to the day. Mandalas can be tricky. You never know when a transformation can take place.

I struggled with the title. Was she a "morning" or a "mourning" demon? It was morning but I could not discard the sensation of "mourning." I mourned that I no longer worked with the inmates—with their great needs, good senses of humor, and charm (also seen as the talent to manipulate). As patients, they courageously shared their lives through words and drawings.

The serpent intrigued me, having appeared in a number of my mandalas. I didn't understand its significance. Snakes frightened me but they seemed positive and healing in my mandalas. I didn't understand their symbolism until recently, when I saw sculptures of an ancient snake goddess. Sure enough, the snakes symbolized the feminine power to me, the totem of women and healing.

Like figure 3, figure 4 started out as a chaotic landscape. I could not leave it that way so I cut the mandala away from its perimeter, which solved nothing. Feeling I had violated the mandala, I put a ceramic snake on top of the reassembled mandala. It fit perfectly within the circumference, keeping the chaotic aspect of the mandala under control. The mandala took on a new satisfying feeling. No amount of chaos and stress was too much for the power of the snake. Although at first the snake appeared spontaneously in my images, I was now sensing when to bring it into the mandala. The snake has an intense spirit and healing power which, in turn, reflected my own growing sense of being healed and empowered.

Figure 5 and figure 6 seemed to pair together. Figure 5, drawn soon after figure 1, seemed less fragmented and more in control. Apparently, I am gaining some stability. It was explosive with vibrant color and shapes—almost out of control. Color went beyond the perimeter of the circle.

Figure 6 was done months later. Kali, a goddess from the Hindu pantheon, who embodieds extremes such as destroyer and builder, appeared in my mandala with the similar shapes and colors of figure 5. In this mandala, however, there is movement, freedom, and absolute focus. Kali was a magnificent figure—wild but centered. Her symbols include signs of physical extermination, such as garlands of skulls. She also represents motherly and feminine attributes, with symbols of life (Zimmer, 1946). She has the potential for aggression, with a snake coiled around her neck and red fingers. In my mandala, she is contained within the embellished border. The more open I became to the mandala process, the richer, more focused and valuable the mandala became to me, letting me actually see my progress in my art. From figure 1 to figure 6, my healing was significant.

Figure 7 was drawn the morning after observing an incident in town. I found myself standing next to two men who were arguing and threatening each other. From what I overheard, I

MANDALA HEALING

Figure 5

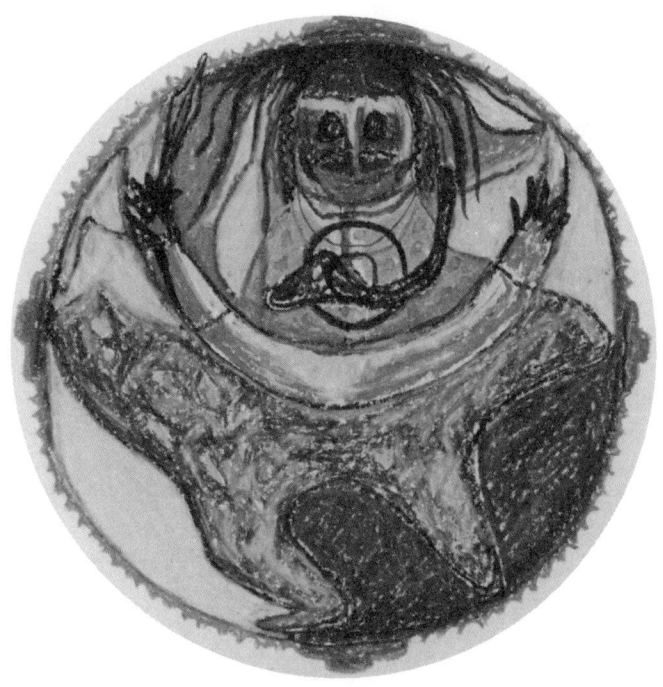

Figure 6

DRAWING TIME

suspected that drugs were involved and this frightened me. I expected a gun to go off. Although I knew my reaction was exaggerated, my fear felt very real to me. The next morning the mandala, figure 7, came to me clearly. Again, a dark shape appeared superimposed on the pastel form which looked like a target.

The more mandalas I drew, the more eager they were to get out on paper. In this last incident, the mandala gave me another opportunity to look at my perception and reaction to events. How am I handling the unexpected? Do I see myself as a target? What is a genuine threat—a time to take cover? The dark side is always there. The mandalas helped me to confront these issues. It might be called mandala wisdom—a mechanism to nudge us forward, away from denial.

The Inmate's Mandala

Although not illustrated, one more mandala bears mentioning—that of the hostage-taking patient. A few weeks before the event, in my art therapy group, he displayed minimal interest in doing any work. I suspected he was reluctant to show vulnerability. However, after some time and without prompting, he picked up a paper with the penciled circle and began working. When he showed it to me, I saw that he had written "love" in the circle's center, with colorful sharp and precise lines. When I asked if he wanted to add anything more to it, he colored the whole background black.

Figure 7

Conclusion

Denial is a considerable, yet necessary, factor of working in a prison. Certain realities of my daily environment remained buried if I wanted to get through each day. I worked with people who were victims and/or perpetrators of horrible crimes. Working with these people/inmates, I wondered how much I could really ignore and how much could I deny to maintain my health and thrive.

Since I was taken hostage, my life has changed. The mandalas have allowed me to heal and learn. My years of working with them prepared me for this time. I did not have expectations and I did not follow a recipe. However, as the process evolved, my openness and faith in it increased. I have been very fortunate.

When I was asked to write about my experience, I was not sure I could do it. In my first draft, I wrote in the present tense. Then the whole episode took on distance and I was less bothered by mysterious aches and sensations. I continued to be vulnerable, but quicker to evaluate an event and how I responded to it. Writing about my experience has been healing. I am regaining freedom.

References

Jung, C.G. (1959). *Mandala symbolism*. NJ: Princeton University Press

Kellogg, J. (1981). *Mandala: path of beauty*. FL: Published by author

Zimmer, H. (1946). *Myths and symbols in indian art and civilization*. (ed.) J. Campbell. NJ: Princeton University Press

Part 5

OTHER ARENAS

What One Museum Does for Prison Art

Carol Wisker, MA

Photographs by Joe Mikuliak and Alex Marchetti

Museums and prisons have much in common. Historically, both are impenetrable fortresses with massive walls, bars and gates designed to secure people and things. To enhance impregnability, both institutions are protected by hundreds of uniformed guards placed strategically every few feet to watch over people and things.

However, the differences between the two institutions are vast. Museums of the 90's seek to educate and sensitize their communities to the cultural arts with the hope that understanding will create a thinking, feeling world. Yet a prison, in the words of William Cleveland, Director of Education at Walker Art Center, "... is a place where truth, beauty, trust, excellence, tenderness, responsibility, vulnerability, color, variety, sensitivity, choice, decisions and physical contact have been banished. It is also a place where violence, corruption and self abuse dominate the lives of the keeper and the kept," (1996).

Inside Out, an outreach program of the Philadelphia Museum of Art, which is examined in this chapter, is making windows in the prison walls.

I have come to this program after many years working as an artist, educator and arts activist in nontraditional arenas. To prepare myself for this task, I have founded a shelter for youth at risk in a correctional setting, using arts as the treatment modality. I have developed award-winning art education programs serving visually impaired and blind adults, those with mental health and developmental disabilities, people with HIV/AIDS, and older adults and incarcerated men. Now, in addition to writing and educating the public about nontraditional ways of teaching art, I curate exhibitions of art created by these populations.

Authority, Credibility and Validation for the Artists

For the past four years, in a partnership program with Frackville Prison, the Philadelphia Museum of Art has provided:

- the services of a professional art educator
- print and slide libraries
- art videos
- special exhibitions with slides, videos, catalogues and audio tapes

- consultants on photography, exhibitions and framing
- a gallery devoted to the art work produced by the students involved in the Museum's programs.

Along with the tangible help, the museum continues to offer authority, credibility and validation for the program and for the inmate/artists, as well.

The Arts in Pennsylvania Corrections

Pennsylvania is about to join the ranks of many other states who now spend more money on incarceration than on education. Statistics show that crime has increased 25% in this state since 1980 and the prison population has quadrupled (Cass, 1996).

Lacking state policies or mandates for any arts activities for the general population, Pennsylvania's twenty-two penal institutions (which house 32,410 inmates) are individually responsible for their arts programs. Their activity directors generally view arts programs as less valuable than sports and religious activities. However, some of the institutions have part time artists-in-residence who are either musicians or visual artists.

Traditionally, state regulations have not permitted the inmates to sell art work. Nor have they encouraged art exhibitions which might increase public awareness of "inappropriate use of funding." The Department of Corrections does sponsor a yearly calendar contest featuring twelve works of art appropriate for calendars which are distributed throughout the corrections system. Also, in honor of Black History month, there is also a state-wide art contest (Parris, 1989).

SCI Frackville

Since the turn of the century, many museums have created programs and exhibitions targeted for special audiences: people of diverse cultures, the economically disadvantaged and/or disenfranchised, and the elderly. Currently, outreach efforts are created around partnering with other institutions in the areas of community service, access and diversity, (Berry and Mayer, 1989).

In 1992, the administration of the new State Correctional Institution at Frackville approached the Philadelphia Museum of Art for help in creating an arts program. The institution is located 110 miles northeast of Philadelphia in an area known as the coal region. During the 1990's, the coal and textile industries were quietly replaced by the new growth industry, prisons. The region has experienced an economic rebirth resulting from the creation of four state and federal prisons within a twenty-mile radius which provide cells for 6,000 inmates.

Frackville administrators became aware of the abundance of art spontaneously produced in their cells. Familiar with the California Department of Corrections and the Federal Bureau of Prisons studies which show that prisoners who make art are less violent while they are in prison and commit less crime when they are released (Cleveland, 1996), the administrators wanted to start a program for this creative activity as well as teach the inmates about art history, art world economics, and the crafts involved in producing exhibitions. The administrators also wanted to help the inmates connect with the surrounding community and with their own communities, including Philadelphia, since Pennsylvania coal regions are virtually without cultural activity.

Initially, there were twenty or more men in the Frackville prison working in their cells, several of them producing sophisticated work. These artist/inmates had little or no contact with each other although some cell mates taught each other. Most had started producing art work since incarceration. Several were tattoo artists transferring their skills to canvas. Others taught themselves formulaic landscape painting from TV shows. Only one could claim any formal high school art instruction.

Many painted animals, while others copied landscapes from magazines. They said their animals and landscapes were painted as symbols of freedom, their only escape from prison life. The paintings expressed a desire for perfection—they were filled with details, attempts at accurately replicating nature. Some of the men said their paintings became real places where they could escape to in their minds. Perhaps this is why they spent so much time perfecting each blade of grass, every leaf on a tree and every ripple in the water. Why not create a perfect world?

After a year's preparation, various prison departments agreed on plans for the exhibitions of art made in the prisons at a nearby shopping mall. The director of the wood shop/arts and crafts department, taught inmates to make frames for the art work, complete with spacers, mats and backings from scratch (rough wood). They also designed and produced large oak portable display boards.

Feedback from the inmates on what they wanted in the arts program influenced the design of the program. Most felt that they wanted more connection with each other as artists and the opportunity to share and show their work. Meetings were scheduled in the music room next to the gym where body builders worked out and observed. Lots of sarcastic remarks and amused smiles came from not only inmates, but staff as well. In fact negative attitudes about the project were expressed all the way from the front gate to the payroll office.

However, as the twenty artists continued to meet, they were transported into a space where prison life could be forgotten for two hours. New rules, commitment, conversation, consideration, respect, responsibility, sincerity, openness and learning had to be created in order for this time to have meaning. As the leader, I was challenged at every turn. One man sat in the back corner behind me at every meeting, twisted into a pretzel, glaring out from under his cap, totally silent. Yet the entire group continued to attend voluntarily.

A common ground was established through the language of art as I introduced form, shape, line and texture. All our exchanges were conducted in "art speak." After several meetings, we started to have meaningful conversations about images. (Our meeting was one of the few places in the institution where extended conversation took place.) Sessions included viewing the work of hundreds of famous artists. Hours of looking at composition, examining space issues, arguing about ideas and learning about color and art history created a group of men who learned how to really look at and connect with art. Their hunger for information on being or becoming artists was exhausting and exhilarating.

Our museum stresses educating visitors to value their own personal response to an art work, rather than relying solely on an "art historian as expert." Since most of the men had never been exposed to galleries, museums or any real form of art, I began the sessions listening to their impressions and experiences.

DRAWING TIME

For the first two years, our meeting room was almost completely dark after the first slide appeared on the screen; the only light came from the projector. The comfort of the darkness which eliminated direct eye contact, allowed the men to let down some of their defenses, to take risks in their conversations about the art work, and to respond with their true feelings. Even after two hours were up and we were all exhausted, they wanted to continue. The corrections officers complained to administration that I was keeping the inmates too long! More inmates, even those who were not making art, began to attend the meetings.

Some of the most dedicated inmates were Red, Bob and George, men who had learned to take risks, be personal, and incorporate techniques and ideas from history into their individual artistic statements.

Red

Red, the silent man who sat behind me, had previously earned himself a reputation as a trouble maker, not able to function with other inmates. His frequent misconduct caused his parole to be repeatedly denied. Slowly he started to contribute to the art discussions and he earned the respect of the group by producing an astounding body of work in six months.

Red, like many inmates who need quiet time in order to create, was not sleeping at night; he was painting. Within a year, something clicked and he started painting and drawing his heart and soul. In painting after painting he let go of his anger and frustration and dealt with deep and disturbing issues. As his anger was released through his art, he began to converse in class; no longer wearing his hat pulled down, and establishing eye contact with me and others in the group.

Two paintings were pivotal in this process, Feline Affection and Clowns (color plates 11 and 12). The lines textures in the man's robe, the cat's fur and the background in Feline Affection were created with such physical intensity that the paper itself almost became textured. Red's aggressive mark-making is in strong contrast to the sensual subject matter which he said came from his head. Although we often discussed the symbolic meaning of the inmates' work in the group, Red became a master of "double speak" when we would get too close. The image of the double clowns is one he repeated in several versions, with different backgrounds. Red would not talk about the content; he always shifted the focus of the discussion back to techniques. When asked to write about this picture, he wrote in third person.

I walked a fine line in this process. Because the class was not "art therapy" and because I am not trained as an art therapist, I was cautious not to delve too deeply for fear of interfering with the creative process and alienating the group. Prison is not a place where emotions are generally revealed.

Several of the inmates learned to work less literally and to use symbols and in order to express their personal "stuff." The mystery and intrigue of symbols was respected and encouraged. Healing comes within the cathartic process of "putting it down." Having other committed artists respect this process is enormously valuable.

Typically, art made in prison is a commodity and its value is determined by its degree of realism or its similarity to cartoon images. The amount of time spent creating artwork is valued, not personal expression. Therefore, when an artist/inmate made a sincere effort at self

Plate 11: Red—"Feline Affection", prisma color on paper

Plate 12: Red—"Clowning Around, 2", prisma color, acrylic on paper

Plate 13: Bob—"Doing Time", acrylic on canvas

Plate 14: Bob—"Adoration", acrylic on canvas

Plate 15: Bob—"Breaker", acrylic on canvas

Plate 16: Bob—"The Ancient", acrylic on canvas

Plate 17: Bob—"Generations", acrylic on illustration board

Plate 18: Bob—"Anatomical Cultivation", acrylic on canvas

Plate 19: George—"Artist's Block", acrylic on canvas

Plate 20: George—"Philadelphia Rush Hour Traffed Jam", acrylic on canvas

Plate 21: George—"U.S. Murderment", acrylic on canvas

Plate 22: George—"George", acrylic on canvas

expression, I was not only pleased, I was honored, even awed at the risk taken, and took care to protect this fragile event.

Watching Red grow and heal was a rewarding teaching experience. His remarkable transformation gave many of the group members permission to trust in their own creative processes; it validated their own perspectives. He started selling his most personal work through the community art shows. Staff treated him with new respect, or at least with new interest. His family responded to him for the first time in years. Red was no longer a number to staff and administration, he now had an identity and a face. He cleverly included self portraits in all of his internal correspondence. He eagerly agreed to be interviewed by the newspaper and TV. He even took part in the creation of a video about the project. Upon learning of his parole, he wrote a letter of thanks to the staff:

> *The art program is perhaps one of the most effective programs the prison has incorporated into its agenda. It allows inmates (including myself) to express themselves freely within the definition of their artwork. It inculcates an impressionable sense of liberation and completion. The program has opened doors to a host of possibilities, encouraging me to make profound modifications in my attitude, behavior and primary objectives, a new lease on life.*

Bob

Of the 28 artists who produced and exhibited their artwork through our program, Bob and George were the two whose paintings were most profoundly affected by the ideas and techniques discussed in the meetings.

Bob has been incarcerated for ten years. He started as a prolific and talented tattoo artist, a maker of fantastic, powerful, horrific imagery on bodies. Ironically, his initial greeting cards, paintings and drawings of animals and portraits on paper, were timid, sweet and sentimental. Bob's desire to become a serious artist drove him to work larger and to do research in order to expand his vision. The art library, which gave Bob the resources to study on his own, was enlarged by the museum's donations to include a variety of art surveys and exhibition catalogues. Although Bob expressed frustration at being restricted to painting in acrylic and water-based media, his experiments within these limitations have served him well (color plates 13-18, figures 1-5).

Risk-taking for Bob has been a way of life and in the past his impulsive nature allowed him to make poor choices. He began to channel this energy into technical experimentation, opening doors that excited him. Methodically, he worked through a number of artistic issues of space, composition, texture and color. Every six months he submitted a variety of landscape, portrait, surrealist, and narrative paintings to be exhibited.

Last year, after a slide presentation of the Barnes Collection which included many impressionist paintings, Bob started a series of pointillist portraits on large canvases. Making the dots of color work optically required that he pace his 6 by 9 foot cell thousands of times each evening. Pointillist painting was a tremendous leap for him in terms of understanding what painting can be. He expressed surprise at discovering how rich his surfaces became.

His portrait subjects are mostly "from his head" —earthy, young women with commanding presence who look directly at the viewer. Another of Bob's ongoing themes is about the

DRAWING TIME

experience of incarceration, an assigned subject which many of the artists have continued to use.

In yet another series, he painted scenes of the prison's surrounding coal region which he based on historical documents. He felt he could contribute something to the immediate community by showing viewers of the mall exhibitions their roots. Although Bob was not present to hear the comments, he created a relationship with a group of mall walkers. Daily, this group of elderly men delighted in arguing about the authenticity of his paintings. Bob's art now has touched his viewers in a personal way. He also has cut back on being the prison greeting card

Figure 1: Bob—"Eagle Colerie", acrylic on canvas

Figure 2: Bob—"Love", acrylic on canvas

Figure 3: Bob—"Metamorphosis", acrylic on canvas

WHAT ONE MUSEUM DOES

Figure 4: Bob—"Wrong Foot", acrylic on canvas

Figure 5: Bob—"Condor", acrylic on canvas

supplier in order to free himself for his serious work.

George

George, another former tattoo artist and inmate of eight years, also successfully transferred his talent to canvas. He was spurred on by his intense interest in surrealist painting and Picasso. His series of paintings about incarceration allowed him to address his anger and frustration with "the system" from a detached and somewhat sinister perspective. In his observations of

Figure 6: George—"Checkmate", acrylic on canvas

DRAWING TIME

prison life he combined remarkable technical skill as a painter of hard edges with a sharp wit (color plates 19-22 and figure 6).

During the first two years of this program, the prison administration was directly involved in every aspect. The commitment to smooth operation and internal cooperation was necessary to meet our proposed goals. Respect for the inmates' art work and for the program has grown with each exhibition. Media coverage, facilitated by both the prison and museum public relations efforts, has attracted wide interest.

Many of the prison's departments and inmates are involved in the creation of display stands, frames, matting and signs. Several of the Museum's employees have contributed support through purchasing art work and providing photographic documentation, posters, educational materials and editing.

The prison administration has added an additional full-time arts and crafts person to assist in supervising the exhibitions. Openings are attended by the Department of Corrections and arts administrators. Public response has been positive. Artist/inmates behavioral records indicate reduced incident reports and lowered recidivism.

One inmate established a friendship with a woman in the community who fell in love with his art work. Several of the inmates have followers in the art world who watch their development as artists. Many professional artists in the community are inspired by the determination of the inmates to keep producing art in an atmosphere that, for many artists, would be stultifying.

Inmates as People

In four years, Inside Out has produced six exhibitions, showcasing several hundred paintings and drawings. Not only have inmates been involved in a process which is inherently healing and continuously validating, they have all learned group cooperation, appropriate interaction and a professional understanding of the real art world. For many of the artist/inmates, this is the first time they have had a series of meaningful, *positive* life experiences.

Inside Out's connections with the community are far reaching, from mall walkers to curators. The ongoing relationship between the art museum, an outside, credible, stable and neutral institution and Frackville prison provides artist/inmates with the opportunity to feel connected with a non-punitive venue. It also allows the viewers of their art to connect with inmates as people.

Public response to the exhibitions indicate that there is real interest in those incarcerated in our country's correction system. Art museum guards report that average musuem visitors viewing exhibitions by artist/inmates, stay for long periods of time and often thank the museum for the opportunity to share the inmates' art work and feelings. Museum employees who gave their time to the exhibition also expressed gratitude for the opportunity to serve humanity in a small way.

In light of these results, we hope that more museums, galleries and art spaces will form partnerships with prisons or correctional facilities and that prisons will recognize that art programs can heal the spirit, serve the ego and teach skills beyond making a pretty picture.

References

Berry N. & Mayer S., (Eds) (1989). *Museum education: History, theory and practice*. Virginia: National Art Education Association

Cass J. (1996). As public fears swell, so do Pennsylvania prisons. *The Philadelphia Inquirer*, (May 20) A1, A8

Cleveland W. (1992). *Art in other places: Artists at work in America's community and social institutions*, Praeger: Connecticut, London.

Cleveland W. (1996) Lessons from the prison planet. *High Performance: A publication of Art in the Public Interest, 29*, (Summer)

Harithas J. (1973). *From within: Selected works from inmates at New York State Corrections at Auburn*, exhibition catalogue, Washington D.C., National Collection of Fine Arts at the Smithsonian

Parris, C.J. (1989). *Prison arts in Pennsylvania Department of Corrections*, (Program Description) Camp Hill, PA: Department of Corrections

Warner S. (1995). *Insight out: A different perspective*, (exhibition catalogue) Washington: Capitol Museum Experimental Gallery Program, Washington State Historical Society.

In The Future
Art Therapy Research in Prisons

Linda Gantt, Ph. D.

Combining my researcher's perspective with my limited prison art therapy experience has suggested some future strategies and ideas for art therapy research in forensic settings.

Two prisoners transferred from the county jail to the hospital where I worked as an art therapist became my patients temporarily. These two men typified those prisoners most likely to be referred for art therapy. One was a man in his thirties who had considerable artistic skill already and enjoyed learning more. The second patient/prisoner was younger, a man barely 19 years old, who was arrested as an accomplice to an armed robbery. He became psychotic in jail and regressed to the point where he smeared his feces on the wall and then ate them.

Two Approaches

When I gave the first young man the limited art materials permitted in the locked hospital cell (pastels and drawing paper) he embarked on a detailed and realistic drawing of a man's face. The style was accomplished but unusual—he divided the face into smaller parts like an illustration from that favorite book of artists, *Gray's Anatomy*. The finished work looked like a rather accurate rendition of muscle groups in the head. His considerable skill was admired by the nursing staff and myself. I asked him if he had ever thought about using this artistic skill in some job or hobby. His reply was direct, "I onlys does this whens I's incarcerated." I was struck by the inclusion of such a large word in a sentence constructed with a decided lack of grammar. But I had (naively perhaps) thought that his artistic talent would have been something he could capitalize on, perhaps to do drafting or sidewalk art.

The second young man was no malingerer. Because I specialized in working with acutely psychotic adults on the hospital's inpatient unit, I was asked to see him. Few of the nursing staff on this unit (which was the locked back room of the detoxification unit) had any experience in working with a mute and floridly psychotic person.

He was shackled to the bed when I first saw him, hardly in a position to draw. I told him who I was and that we would be doing art therapy together. I saw him for five sessions. He was treated with anti-psychotic medications and transferred back to jail.

During the first session he could not draw because of the shackles so I did a modification on what I usually do with my psychiatric patients. Typically, I would use a life-sized portrait as a means of reality orientation. But since this technique was impossible, I drew a head-and-shoulders portrait of him. I assumed that in his psychotic state he did not know who or where he was. While he did not respond in more than grunts and gestures, I assumed he could hear and understand a little of what I was saying. There was, of course, nothing wrong with his hearing but he was seriously disturbed.

As the medication took effect, the doctors unshackled him for our sessions. Over the five sessions he drew more and more. Finally, in his last session, when we both knew he would return to jail, we reviewed what he had done. He said he remembered when I did his portrait and he wanted to return the favor. His drawing of me was sensitively done with a great economy of line—a contour drawing done only with black chalk. Obviously, that first session had made a great impression on him.

Clearly, these two men were at the ends of the continuum one sees in most prisons. The first was just short of being a career criminal—in and out of the penal system with some regularity, adaptable and charming, with skills to ingratiate himself with others or get specific favors. Above all, he knew "the system" and could usually manipulate it.

The other was a first-time offender with a bona fide (if short-term) mental illness who needed specific psychiatric treatment. The art therapy approach I used with each was different because I tailored my interventions to their respective needs.

Tailoring Research

Similarly, there are quite different types of research questions these two prisoners raise. Following are some of the ideas both types suggest to me, providing contrast in both methods and topics for investigation.

If an art therapist were the first art therapist to be hired at a prison, she or he would have to research the kinds of art inmates had been doing without any special instruction or materials before her or his arrival. Hans Prinzhorn used this approach. He and other psychiatrists, who were "keepers" of the insane and of prisoners, have long noted that some people will turn to artistic expression or pursuits when locked up. They essentially employed an ethnographic approach with the goal of carefully describing what kinds of art prisoners do when left on their own. It is unfortunate there is no English translation of Prinzhorn's book, *Bildnerei der Gefangenen*, on the art of prisoners. What an interesting comparison we could make over a half century's time.

One might start with systematic portfolio reviews, making careful notes to compare specific groups of prisoners not only across units (such as solitary confinement or death row) but across prisons. Not only could one chronicle subjects of spontaneous art but one could record details of the visual environment such as tattoos, posters, books, and magazines that influence the art. How do cultural or gang styles influence what is done? What are the gang symbols or colors commonly used? Are there shared meanings for certain symbols or are there idiosyncratic ones? What are the typical styles? Are they super-realistic, abstract, or non-representational? Is one style favored by a particular prisoner or age group?

If several art therapists in different prisons collect similar information, this cataloging can lead to a taxonomy of prison art. Also, it could provide a useful means of understanding the use of covert symbolism as a means of communication. Perhaps nowhere else is there as strict a code of language and gesture as in a prison system, with an elaborate mechanism for keeping certain information from others. The decoding process is a slow one, with changes in terms gradually becoming commonly known and then abandoned as new terms are adopted. If art therapists can investigate and write about how to decode the covert symbolism, they may contribute to the safety of staff in other prisons.

Such an ethnographic approach has been the foundation of anthropological research which strives to capture as much detail as possible from the perspective of the person living in a culture. But this approach, which is fundamentally qualitative, has been often seen as a poor substitute for experimental research. Anthropologists have recently struggled with whether the discipline is truly scientific because of its reliance on ethnographic methods which are qualitative rather than quantitative (Benfer, 1996; American Anthropological Association, 1996). But there should not be a hierarchy of methods within research, simply a matching of the best methods with the question one seeks to answer. Qualitative approaches give a richness of detail and a sense of the potential domain in a way that quantitative studies do not. Ideally, the two types play off each other, with a good qualitative investigation leading to more specific hypotheses. Only by developing a taxonomy or classification system can one even begin to amass any statistical data. With a foundation laid on careful description, we can begin quantifying that description.

In the first case we are concerned with a naturalistic study of the sociological factors, the meaning of specific symbols, and the context in which the art is produced. For the second, a different model is more suitable. What takes priority here is researching the effects of psychiatric illness on art and vice versa. Here we are concerned with isolating particular variables and determining how changing levels of these variables are manifest in the art. For example, one could examine the correlation of formal variables in art with changes in behavior or with diagnostic information. Once that relationship is better understood, specific changes can be studied.

The second model is a correlational one in which the art therapist keeps a record of certain behaviors to see if they are associated with certain aspects of the art. For instance, are there specific features in the art which seem to predict outbursts of violence? In the first phase of such a study, art therapists would collect art which had been done prior to such outbursts. Then they would see what if any features seemed to be common such as quickly drawn lines, scratching out, disorganized compositions, or disguised themes of aggression.

The researchers would then set up testable hypotheses for a prospective study. Using this model, they might also study response to or need for psychiatric medication. Suicidal gestures or intentions may be included in art in a direct way or in a disguised form. Often, however, that material is not recognized as having suicidal content until after a person makes an actual attempt. If a number of art therapists collect and write about such examples, they will be training others to be alert for such material.

Many Variables can be Correlated with Art Work

One advantage for researchers is that the corrections systems keep inmates for a long time. Few psychiatric or psychological studies can be done longitudinally with the ease that one can in prisons. Also, prisons collect data on specific behavior both inside and outside the facility. Recidivism, suitability for job training, and the stages of psychological adjustment to confinement are other variables which could be correlated with artwork.

Well-done research, regardless of the specific method used, is crucial to further the development of any discipline. We are ready to advance beyond the generalizations of our earlier literature and build on a more solid foundation constructed on empirical evidence. John MacGregor, who chronicled the "discovery" of the art of the insane, states that "So long as a group of people is seen as less than human, an endeavor that seriously undermines our own humanity, we feel justified in ignoring their efforts to inform us about themselves and seek instead to understand them from the outside," (MacGregor, 1989, p. 309). Art is a way to understand people from the inside and research is a way to overcome our biases and look carefully at what is really there.

References

American Anthropological Association (1996). Science in anthropology. *Anthropology Newsletter, 37 (4)* p. 10-12.

Benfer, R. (1996). Science and anti-science in anthropology. *Anthropology Newsletter, 37 (4)* p. 76, 74.

MacGregor, J. (1989). *The discovery of the art of the insane.* Princeton, NJ: Princeton University Press.

Prinzhorn, H. (1926). *Bildnerei der gefangenen* [Artistry of convicts]. Berlin: Verlag Juncker.

About the Editors

David E. Gussak, MA, A.T.R.-BC
David Gussak received his Master of Arts in Art Therapy at the Vermont College of Norwich University Graduate Art Therapy Program. He is a Rehabilitation/Art Therapist for the mental health department of a prison in northern California, providing services for the mentally ill in prison. He has presented papers, lectured and provided classes about art therapy in prisons for conferences and art therapy graduate programs. He is currently the chairperson of the American Art Therapy Association's Governmental Affairs Committee. He is also the president-elect for the Northern California Art Therapy Association and the co-chair for the California Creative Arts Therapies Coalition.

Evelyn Virshup, Ph.D., A.T.R.
Evelyn is author of *Right Brain People in a Left Brain World*, editor of *California Art Therapy Trends*, and co-editor of *Creativity and Madness: Psychological Studies of Art and Artists*, as well as a dozen articles on creativity and art therapy for professional journals. She has conducted creativity workshops in Canada, London, Stockholm, Moscow, and the United States.

Dr. Virshup has produced and hosted over two hundred public access programs, including *Your Art As Language*, *L.A. Psychology*, and *National Women's Political Caucus Presents*.

A faculty member of Art Center College of Design in Pasadena for 16 years, she teaches courses in creativity and self-awareness. She has been on the faculty at California State University at Los Angeles, teaching art therapy since 1984. She is also past president of the Southern California Art Therapy Association and has been their newsletter editor for seven years.

Contributors

Jack Cheney, MA, A.T.R.
Jack received his BA in art from the University of California, Santa Barbara, and he received his MA in Art Therapy from Cal State Los Angeles. He is also a multimedia artist/musician, and was a community arts leader. Mr. Cheney founded and directed the Art Therapy/Fine Arts Discovery Program at Camarillo State Hospital and Developmental Center, which served over three hundred patients a week before the hospital closed, In 1993, Mr. Cheney was awarded the prestigious AMGEN award, the only therapist ever to receive this Excellence in Education honor. He currently works for a mental health program at a prison in northern California.

Elizabeth Day, MA, A.T.R.-BC
Elizabeth is the director of Rehabilitative Therapies at Silver Hill Hospital in New Canaan, CT. She has experience with various aspects of the abuse cycle having initially worked with battered and sexually abused children. Ms. Day later worked as an art therapist with male pretrial detainees, many of whom were both victims and perpetrators of sexual violence. Presently her experience with trauma survivors is drawn upon practicing art therapy with hospitalized psychiatric patients as well as with female inmates in a prison treatment program.

Pamela M. Diamond, Ph.D.
Pamela is the Regional Director of Program Evaluation for Texas Tech Health Science Center's Division of Correctional Care. She received her doctorate in Educational Psychology with an emphasis in Quantitative Methods from the University of Texas at Austin. Dr. Diamond served as a Senior Research Assistant for the Hogg Foundation for Mental Health at the University of Texas for several years prior to assuming her present position. Her current research interests focus on the mentally impaired offender and she has published and presented widely in this area. In addition to her research work, Dr. Diamond's early training and clinical work was as an art psychotherapist. She was founder and director of the Art Psychotherapy of Cleveland during the late 70's and served on the Education and Training Board of AATA under the direction of Elinor Ulman.

William Fox, M.S.W., L.C.S.W.
Bill has worked for thirty years as a psychotherapist, teacher, writer and administrator in California and Arizona. He has delivered services to and written about such diverse and stigmatized populations as borderline adolescents, exhibitionists, methamphetamine and heroin addicts, the elderly and mentally ill criminals, in a variety of public and private agencies, as well as private practice. He is currently a licensed clinical social worker for a California prison and is expanding his article in this collection into a book as well as finishing a collection of his poetry for publication.

Linda Gantt, Ph.D., A.T.R.-BC, HLM
Linda has a master's degree in Art Therapy and a doctorate in Interdisciplinary Studies. Currently, she is the art therapist for the Trauma Recovery Institute, Morgantown, West Virginia, and is doing research on the correlation of psychiatric diagnosis and art work. During the past 20 years Dr. Gantt has taught in both graduate and undergraduate art therapy and served in numerous elected positions in the American Art Therapy Association (including president) and the National Coalition of Arts Therapies Associations.

Deborah Good, Ph.D., A.T.R., LPCC, LPAT
Deborah, President-Elect of the American Art Therapy Association, received her doctorate from the University of New Mexico in Counseling Education with a minor in Art Therapy. A licensed professional clinical counselor and licensed professional art therapist in New Mexico, Deborah practices at Family Therapy of Albuquerque and is the Art Therapy Program Chair at Southwestern College in Santa Fe.

David E. Gussak, MA, A.T.R.-BC
David received his Master of Arts in Art Therapy at the Vermont College of Norwich University Graduate Art Therapy Program. He is a Rehabilitation/Art Therapist for the mental health department of a prison in northern California, providing services for the mentally ill in prison. He has presented papers, lectured and provided classes about art therapy in prisons for conferences and art therapy graduate programs. He is currently the chairperson of the American Art Therapy Association's Governmental Affairs Committee. He is also the president-elect for the Northern California Art Therapy Association and the co-chair for the California Creative Arts Therapies Coalition.

Nancy Hall, A.T.R.-BC, CRC
Nancy, graduate of the Rhode Island School of Design and Goddard College, has been practicing art therapy for 18 years, working in a state developmental center, a hospital for physical rehabilitation, a school for emotionally disturbed girls, a state psychiatric hospital, and medium and maximum security state prisons. President of the New England Association of Art Therapists, Governmental Affairs Chair and Board Member for the American Art Therapy Association, and President of the Art Therapy Credentials Board, she has been a lifelong resident of the Northeast. Currently, she is moving to California.

Ann Hanson Howe, M.S.W., L.M.S.W.-A.C.P.
Ann has specialized in group therapy in psychiatric settings and established the group therapy program at the Montford Unit. At present, she is the director of habilitation therapy at the Texas Department of Criminal Justice J.T. Montford Unit and an instructor in the department of psychiatry at Texas Tech University Health Science Center.

CONTRIBUTORS

Beth Merriam, A.T.R.
Beth has a private practice in Kingston, Ontario. She worked at the Kingston Prison for Women for five years. Her short story "Red Rope and Blue Veins" won an award for outstanding achievement in the arts in the 1995 Kingston Literary Awards. She has presented papers on art therapy in correctional settings at the Canadian and Quebec Art Therapy Conferences. Currently she is coordinator of Project Art Lab, which provides opportunities in art expression for children of prisoners.

Linda Milligan, MPS, A.T.R.
Linda, artist and graduate of Pratt Institute with a degree in art therapy and creativity development, is an art therapist at the Youth Development Center in Bensalem, PA., a maximum security facility. She works individually with 14 to 18 year old males. Ms. Milligan has published articles in the Pratt Institute Creative Arts Therapy Review, in AATA's Journal, Art Therapy, and Railing Against the Rush of Years, by Ridker and Savage, in 1996. She lives with her husband in Voorhees, NJ.

Dorrie Mosel-Gussak, MA, A.T.R.
Dorrie is a graduate of the Vermont College of Norwich University Graduate Art Therapy Program. She has worked as an artist/art therapist in Canada, France and the United States. She has developed rehabilitation programs, taught psychiatric rehabilitation classes and lectured for various professional conferences, hospitals and schools. She currently works for a partial hospitalization program in northern California.

Greg Onorato, Psy.D.
Greg is the Program Coordinator of the Trauma Program of a low level security female prison. He graduated from the Illinois School of Professional Psychology. Dr. Onorato has worked in corrections since 1979. He worked a Cook County Jail in Chicago with mentally ill detainees and later with offenders found not guilty by reason of insanity at a forensic unit within a state hospital.

Joan Pakula, MEd, A.T.R.
Joan received her Masters degree in Special Education at the University of Missouri, and her art therapy certification at the College of Notre Dame, in Belmont, California. She worked for six and a half years as an art therapist at the California correctional facility where the hostage incident occurred. Currently, she is a disability analyst for the state of California. Despite her change of occupation, she has "never left art therapy."

Stephen Rojcewicz, M.D.
Dr. Rojcewicz balances the private practice of psychiatry with his duties as a forensic psychiatrist for the state of Maryland. An Associate Clinical Professor of Psychiatry at Georgetown University, he has numerous publications on such topics as psychotherapy, hallucinations, and suicide. Enchanted by literature and fascinated by the integration of mental health and the humanities, he will serve as president of the National Association for Poetry Therapy for 1997-1999.

Claudia Ronaldson, Ed.D., A.T.R.-BC
Claudia received her doctorate in Counseling Psychology from the University of San Francisco. She has been an administrator and art therapist at Timothy Murphy School in San

Rafael, CA, for the past eleven years and is a credentialed art teacher and board certified art therapist. Dr. Ronaldson also has a M.A. in psychology from Sonoma State University and an M.F.A. from the School of the Art Institute of Chicago. She was an Assistant Professor at Oregon State University and Northern Illinois University and taught design, drawing and textile design. She also is an exhibiting artist.

Renu Sundaram, Ph.D., A.T.R.-BC
Renu is an art therapist and counselor at the John Tracy Clinic in Los Angeles, California, which serves families of hearing-impaired children. She has also completed her Ph.D. at UCLA in Special Needs/Educational Psychology.

Marcia Taylor, Ph.D., A.T.R.
Marcia is Associate Professor of Art and co-chair of the Art Department at the College of New Jersey. She received her MS in Art Therapy from Hahnemann University and Ph.D. in Behavioral Science from the Florida Institute of Technology. Most recently she has coordinated several projects with the New Jersey Department of Corrections including the conference, *Art in Prison: "It's More than Just Killing Time."* Her volunteer work with the Senior Men's Group at the Trenton State Prison was supported by a Faculty Research grant from the College of New Jersey.

Will Ursprung, A.T.R., NCS
Will is a registered art therapist affiliated with the Commonwealth of Pennsylvania Department of Corrections/State Correctional Institution at Graterford. He also serves as liaison between the American Art Therapy Association and the International Correctional Arts Network, and affiliate of the American Correctional Association. An accomplished exhibiting artist/collagist, member of the National Artists Equity Association, and the National Collage Society, his artwork has been the cover design for the International Journal of the Arts in Psychotherapy since 1980.

Carol Wisker, MA
Carol is a artist, educator and arts administrator and has worked with a variety of populations in nontraditional settings. In the 70's, while working within the corrections world, she founded a shelter for "youth at risk" using the arts as a treatment modality. As the special audiences coordinator in the Division of Education at the Philadelphia Museum of Art she has developed award-winning, world-renowned art education programs serving visually impaired and blind adults, those with mental health and developmental disabilities, HIV/AIDS victims, the incarcerated and older adults. In addition to teaching, writing and training about art and nontraditional art education, she curates exhibitions of art created by these populations.

Janis St. Clair Woodall, A.T.R., L.M.S.W.-A.C.P.
Janis received her masters degree in Art Therapy from Emporia Kansas State University. She has eighteen years experience in art therapy and counseling. Her current treatment population is with the adult male mentally ill inmate/patients of the Texas Department of Criminal Corrections in the J.T. Montford Psychiatric Prison facility.

Index

Act of Transportation   xvi
action figures   170
adolescent   167, 175-185
    —cognitive distortions   182-183
    —profile   176
aggression, characteristics of   167, 175, 177, 190
    aggressive impulses   49-50
    catharsis of—   172
    "secret"aggression   51-53
    symbols of—   105, 224, 233, 243
    —as a drive   82-84
Allen, Bud   48
American Correctional Association   14
anthropology   243
APA Task Force on Psychiatric Services
    in Jails and Prisons of the Council on Psychiatric Services   xviii
Apollinaire, Guillaume   77, 79
Art Brut   15-18, 22
art directives:
    Accumulative Drawing   124
    Create A World   160
    Feelings Chart, The   159
    feelings exercise   121
    Here and Now tasks   189
    life-sized portrait   241-242
    Lifeline Task   122
    Paint Blot Projection   124
    Self-Image Collage   123
    string and ink art   91-92
    Tree That Would Be Like You   112, 122
    Where Am I Going?   105, 123
    wood box decorating   182

Art Therapy Full Value Contract 103, 105, 106, 121, 125
Arts In Corrections program xix
assessments and diagnostic tests:
    Brief Psychiatric Rating Scale (BPRS) 100 *(fn)*
    Buss-Perry Aggression Questionnaire (BPAQ) 100 *(fn)*
    Center for Epidemiological Studies-Depression Scale (CES-D) 104, 105, 119-121
    Diagnostic Drawing Series 177-178
    Executive Interview (EXIT) 100 *(fn)*
    Mari Mandala Assessment 220
    Mini-Mental Status Exam (MMSE) 100 *(fn)*
    Penn State Worry Questionnaire (PSWQ) 104, 105, 119-121
    Personality Assessment Inventory (PAI) 99
    Qualitative Evaluation of Dementia (QED) 100 *(fn)*
    Structured Clinical Interview for Diagnosis-Clinical Version (SCID-CV) 100 *(fn)*
    Structured Interview for Reported Symptoms (SIRS) 100

Bipolar disorder 26, 65
Blake, William 81
Borderline (personality disorder) 4-10, 27, 104,111,129
Brewster, Larry xix, 232
Brooks, Gwendolyn 80
California Department of Corrections studies xix, 232
Cane, Florence 2
Cardinal, Roger 15-16
career criminals 197
catharsis 132, 172, 199-200
classification (of inmates) xvii
classroom 169-174, 200
clay 18, 39, 62, 121, 132, 161, 171, 172, 180, 189, 202
Cleveland, William 231
collage 121, 123, 156-159, 178, 190-191, 202   COLLAGE PHOTOS
Compromise Option 59-60, 62
conduct-disordered 167-169, 171
✓ containment 136, 138-141
contraband, defined 18
coping skills 10, 87, 89, 102, 103, 199-200
counter transference 175, 184-185
creative writing 87, 204, 213
criminal (early definition of), xvi
criminalized xviii
custody 15, 89, 199
Darth Vader 82
"dead time" 198
deafness (see *hearing impairment*)
debt to society 46, 54

INDEX

defense mechanisms, general: 44, 178
    denial as a—   9, 44, 47, 71-72, 137, 159, 178-179
delinquency, juvenile delinquents   168
depravation, sensory   17, 94-95, 98
    movement—   94-95, 98
depression   26, 34, 63, 67, 100, 103-110, 110-116, 130, 199
developmental delays   154
Dickinson, Emily   80
Dissanayake, Ellen   60
dissociation, state of   35, 46, 114, 138, 141
    as an Identity Disorder   130, 142
Dostoevsky, Fyodor   76
drug-related crimes   27, 69, 148, 88-96, 176
Dubuffet, Jean   15-16
dyadic relationship   44-49, 60
Dysthymia   3-10, 168
egocentrism   172
empathy   47, 62
    lack of—   177-178
empowerment   137-138
envy, defined   52-53
episteophilic impulse   50

Erikson, Erik   175, 178-182
    Erikson's Developmental Stages:
        autonomy vs. shame and doubt   202-181
        identity vs. role confusion   178, 182
        industry vs. inferiority   178, 181
        initiative vs. guilt   178, 181
        trust vs. mistrust   178-179
ethnography   242-243
escape, making art to   2, 10, 31-32, 60-61, 68, 98, 194, 233
exclusion and inclusion criteria   102
execution, as a punishment   xvi
Federal Bureau of Prisons Studies   232
female offenders   128-150
5150 (California Welfare and Institutions Code)   153
found object, as medium   19-20
Frackville Prison   231, 232-234
Freud, Sigmund   44
gerontology   197-208
gestalt   196
Giovanni, Nikki   82
Gorecki, Henryk   77
graffiti   18, 20, 30, 181-182
grandiosity, delusions of   153, 155, 192

Gray, Martin   13
Greenberg, Jay   43
hallucinations, as symptoms   27, 63, 67, 104, 105-109, 119, 155, 188, 192-195
"hard time"   197-203
health care, the right to   xviii-xix
hearing impairment, in the clients   188-189, 190-196
     in the therapist   188
"hidden weapon" exercises   51
hulks   xvi
human rights   xvii
humor, the importance of   54-55
hypervigilance, in clients   90, 92, 97, 179
     in staff   xv, 45, 188, 220
identity, sense of /loss of   4-10, 35, 38-40, 49, 235
incapacitation, as a prison objective   130
incident reduction   xix, 238
infantilization   47-48, 61
inmate/correctional subculture   1,133
"insane"   xviii, 244
     "criminally insane"   187-196
insider art   18-25
institutionalization   27, 155, 208
Internet   17, 77
invisibility (of inmates)   49-50
isolation, forced   xvi
     sense of—   67, 109, 141-142
Jonas, Hans   51
Jung, C.G.   8, 220
Kernberg, Otto   44
Klein, Melanie / Kleinian theory   43-55
Kramer, Edith   2, 60, 169
learning disabled   167, 169
level system   154-155
libido   53, 60
"locked down"   198-199
lupus erythematosus   71
malingering   3, 47, 100
managed care   99-116
mandalas   7-8, 109, 184-185, 220-226
mandatory sentences   200
mask making   68-72, 182, 202
     masks, as a defense   1, 7-8, 137, 169, 184
mirroring   98
Mitchell, Stephen   43
Morrison, Andrew   43
murals   34-36, 194-195

INDEX

murderers, cases of   62, 67-68, 69-71, 103-110, 130, 204-208
music, use of   87-98, 112-114, 137-148
      music therapy   99, 101-103, 111-112
Nachmanovich, S   17
narcissism, as a personality disorder   111, 192
object relations   43-54
outcome measures, studies   101
outpatient services   26
outsider art   (see *art brut*)
overcrowding   xvii, 198, 200
"overfamiliarity"   49
paper making   65-67
paranoia   59, 60, 109, 179
    —basic dynamic of   43-44
paranoid
    —"brainstorming"   45
    —myth of a stabilized system   52
    —projection   44-53
    —"rush"   47
    —vigilance   45
Pennslylvania Department of Corrections:
    —art in   14-22
    —population statistics   14
    —sales of art   16
Perrine, Van Dearing   17
Petronius   75, 84
Philadelphia Museum of Art   231-240
Plaster-of-Paris/plaster   62-65, 132
Plato   76
Poetry Therapy/Bibliotherapy   77-84
portfolio review   242
Post Traumatic Stress Disorder (PTSD)   27, 177
primitive art   14
Prinzhorn, Hans   242
prison "taboos"   87-98
prison standards, adaptation to   2
prisonization, symbolic of   19
prison, history of   xv-xx
    —reform   xvii-xviii
probationary students   167-169, 171
professionalism (correctional)   48
Progressives   xviii
projection   44-53, 61, 178
pseudoempathy   47, 62
psychiatric rehabilitation   153-154, 155
punishment, early forms of   xvi-xviii

DRAWING TIME

ready-made 19 ✓ *Photos*
rebirth, symbols of 207
recidivism, reduction in xix, 238
rehabilitation, intent of xvi-xviii
rejuvenation (see *rebirth*)
reparation, in Melanie Klein 53-55
research methods 241-244
residential treatment facility 153, 168
Rubin, Judith 172
schizophrenia, various diagnoses of 26, 43, 45, 104, 153, 155
segregation 213-218
self:
    —care 213
    —esteem 14, 102, 103, 199, 208
    —exploration 213
    —monitoring (for the therapist) 213 ✓
    —mutilation 10, 27, 129, 133
separation /individuation 156
seriously emotionally disturbed (SED) 167-168, 171-172
sex offenses 3, 190, 197, 201
sexual abuse 3, 129, 130, 160
    symbols of 8-9, 107
shame, transformation of 142-144

sign language inc. Signing Exact English (SEE) and American Sign Language (ASL) 188
socialization,
    building these skills through art therapy 124, 155
sociopathy xviii, 1, 153, 154
Socrates 76
Special Education 167-168
splitting, defined 50
stimuli, externalized 172
    internal 155
sublimation 60, 169
substance abuse
    alcohol 62, 88, 105-110, 155, 204-205
    drug use 3, 6, 18, 27, 47, 69, 88-96, 105-110, 110-115, 148, 155
suicidality, as a symptom 3-10, 63-65, 67-68, 88-95, 103-110, 130, 190
    symbols of 122, 243
"supercop and supercriminal" 50
tattoos, tattoo artists xix, 30, 38-39, 233, 235, 237
taxonomy (of prison art), the importance of 242-243
Thich Nhat Hahn 91
"three-strikes" law xvi, 46
transportation (see Act of Transportation)
trauma in clients 93-94, 112, 127-150

258

INDEX

       in therapists   219-220
"ultimate hidden weapon"   61-62
vagrancy, crime of   xvi
Villon, François   77
"walked out"   59
wheat paste, as medium   94-97
Wilde, Oscar   77
wood, as medium   19, 21, 34, 171, 172, 180, 182
workhouses   xvi

Magnolia Street Publishers

Supervision and Related Issues: A Handbook for Professionals   MALCHIODI & RILEY

A highly informative guide to the complexities of supervision in the 90's. Supervisors, educators, and students will find it indispensable in their sessions, the classroom and in work with clients. An extensive appendix includes ethics and standards of practice, sample forms for use in supervision, laws effecting supervisors and many more references and resources. (300 pages)

California Art Therapy Trends   Ed. EVELYN VIRSHUP

This book is hands-on, clinically oriented, how 30 art therapists who live in California practice—a day in their life, so to speak. (431 pages)

The Gestalt Art Experience: Patterns That Connect   JANIE RHYNE

Based on gestalt psychology and therapy, the focus of this book is on direct and immediate experiential insights gained through creating art that expresses and clarifies personal problems and potential. Emphasis is on exploring present life style and discovering possibilities for self-actualization. (revised edition, color illustrations, 225 pages)

Art Therapy in Theory & Practice   ed. ELINOR ULMAN & P. DACHINGER

Since its first publication, this volume has been used continually as both a textbook and a resource. Many of the chapters have become indispensable classics which continue to define the field of art therapy. Elinor Ulman shows great skill, perception and eloquence as both a writer and editor. (color illustrations, 414 pages)

Integrative Approaches To Family Art Therapy   SHIRLEY RILEY & CATHY MALCHIODI

This important new book by noted family art therapist Shirley Riley is designed for both the beginning practitioner as well as the advanced family therapist. An important source of ideas, this text provides not only examples of integrative approaches to family art therapy, but also offers practical ways to utilize art therapy with individuals, families and couples. Chapters cover a wide range of theoretical viewpoints, including structural, systemic, narrative, family of origin and social constructionism. (262 pages)

Art As Therapy With Children   EDITH KRAMER

Kramer's discussions of sublimation, art and defense, aggression, and the role of the art therapist have not been surpassed by later volumes or by other authors. This profoundly wise volume offers inspiration and genuine assistance to the fledgling clinician as well as to anyone else working with children who wishes to understand how and why art can have such a profound effect. (color illustrations, 238 pages)

Shattered Images: Phenomenological Language of Sexual Trauma   DEE SPRING

Dee Spring has specialized in the treatment of post-traumatic stress and dissociative disorders for more than twenty years. Her pioneering efforts in this field have gained international recognition because of her unique treatment style which includes art therapy, imagery and hypnosis. She presents a treatment model that simultaneously helps the therapist stay on track amid the myriad crises encountered with sexual trauma victims and creatively explains the complex, multi-level treatment process. (305 pages)

Dynamically Oriented Art Therapy: It's Principles & Practice   MARGARET NAUMBURG

As a pioneer in this field of psychotherapy, Margaret Naumburg's approach to art therapy is psychoanalytically oriented; she recognized the fundamental importance of the unconscious as expressed in the patient's dreams, daydreams and fantasies. In this work, three case histories of emotionally disturbed women are used to illustrate the various ways in which the process of dynamically oriented art therapy can function in the treatment of depression, ulcers and alcoholism. (color illustrations, 168 pages)

1250 West Victoria, Chicago, IL 60660, 773-561-2121, fax 773-477-6096